·033

This book is due for return on or b

D0487679

FOR ALL THE
TEA IN CHINA

FOR ALL THE TEA IN CHINA

Espionage, empire and the secret formula for the world's favourite drink

Sarah Rose

HUTCHINSON
LONDON

Published by Hutchinson 2009

4 6 8 10 9 7 5

Copyright © Sarah Rose 2009

Sarah Rose has asserted her right under the Copyright, Designs
and Patents Act 1988 to be identified as the author of this work

This book is sold subject to the condition that it shall not,
by way of trade or otherwise, be lent, resold, hired out,
or otherwise circulated without the publisher's prior
consent in any form of binding or cover other than that
in which it is published and without a similar condition,
including this condition, being imposed
on the subsequent purchaser

First published in Great Britain in 2009 by
Hutchinson
Random House, 20 Vauxhall Bridge Road,
London SW1V 2SA

www.rbooks.co.uk

Addresses for companies within The Random House Group Limited can be found at:
www.randomhouse.co.uk/offices.htm

The Random House Group Limited Reg. No. 954009

A CIP catalogue record for this book
is available from the British Library

ISBN 9780091797065 (HB)
ISBN 9780091921309 (TPB)

The Random House Group Limited supports The Forest Stewardship
Council (FSC), the leading international forest certification organisation. All our
titles that are printed on Greenpeace approved FSC certified paper carry the FSC logo. Our paper
procurement policy can be found at www.rbooks.co.uk/environment

Mixed Sources
Product group from well-managed
forests and other controlled sources
www.fsc.org Cert no. TT-COC-2139
© 1996 Forest Stewardship Council

Typeset by Palimpsest Book Production Limited,
Grangemouth, Stirlingshire

Printed and bound in Great Britain by
CPI Mackays, Chatham ME5 8TD

For Scott

'The greatest service which can be rendered to any country is to add a useful plant to its culture' — Thomas Jefferson

'Tea is exceedingly useful; cultivate it, and the benefit will be widely spread; drink it and the animal spirits will be lively and clear' — Robert Fortune, quoting a Chinese proverb

Prologue

There was a time when maps of the world were redrawn in the name of plants, when two empires, Britain and China, went to war over two flowers: the poppy and the camellia.

The poppy, *Papaver somniferum*, was processed into opium, a narcotic used widely throughout the Orient in the eighteenth and nineteenth centuries. The drug was grown and manufactured in India, a subcontinent of princely states united under the banner of Greater Britain, in 1757. Opium was marketed, solely and exclusively, under the aegis of England's Empire in India by the Honourable East India Company.

The camellia, *Camellia sinensis*, is also known as tea. The Empire of China had a near complete monopoly on tea, as it was the only country to grow, pick, process, cook, and in all other ways manufacture, wholesale and export 'the liquid jade'.

For nearly two hundred years, the East India Company sold opium to China and bought tea with the proceeds. China, in turn, bought opium from British traders out of India and paid for the drug with the silver profits from tea.

The opium-for-tea exchange was not merely profitable to England, it was indispensable. Nearly one in every ten pounds sterling collected by the government came from the import and sale of tea – about a pound per person per year.

Tea taxes funded railways, roads and Civil Service salaries, among the many other necessities of an emergent industrial nation. Opium was equally significant to the British economy, for it financed the management of India – the shining jewel in Queen Victoria's imperial crown. While it was always hoped that India would pay for itself, by the mid-nineteenth century England was waging a series of expansionist wars on India's North West Frontier that were swiftly draining whatever profits could be derived from the rich and vast subcontinent.

The triangular trade in flowers was the engine which powered a world economy and the wheels of Empire turned on the growth, processing and sale of plant life: poppies from India; camellias from China; with a cut from each for Great Britain.

The British-Chinese relationship was tragically unhappy. The Exalted and Celestial Emperor in Peking 'officially' banned the sale of opium in China in 1729, but regardless it was smuggled in for generations afterwards. (Notably, the sale of opium was also forbidden by Queen Victoria within the British Isles. She, however, was largely obeyed.) Opium sales increased quickly and steadily; there was a fivefold growth in volume in the years 1822–37. Finally, in 1839, the leading Chinese court official in the trading port of Canton, rankled by the profligacy of the foreigners and the pestilence of opium addiction among his own people, held the entire foreign encampment hostage, ransoming the 300 Britons for their opium, then worth $6 million (about $145 million in today's dollars, or £290 million). When the opium was surrendered and the hostages released, the Mandarin ordered 500 Chinese coolies to foul nearly 3 million pounds of the drug with salt and lime, and then wash the filthy mixture out into the Pearl River and thence to the South China Sea. In response, young

Victoria sent Britain's navy to war, to keep the lucrative opium-for-tea marriage alive.

In battle, Britain trounced China, whose rough wooden sailing junks were no match for Her Majesty's steam-powered modern navy. As part of the peace treaty England won concessions from the Chinese no one had previously thought possible in a century of diplomatic entreaty: the island of Hong Kong, plus the cession of five new treaty or trading ports on the mainland.

Few Westerners had penetrated the Chinese interior since the days of Marco Polo. For two hundred years prior to the First Opium War British ships had been restricted to docking at the entrepôt of Canton, a sliver of a trading city at the mouth of the Pearl River. No Englishman had been granted permission to leave that southernmost port to explore the centre of the Yellow Country. Britons could not officially step foot outside their warehouses, and many had never even seen the city walls, 20 foot thick and 25 high and only 200 yards away from the foreigners' district. Now, with their triumph in the war, the interior of China was opened to the British – just a crack – for business.

With five new cities in which to trade, British merchants were dreaming of the lush silks, delicate porcelains and perfumed teas stockpiled in the Chinese interior, just waiting to be sold on to the wider world. Sitting before their ledgers, businessmen imagined dealing directly with Chinese manufacturers, rather than the cantankerous middlemen or compradors who commanded the Canton warehouses. Bankers had visions of untold riches, of mineral wealth, and of crops, plants, flowers – a giant country of unmonetised commodities.

The new order established by the first Opium War was an unstable one, however. Forced by British gunboats to sign intolerable treaties, a wounded China seethed. The once proud and self-contained nation had been thoroughly shamed. British politicians and traders worried that the humiliated Chinese Emperor might upset the delicate balance laid out in the peace accords by legalising opium production in China and breaking India's (and thus Britain's) monopoly on the poppy.

An idea took hold in the City of London: tea could and must be secured for England. The Napoleonic Wars were long over by the time of the Opium Wars, but the brave men who had fought at Trafalgar and Waterloo still held enormous sway over foreign policy and opinion. Henry Hardinge, a great general who had helped defeat Napoleon beside Nelson and Wellington, warned of the risk posed by a defiant China when he was Governor General of India:

It is in my opinion by no means improbable that in a few years the Government of Pekin, by legalising the cultivation of Opium in China, where the soil has been already proved equally well adapted with India to the growth of the plant, may deprive this Government of one of its present chief sources of revenue. Under this view I deem it most desirable to afford every encouragement to the cultivation of Tea in India, in my opinion the latter is likely in course of time to prove an equally prolific and more safe source of revenue to the state than that now derived from the monopoly on Opium.

If China should legalise the opium poppy, it would leave a crucial gap in the economic triangle: England would no longer have the money to pay for her tea, her wars in India, or public works projects at home. Chinese-grown opium would put an end to the shameful economic co-dependence between the two Empires, the unhappy marriage sealed by the exchange of the two flowers. It was a divorce that Britain could ill afford.

The Indian Himalaya mountain range resembled China's best tea-growing regions. The Himalayas were high in altitude and richly soiled, clouded in mists to water tea plants and shade them from the scorching sun, while frequent frosts would help sweeten and flavour the liquor, make it more complicated, delightful, delicious.

As flowers swelled the balance sheets of the Oriental trade, they became so important to the world order that the men who understood them – men who were once called gardeners – were now regarded as members of a new profession: botany. By the mid-nineteenth century gardeners were no longer humble men in hats and hob-nailed boots, tending to their bulbs, flowers and shrubs. Furthermore, the emergent botanists were becoming swashbucklers and world-changers. Foreign plants were collected and studied for the sake of the potential scientific, economic and agricultural advances they might bring about in England and throughout the Empire. Gardeners, freed from the tyranny of restriction to their home ground, became plant hunters in the wild. Flowers, too, became travellers as new technology for transplanting live flora grew ever-more sophisticated. Whether a plant specimen was rare or as commonplace as grass in its native land meant nothing to the professional plant hunter; only that it was new and useful to England and her budding colonial economies.

No longer confined to China's southernmost coast, Britain now had greater access to the areas where tea was cultivated and processed. If the manufacture of tea in India were to be successful, Britain would need healthy specimens of the finest tea plants, seeds by the thousand, and the centuries-old knowledge of accomplished Chinese tea manufacturers. The task required a plant hunter, a gardener, a thief, a spy.

The man Britain needed was named Robert Fortune.

I

Min River, China, 1845

On an autumn afternoon in 1845, long before Robert Fortune made his name as one of the world's great plant hunters, it seemed very likely that he would die in China. For two weeks he had been confined on a listless junk near the city of Fuzhou, at the mouth of the Min River. His ordinarily robust constitution was near collapse. With a raging fever, he took to his bunk in the cabin of a seagoing cargo boat, dizzy from the smell of bilgewater and rotting fish. The junk's deck was laden with timber from the countryside. Also on deck was Fortune's cargo, which included trunk-sized glass boxes filled with flowers, shrubs, grasses, vegetables, fruits, and all matter of exotic plant-life. These glazed cases, known as Wardian or Ward's cases after their inventor, were on their way, with Fortune, to London – if he ever made it that far. With his long legs dangling off a bunk made for shorter, Chinese men, Fortune, only thirty-three years old at the time, imagined himself dying in the boat's hold, being swaddled in his grimy bedclothes, then unceremoniously hurled overboard. A watery grave in China would be the end of him.

He was in the last days of a three-year expedition to China, conducted at the behest of the Royal Horticultural Society of London. He was there to find and collect samples of the Orient's botanical treasures, the remarkable breadth of which promised wealth and fame to anyone who could determine what a plant could be used for in the West. (And could return to England with the specimen – and himself – alive.) Fortune's assignment included procuring 'the peaches of Pekin, cultivated in the Emperor's Garden and weighing 2 lbs', among other imagined delicacies. Untold thousands of species awaited discovery by Fortune. In addition to living flora, he would take home a pressed herbarium and intricate botanical drawings penned by the finest draughtsmen in China. With every seed, plant, graft and clone collected, Fortune was advancing Western knowledge of the East and of botany.

Each new plant he catalogued was significant, not only for its novelty value but for its possible utility to the British Empire. The nineteenth-century world was revolutionised by the mechanised manufacture of natural products into refined goods; cotton became cloth on automated looms, iron ore was transformed into train tracks and steamships' hulls, clay became stoneware and porcelain. China was a frontier of agricultural riches and industrial possibilities.

But, lying feverish in his bunk, Fortune could not believe he or his plants would ever find their way safely back to the gardens of Britain. He was in the greatest danger he had ever known, even after three years living in China as a foreigner.

'It seemed hard for me to die . . . without a friend or countryman to close my eyes, or follow me to my last resting place; home, friends, and country, how doubly dear they did seem to me then!' he later wrote.

But Fortune was too young to be picked prematurely off the vine, and too promising. His life was emblematic of the many opportunities being opened up to entrepreneurial Britons with the expansion of the Empire. His roots were modest, his early education in rural horticulture learned at the elbow of his 'hedger' father, a hired farm worker. Yet he rose to a place of status and stature in the new world of professional botany. The younger Fortune had no formal higher education beyond his parish schooling in the tiny town of Edrom, in the Scottish borders; his knowledge of Natural History was not won at the universities of Oxford or Edinburgh, but from folk practice and professional apprenticeship. He gained a first-class certificate in horticulture, a trade qualification, but lacked the degree in medicine which was a common accompaniment to an interest in botany among those he aspired to join as a peer. For all that, Fortune was ambitious, with a colonialist's striving for achievement. For many nineteenth-century Scots as well as English second sons of some talent and no sinecure, seeking an opportunity abroad was the only way to advance in the rigid Victorian social hierarchy. There were untold opportunities to make a decent living exploiting the untapped resources of the Empire.

With his lively mind, Fortune rose quickly through the ranks of horticulture, first in the Botanic Garden at Edinburgh and later at the Royal Horticultural Society's gardens in Chiswick. Based on his skills at cultivating orchids and hothouse ornamentals – the showy, rare plants from the Orient – Fortune was the Society's first choice to explore China at the close of the First Opium War. The Society was the arbiter of all things green and growing in England. At lively meetings, botanists and zoologists presented papers and discussed new developments in their fields, coming thick and fast with the increase in British global dominion. The Society was founded in 1804 by John Wedgwood, Charles Darwin's maternal uncle. Its journals detailed the classification of the newest plants from the farthest reaches of Her Majesty's Empire. The Society's botanists were busily engaged in the great project of naming and describing every species according to the methods by which they reproduced, a system recently introduced in Europe by the great Carl Linné, known as Linnaeus.

Victorian England had a great passion for natural exotica, for the insects, fossils, and plants collected by its missionaries, officers and merchants on the high seas. At home the rural peasantry was moving off the land and into the city as industrialisation took hold and farmland was enclosed by the gentry. Britons yearned for nature, in all its forms, and a new market evolved to supply British households with plants. Potted ferns of all varieties became a national obsession and soon were seen everywhere: on decorative porcelain, wallpaper and textiles, in the conservatories of the rich and on the windowsills of the poor. Easy to grow and propagate, hardy enough to transplant, ferns had a wild, uncultivated look that reflected a broader national pastoralism.

In pursuit of a more exotic trophy, the Sixth Duke of Devonshire paid a hundred guineas, about $12,000 today, or £6,000, for the first imported example of the Philippine orchid, *Phalaenopsis amablis*. The Duke nearly squandered his fortune on his passion for flowers. The amabilis orchid, with its snow white oblong petals and yellow lips, was striking and delicate, hence its name. It was beloved by Society members and hugely profitable to its discoverer. A British plant hunter could make a mint feeding England's craving for greenery.

Since China had been closed to Westerners for centuries, it remained a blank on plant-hunting maps, a place once marked 'Here be dragons'. China considered itself the Centre of the World, but the Middle Kingdom was almost entirely removed from the global stage, albeit Chinese civilisation was more than 5,000 years old, compared to modern Europe's meagre

500 years, and China's borders could easily contain the entire Western continent. The West, with little real knowledge of China, projected on to it a million fantasies of paradise, danger and exoticism. All the yearning reflected in England's desire for gardens was met and magnified by its perception of China as the untouched Shangri-La of horticulture.

Had Europeans been permitted a closer look at China, they would have found a country seething with internal unrest and governed by hated foreigners. The Manchus had crossed the Great Wall from the north and for two hundred years had ruled the capital of Peking (now Beijing) and the ethnic Han Chinese, demanding fealty and taxes. Secret societies abounded in the south, sworn to combat the alien emperors of the Manchurian Qing (pronounced *ching*) Dynasty. The countryside was full of thieves and highwaymen, the seaways plagued by pirates. Famines blighted the lives of the rural peasantry, as did corrupt officials, the Confucian-educated scholar class known as Mandarins, while squalor overwhelmed the cities.

The British had some knowledge of China's affairs through trading contact over the centuries – the East India Company had been doing business in Canton for almost two centuries – but the interior of China was simply unfathomable. There were two things England did know, however: there were bound to be marvellous plants in China, and the economic future of Great Britain might well depend upon them.

The Emperor of China, however, took pains to prevent interlopers from exploring his territory and capitalising on its resources. In the wake of the First Opium War, the Treaty of Nanking had granted Britain rights to trade in Fuzhou and four other 'treaty ports', walled coastal cities previously forbidden to outsiders. But suspicion of the British and their intentions was widespread, with white men officially forbidden from travelling beyond the newly constructed foreign concessions in the port cities. And if Chinese laws could not keep foreigners inside the city walls, the realities of life in China might: it was a hostile environment to Britons unaccustomed to the humidity, insects, vermin, disease, and rotten sanitation of even the most civilised outposts. China was nowhere a sane man would wish to live, or die.

In the autumn of 1842, news of the peace between China and England reached the halls of the Royal Horticultural Society which saw its opportunity to send an expedition into deepest China. Plants were now widely recognised as a British priority. So much so that Robert Fortune was the first person given leave by the Foreign Office to travel to China at the end of hostilities.

The Society was a gentlemen's club, yet Fortune was chosen for the China expedition despite lacking the usual background that would fit him for such a job. The Society paid him wages of only £100 a year (about $10,000 in today's money, or £5,000), a paltry sum on which to raise a family, and one that would not be increased during Fortune's entire three-year tenure. When he dared to try and negotiate for a better stipend, the Society sharply rebuked him. 'The mere pecuniary returns of your mission ought to be but a secondary consideration' next to 'the distinction and status which you could not have attained any other way', he was told.

Fortune was neither a gentleman nor a man of property, and so in the Society's eyes was entitled to none of their perquisites, including such niceties as a rifle, pistols, bullets and powder. His mission was to study and expropriate the rare plants of the Orient, which did not, they maintained, require weaponry. It was not for the plants, Fortune argued, but for his own skin that he needed weapons. His fellow professional botanists were sympathetic. When gentlemen plant hunters needed guns, they had the means with which to purchase them. But Fortune was not a rich man.

Eventually, the Society members agreed that their investment in the China expedition would be forfeit, or at least greatly reduced, if Fortune were killed before its completion. The Society refused to raise his salary but reluctantly gave him some guns.

As it turned out, their choice of Fortune to lead the expedition was a triumph. He faithfully reported back to them all the details of his botanical finds, shipping to England as many living examples of the new and wonderful plants of China as he could. He took cuttings, made grafts, kept notes, and wrote detailed letters for the botanical gardeners of the world, many of whom received the fruits of his discoveries as part of a programme of global, imperial plant exchange. Already, by the end of his first trip to China, Fortune was considered a success in the circles of scientific exploration, the first of his shipments having been received, propagated and duly celebrated.

It helped that he had a collector's eye for the rare and wonderful, as well as for the expensive and ornate; he plumbed the reaches of China's natural wonders, keeping his eye trained on the flowers that, while not of immense significance to science, might fetch a high price under the gavel. Over three years, Fortune discovered the winter-blooming jasmine, to brighten dreary days in the gardens of the West; the bleeding heart, a floral image of broken-heartedness to play to Victorian romanticism; the Chinese fan palm, a gift of colonial exotica to Queen Victoria on her thirty-second birthday; the white wisteria; the corsage gardenia (*Gardenia fortunei*); and the lilac daphne (*Daphne fortunei*). Fortune found the fabled double yellow rose in a Mandarin's garden, climbing walls 15 foot high, (it is commonly known as 'Fortune's Double Yellow' or 'The Gold of Ophir'). One discovery in particular – the kumquat, *Citrus fortunei*, or commonly *Fortunella* – the miniature citrus fruit with edible skin, would make him immortal. Though Fortune did not own the property rights to any of his botanical finds, he would travel home with many other curiosities and trinkets, rare gems, pottery and pieces of jade, with which to increase his bank balance.

Beyond his scrupulously observed field notes, Fortune kept a diary of his exploits and derring-do, a first-hand account of the exotic people and customs of China as he encountered them. He wrote about his servants and interpreters, officials, merchants, herbalists, artists, fishermen, gardeners, monks, prostitutes, street pedlars, women and children. Like other travellers of the Victorian era, upon his return in 1847 Fortune published his experiences in the form of a travelogue. *Three Years' Wanderings in the Northern Provinces of China* is liberally sprinkled with the geographical and botanical descriptions one might find in any horticultural study, but it also contains his jaunty and unstinting reminiscences of meeting fellow British expatriates in the treaty ports, of the temples and priests and shopkeepers he encountered, of the dangers of bandits, and the many jaundiced zombies he observed, in thrall to the scourge of the opium poppy.

Fortune's trip began in Hong Kong, Britain's newest colonial possession, during the typhoon season of 1843. He declared the island to be 'in lamentable condition', suffering from the bad air, the *mal aria*, which laid waste to its European inhabitants. 'Viewed as a place of trade, I fear Hong Kong will be a failure,' he wrote, none too prophetically. Sailing up the coast towards the most northerly trading port at

Shanghai, Fortune was nearly shipwrecked in a typhoon. 'Some idea may be formed of the storm when I mention that a large fish weighing at least 30 pounds was thrown out of the sea on to the skylight upon the poop, the frame of which was dashed to pieces and the fish fell through and landed upon the cabin table.' While plant hunting on mainland hillsides, Fortune was pickpocketed, chased and beaten by thieves, who threw a brick at his head. 'I was stunned for a few seconds and leaned against a wall to breathe and recover myself . . . The rascals again surrounded me and relieved me of several articles,' he wrote.

Fortune also visited opium-trading dens and held forth on the perils of addiction. 'I have often seen the drug used and I can assert, in the great majority of cases it is not immod-erately indulged in. At the same time, I am well aware that, like the use of ardent spirits in our own country, it is frequently carried to a most lamentable excess.'

He hunted for living treasure in the gardens of Mandarins. Seeking access to the gardens of Suzhou, a forbidden city, he donned a disguise. 'I was, of course, travelling in the Chinese costume; my head was shaved, I had a splendid wig and tail, of which some Chinaman in former days must have been extremely vain; and upon the whole I believe I made a very fair Chinaman.' He fooled the gatekeepers of Souzhou into believing he was himself Chinese, rich and elegant. 'How surprised they would have been had it been whispered that an Englishman was standing amongst them.'

Three Years detailed Fortune's evolution as a man confronted with an inscrutable society. At first he approached China with all the arrogance of a colonialist; it was a country full of 'wretched Chinese hovels, cotton fields, and tombs'. Fortune was, on arrival, a missionary for the Western way of life, mocking any Chinese notions of superiority.

European expatriates would be examples to the Chinese, any 'peeps at our comforts and refinements may have a tendency to raise the "barbarian race" a step or two higher in the eyes of the "enlightened" Chinese'. Yet after three years, his opinion had softened, for he could not have successfully completed his mission without close contact with everyday Chinese, and, in so doing, the country assumed a human face for him.

The barriers to penetrating China were enormous: linguistic, social and official. Fortune was almost entirely dependent on his Chinese servants to help him transcend his outsider status. The success of his attempts to collect plants and shrubs required at least the assent and often the assistance of Chinese peasants, boatmen, coolies, guides and porters. He found many enablers willing to help him sidestep national and cultural boundaries – for a price. He had contact with ordinary Chinese people in a way that few Westerners had or wanted. Fortune grew to hope for unity and reconciliation between the two nations. 'Nothing,' he wrote, 'can give the Chinese a higher idea of our civilisation and attainments than our love for flowers, or tend more to create a feeling between us and them.'

Three Years' Wandering was a critical and popular triumph. A reviewer for *The Times* of London, the paper of record, wrote:

When readers have recovered from the intoxication produced by the exciting drink of *Uncle Tom's Cabin*, we seriously recommend them . . . to 'try Fortune's mild Bohea'. There is no adulteration in the article. It is pure – almost to a fault, and has to be taken, as the Chinese themselves drink tea, without the admixture of milk and sugar, for luscious ornament and superfluous additions our singleminded author has none. Concerning the flavour there can be no mistake. One trial will prove the excellence of the commodity, and he that sips once will be soothed and sip again.

The book was avidly enjoyed by an audience of armchair botanists and starry-eyed colonialists, but also with those who simply liked a gripping tale. Fortune rendered his experiences into the Victorian *Bildungsroman*: living by his wits and full of improvisation, the young man from the provinces makes his name in the unlikeliest of ways and is celebrated on his return to London.

But if one vignette in particular stood out, and made Fortune's name as a hero, it was the tale that began with him in his fevered state, lying in a cabin belowdecks on the treacherous River Min.

Fortune's flat-bottomed ship made a turn north from the rocky mouth of the river, out into the South China Sea. The small wooden craft sailed on an early-morning wind, her rattan sail full, patched together like a quilt and pouching out between bamboo stays.

The cabin door burst open and a breathless captain and pilot began to prattle in a spirited Fukienese, the dialect of the coast.

'Pirates!' they announced. *Feitu!*

On deck it was a scene of mad chaos. The captain started ripping up floorboards in order to stash his valuables away while crew members likewise sought places to hide the few pieces of copper money they had managed to set aside in a life of hard sea labour. Fortune took out his telescope: he could see five ships on the horizon, unmarked, flying no imperial flags. They could only be pirate ships.

As the first enemy ship bore down on them, its crew, some fifty or so strong, gathered along the gangway and began 'hooting and yelling like demons'.

'Their fearful yells seem to be ringing in my ears even now, after this lapse of time, and when I am on the other side of the globe,' Fortune later wrote.

Looking again at the crew of his own ship, he saw a subtle transformation in them; the men had made themselves look like beggars, as if they had been at sea for forty years or more, now wearing only the suggestion of clothes, torn rags and shreds of rice sacks. With enemies about to board, it was idiocy to look prosperous.

Piracy was the scourge of China. Trade with the West brought in untold foreign wealth and so the coasts had become a battleground between the Mandarins who sought to win official control and a mutinous waterworld of thieves. Life in a pirate gang was a frenzy of sodomy, gang rape, torture and cannibalism, but mostly it was a way to make a living outside the rigid structure of Qing society. There was little booty in taking a small boat like Fortune's – a few captives to sell as slaves, a vessel to commandeer or sink – but there was also very little risk. The pirate ship could easily outgun, outclass, outman and outmanoeuvre Fortune's cumbersome cargo junk.

His crew hauled up baskets of stones from the hold, emptying the rocks all over the deck. In peacetime, these stones functioned as ballast; in war they were the most rudimentary of weapons. As Fortune noted, however, 'All the pirate junks carried guns, and consequently a whole deck load of stones could be of very little use.'

'Bring the junk round,' one of his crew yelled.

'Run us back to the cliffs and hide among them,' another argued.

'Fight!' cried one. *Da!*

'Flee!' yelled another. *Zou!*

'Job's comforters', Fortune called them, though no one could understand his English or the biblical reference.

The fate of a Westerner taken by pirates was often a bloody one: the brigands would hold Fortune for ransom and torture him. Under duress, he would be forced to write letters to the British missions, begging for impossible sums to be paid on his behalf. One English captive held in such circumstances wrote, 'I saw one man, nailed through his feet with large nails, then beaten with four rattans twisted together, till he vomited blood; and after remaining some time in this state, he was taken ashore and cut into pieces.' Another 'was fixed upright, his bowels cut open and his heart taken out, which they afterwards soaked in spirits and ate'.

Pirates would not shrink from cruelty when their own death sentence was assured. The state's punishment for piracy, was worse than the pirates' punishment for captives: in China, they were sentenced to death by slicing. Nailed to a cross, pirates were sliced with a sharp knife, cut into either 120, 72, 36, or 24 pieces. Of the lightest sentence, 24 cuts, one observer wrote:

The first and second cuts remove the eyebrows; the third and fourth, the shoulders; the fifth and sixth, the breasts, the seventh and eighth, the parts between each hand and elbow; the ninth and tenth, the parts between each elbow and shoulder; the eleventh and twelfth, the flesh of each thigh; the thirteenth and fourteenth, the calf of each leg; the fifteenth pierces the heart; the sixteenth severs the head from the body; the seventeenth and eighteenth cut off the hands; the nineteenth and twentieth, the arms; the twenty first and twenty-second, the feet; the twenty-third and twenty-fourth, the legs.

As Fortune himself would be the choicest of the pirates' prizes, he mustered his depleted strength and rallied from his fever, imposing what order he could on the pandemonium. He raised his pistol, taking aim at the head of his own helmsman.

'My gun is nearer you than those of the pirates,' he threatened. 'And if you move from the helm, depend upon it, I will shoot you.'

The enemy ship fired a broadside cannon. The crew, every man but Fortune's terrified pilot, fled belowdecks. The cannonball whizzed over Fortune's head, directly between the sails.

The pirate ship was at least half the size again of Fortune's but her guns were fixed along her gangway, the passageways along either side of the ship, which meant that if the ship was approaching head on, she had to turn at a sharp angle in order to fire. As the cannon volley continued, Fortune settled on his plan: he would not retaliate from a distance but would allow the pirates to believe his ship could be easily boarded. Bringing them into close range would give the advantage to Fortune's precision weaponry over the pirates' heavy and clumsy cannons. The Chinese did not have rifles or pistols, only locally made muskets, or matchlocks, which were as likely to blow up on the marksman as fire a shot.

The pirates bore down on Fortune, guns ablaze. When they were twenty yards off he took his chance. Belly to floor, he crawled towards the high quarterdeck at the stern. Rising abruptly, he let loose with his rifle – both barrels.

In an instant the terrified crew of the pirate ship disappeared, hiding behind bulwarks. Fortune's shot was true. Someone was injured, probably dead. The pirate ship was suddenly a ghost vessel: no one was steering her; her sails luffed helplessly into the wind.

Fortune's craft, on the other hand, had its pilot and a full sail.

Pirates travelled in packs, however, and shortly afterwards

the second ship gained on them. There were three more in the distance.

Fortune then hit upon an idea prompted by his rag-bedecked crewmen and his own experiences visiting the Mandarin gardens of Suzhou in disguise: borrowed clothes, cultural cross-dressing, transvestism. He still had several changes of Western clothing stored in his cabin below. What if he dressed up the crew as white men? 'It now struck me that perhaps I might be able to deceive the pirates with regard to our strength,' he wrote. The Chinese were essentially blind at sea: where all British ships carried telescopes, and some even binoculars, few Chinese vessels had them. Fortune's weapons were superior at close range. If the pirates believed there to be a full European arsenal aboard, they might be less enthusiastic about running down the junk.

Fortune dressed the 'least Chinese-looking Chinamen' from the crew in his remaining Western finery. Out of their rags, the crew began to look like Victorian travellers, in frock coats, trousers, and heeled shoes. He instructed the costumed men to take up sticks that might look like rifles at long range, sticks such as the short levers used for hoisting the sails.

The crew looked smart and, perhaps from a distance, even British; but with pirates at close range they were petrified. When a cannon volley began, every man fled belowdecks, leaving the true coin, Robert Fortune, alone.

The second pirate ship began to fire: more shrapnel, more terror, more cries. But before the brigands had time to reload, Fortune was on his feet.

He let loose the contents of his rifle: two shots, fore and aft. Then he fired his revolvers.

He killed the pirates' helmsman.

For want of a pilot, the vessel heeled under the wind.

On the horizon, the remainder of the pirate fleet began to turn about.

Fortune's crew emerged from below, shouting and screaming in victory as the pirates had done before them. Some were in English finery, with tight trousers and nipped jackets, others in tattered Chinese rags, their long hair flying loose. They screamed taunts at the retreating pirates.

'Come back and fight like men!' they called.

The crew picked up the stones littering the decks and pitched them into the water after their retreating enemy.

'A stranger who had not seen these gentry before would have supposed them the bravest men in existence,' Fortune later commented. 'Fortunately the pirates did not think it proper to accept the challenge.'

'With the captain, pilot, crew and passengers, I was now one of the greatest and best men in existence,' he wrote. 'They actually came and knelt before me, as to some superior being.'

His seagoing escapade, and the attention it attracted upon publication of his book, was to become an essential first move in an unfolding global game of risk, revenge and espionage.

The interior of China was within reach of the West. Fortune had become a seasoned China hand, an expert, revered amongst the locals in a way that no tradesman, military man or missionary could ever be. His arrogance was transformed into real expertise.

When Robert Fortune returned to China on his next expedition, much more than the fate of a few orchids would be at stake. He would change the fate of nations.

2

East India House, City of London, 12 January 1848

East India House occupied a prestigious site on Leadenhall Street in the centre of the City of London. The building was grand. Its façade had Ionic columns supporting a triangular tympanum decorated with emblems of global commerce: at the corners, a figure representing Europe rode a horse and the figure of Asia sat astride a camel; between Europe and Asia rode King George in flowing Roman dress. The mad king, who famously lost the reins of thirteen profitable colonies in the Americas, brandished a sword in defence of international trade. Though the architectural pediment faced north, every man who walked beneath it into the bustling East India Company offices below faced due east, towards the Orient, the centre of profit for the venerable Company.

Amidst the hubbub of the trading house whose day-to-day activities included the recopying of letters, the serving of breakfast and the distribution of favours, perquisites and privileges in assemblies that lasted from dawn to dusk, a wooden chest arrived from India. It was carried through panelled hallways sumptuously adorned with portraits, statues and memorabilia, beyond a vast library and a museum filled to brimming with models, coins, medals, fossils, stuffed birds, sculptures and reliefs. Shouldered by porters from the dockyards, the chest passed before a clockwork tiger, which, when wound up, would 'eat' a wooden British soldier – once the property of an Indian sultan before his defeat at the hands of the Company.

Light but large, the chest was delivered to a young clerk who pried off its tin-lined lid. From the contents of the chest, he was to prepare several packages of small size but great importance. With a scale before him, brass weights lined up by size, he began to measure out uniform quantities from the box, carefully depositing each into a wax-dipped cloth bag. He was readying parcels of loose tea – dry, fragrant, herbal, and portentous – to be delivered to the best tea distributors in London.

The task of tea allocation was hardly among the clerk's usual duties which were normally those of any secretary: writing out triplicates of every document, letter and bill of lading that reached the offices of the Company from the Orient. This particular chore was therefore as unusual as it was critical. To a man making a decent wage of £300 a year for work that was neither taxing nor glamorous, this task of doling out some packets of tea would be among the most significant actions he would perform in his lifelong career. It was no exaggeration to say that his employer's survival hinged on whether the tea he was dispatching made a favourable impression on its distinguished recipients.

Officially titled the United Company of Merchants of England Trading to the East Indies, sometimes referred to as 'John Company' or, even more incongruously, 'The Honourable Company', the clerk's employer was a global corporation that had weathered three hundred glorious and mostly profitable years in trade with the East. It colonised nearly as much of the world as it left free, unifying and governing the subcontinent of India to become the world's first and largest multinational company. For very good reason, it was called the 'Grandest Society of Merchants in the Universe'.

When Queen Elizabeth granted her royal charter to the East India Company in 1600, the Virgin Queen gave the Company all trading rights in the East Indies, a mandate as broad and valuable as any a public concern has held. For the first hundred years of its existence, it largely bought spices and fabrics in the Orient and sold them in London. To fund the expeditions eastwards, the Company sold shares and stockholders received a dividend on profits. The operation was enormously successful for England and the Company prospered.

As profits and opportunities grew, however, trade with the East became more and more complicated. John Company became the *de facto* government of many of the lands in which it did business: it could acquire territory, mint money, command armies, sign treaties, make war and peace, and develop its own judicial and taxation systems. It became a peer to empires and states, and as such was something entirely new under the sun.

The East India Company gave birth to so much for so many: the fortunes of the Pitt Family, the military reputation of Wellington, the Empire of Hastings. One Company governor, Elihu Yale, funded a college of some apparent renown. The club-like offices at Leadenhall Street employed such fine minds as John Stuart Mill and Charles Lamb. With nearly 350 employees in the London house, it was the single largest private employer in Britain. In many ways, the Company acted as an immense employment opportunity for the nation, hiring as many soldiers as did the Crown and thus doubling jobs in the military, while increasing Civil Service positions by 50 per cent. The Company extended a gentle-manly capitalism to England's otherwise property-less leisure class, largely southern English and public school-educated, 'Some of the best working blood of England is in India,' commented one Company man.

Managed in London by its Court of Directors, the organisation of the East India Company looked very much like the management structures of our modern corporations. Before the days of the East India Company, businesses were generally owned by the same people who managed them. But the shareholders of East India Company had no say in its day-to-day operations. A professional managerial class arose in England and becoming a member of it became synonymous with middle-class success. The Company's international ambitions were so extensive and its structure so complex, it developed elaborate international banking and inventory systems to track goods, services and debts across oceans. Managers were empowered to make high-volume transactions in several markets all at once, using whatever technology and information was available: from the letter to the telegraph to the hunch. In its reach and rationale, the East India Company rivalled any of our modern-day multinationals; it was the first truly global company. And, like today's international businesses, the Company would do anything to get ahead of the game.

It was believed that tea was the very commodity to keep the Company pre-eminent. Tea was first introduced into England in the 1660s as part of the dowry of Portuguese princess Catherine De Braganza when she married Charles II. As a commodity, it was perfect for the East Indiamen merchant boats in that it was lightweight, packed easily, and could withstand the vagaries of many months spent in an ocean crossing. An exotic luxury, tea rapidly became a favourite way amongst the upper classes of signifying civility and taste in the chilly, wet climate of Britain. Of course, once the upper ranks latch on to anything, it rapidly percolates downward through society, and so by the mid-eighteenth century tea was the most popular drink throughout Britain, outselling beer.

Previously just another trading commodity to the Honourable Company, tea had become a staple of British life. To be English was to drink tea: wives put tea on the breakfast table; the British Government paid for an empire with Tea Tax revenue; and the bankers of the Empire understood for two hundred years that it was tea that made the Far East trade go round. Tea was an 'essential' and 'necessary' to British life. It was also a significant profit centre for the government, a multi-billion-pound industry, accounting for as much as 10 per cent of the total British economy as measured by tax revenues to the exchequer. And the East India Company had its stamp on every single case shipped into England.

The financial situation of the Company began to be threatened when Parliament made a series of moves in the early-nineteenth century to withdraw their licence to trade with Asia. The Company's royal charter initially gave it a total monopoly on trade with the Orient at a time when no one really understood the implications of what that meant. Monopolies, by definition, have a way of squelching competition and innovation. As the Company became the behemoth of the Orient, Parliament in London moved to curb its domination. Rival firms objected to the high barriers to trading in foreign ports. A sense of populism in England extended to the business practices of the Empire – as the men of Britain became increasingly enfranchised politically, why couldn't every British trading firm have the same rights to trade in the Far East? In 1813 Westminster withdrew the Company's monopoly on trade in India; it was left to rule the sub-continent as the *de facto* government, but necessarily had to allow other corporations to do business in Indian ports and profit on Indian-made goods. Despite this check on Company power, it collected tax revenues in India equal to half of the total tax revenues of Britain and remained financially healthy. It also retained its most valuable monopoly: on trade in China.

China had once been a source of pure profit to the Company; tea's margins were deliciously high, and its value by the turn of the nineteenth century equalled that of all other Chinese goods combined. But free trade advocates, including Adam Smith, continued to rail against the Company's dominance in the China trade. The Company had the run of Cathay, every chest of tea, silk or porcelain out of Canton travelled on East Indiamen ships, and money practically minted itself. An 1834 Act of Parliament ended the artificially imposed supremacy, stripping John Company of her long-sanctioned monopoly over China. She would now have to compete to win. Free trade sentiments and mercantilist tendencies stirring in England ensured that there was fierce jostling to take part in the lucrative tea business. Leaner, younger trading firms were docking in Canton, offloading opium and uploading tea for England. With newer ships, these firms could sail between continents in record time. The triple-masted East Indiamen looked old, bloated and slow, much like the East India Company itself. It seemed as if the Company's days of supremacy in the East were numbered.

After the loss of her last trade monopoly, China became mostly a headache for the Company due to a series of unsolved problems. The Empire of Great Britain owed its entire acquaintance with tea, not to mention its continuing fix, to the Empire of China. The Chinese picked tea, roasted tea, blended tea, and then sold it to England at a painful mark-up. China was in complete control of the drink that had dominated British taste for two centuries. Dependence on another country was a recurring blow to Imperial Britain's sense of self-sufficiency. It was galling to be so reliant on an often churlish and disobliging nation. The Chinese tea monopoly frustrated the Company, for China would raise prices on inferior goods whenever it pleased and the mighty will of Great Britain could do nothing to stop it.

To East India House, it had long seemed preposterous that any country, let alone one of 'backwards Orientals', could so thoroughly ignore trade initiatives from a nation whose mighty navy was, at the time, painting the world pink. Yet isolationist China successfully kept Great Britain at arm's length for two centuries or more, even though Britain purchased one out of every five chests of tea manufactured in China. Tea was a mere plant, yet it remained as enigmatic and fiercely protected as the Chinese who harvested it. Despite a century of diplomatic approaches, the Chinese had yielded absolutely no secrets about the manufacture of tea to the British. How it was grown, by whom, and in what conditions remained a mystery to the West. Even the very names for tea were inscrutable: *Lark's Tongue, Dragon's Well, Jade Girl Peak, Looking Glass Rock, Water Tortoise Stones, Rock of Three Monks*. Were these green teas? Blacks? How could one label them with such nonsense? How could the Company be sure the teas would taste the same from year to year? Its Court of Directors grew tired of dealing with grasping middlemen and did not want to share any part of their profits with the infuriating Chinese. Tea had become a symbol of the one major country on earth that still resisted Britain's Empire.

If the tea trade had been the greatest boon for the East India Company in its prime, by the mid-nineteenth century the Company was reeling; its tea trade was both in retreat while simultaneously its last, best hope for survival. In India, the Company presided over a parade of human catastrophes:

a famine that killed more than 10 million, heavy death tolls from warfare between states, corruption, expansionism, drug-dealing and ethnic cleansing. And governing a subcontinent was an expensive business. To safeguard its territory the Company was mounting military campaigns in Afghanistan and the Punjab, with scant resources to pay for them. New colonies were supposed to create new markets for British-manufactured goods, but there was little desire amongst the Asian peasantry for British woollens.

In the shadow of these international tempests, the Company clerk kept his hand steady and deliberate as he measured out the chest of Indian tea in the dark-panelled confines of East India House. This was Himalayan tea, never before seen in England. It had been sent on the orders of Viscount Hardinge himself, from Calcutta, as part of a plan to save the Company.

Hardinge, a one-handed former soldier, had battled Napoleon side by side with Nelson and Wellington. He missed Waterloo by a mere two days after losing his hand at the Battle of Ligny. The Viscount was such a favourite of Wellington's that he was nevertheless presented with the gift of Napoleon's sword. Hardinge went from the military to a life in politics, serving and a Member of Parliament and later at Cabinet level as Secretary for War, in both Whig and Conservative administrations. He was an able hand at the tiller – even if he only had one – and the Honourable Company counted itself lucky to have such a trusted soldier helming India as Governor-General from 1844–8. When he suggested that this Indian tea ought to be sent to London's tasters and blenders, the finest practitioners in the entire world, the Court of Directors of the East India Company hastily and heartily agreed. The tea was sent.

Himalayan tea was not the first tea produced on Indian soil. The Company had been growing tea there for at least ten years, propagated out of native Indian tea plants in Assam Province. Indian tea was initially discovered in Assam by Company Medical Corps surgeons as early as 1815, but was not formally acknowledged as such until 1831. Indian tea grew well in its sea-level home soil, near Burma, where the natives chewed rather than drank it. In the following years, the Company invested millions in the experimental cultivation of native tea, to see if it could be grown in Indian gardens for the domestic market. To an extent, the plan had worked. The Company discovered it could grow native tea; it could produce a leaf that looked like the tea leaves of China; it could train natives to pick and prepare tea. But the Company could never make Assam tea taste good – or at least not as good as China tea, the finest in the world and the only one that mattered to a thirsty English market.

Assam tea had a terrible bite to it, with a hot sooty taste. Even today, Assam is seldom graded fine at auction and is appreciated only by those who desire a strong nose and a certain maltiness to their brew. It doesn't grow well either, giving a poor return per acre. Now as then, Assam tea is largely used in blends when the prevailing notes of dainty florals require a slight undertone of heft, or of old shoe. Within a few years of their tea experiment, the Company saw that Assam would never fetch the high prices of its rival, and would certainly never overtake China tea in the world marketplace. There was not enough profit to be had from Assam tea, so the Company begrudgingly divested itself of its tea assets there.

Himalayan tea was the Company's next big hope. 'I consider it highly probable that in the course of a few years, the cultivation of [Himalayan] tea is likely to prove a highly valuable source of revenue for the state,' enthused Hardinge in a letter to the Court of Directors dated 20 September 1847.

No apparent difficulties exist to the spread of Tea cultivation in the Hills to an almost unlimited extent and I have every confidence that at no remote period Tea will be produced in sufficient amount not only to meet the probably large demand in India but also in quantity and sufficient fineness in quality to enable it to compete with the Tea of China in European markets and to render England in some degree independent of a foreign Country for its supplies of this necessary of life.

The Himalayas possessed the same growing conditions as China's best tea regions. They were sub-tropical, on roughly the same latitude as Cairo, but high and cool so the tea would be slow-growing and retain its pungency. There was infinite space in the Himalayas for tea production – the natives seemed neither to want nor to make use of most hillsides, for food or profit. Under Hardinge's orders, the Company made elaborate plans: experimental plantations, a minimum of 500 acres each, would allow for economies of scale, capital investment, and the European efficiency that Chinese tea production lacked. British laws and British investors would oversee the sale and merchandising of Himalayan tea; there would be no middlemen, no double-dealing, no Chinese-style obfuscation. Labour in India was at least as cheap as in China, both countries having a surfeit of manpower. The quality would improve and the prices would drop. Growing tea would be like printing money – leaves that were picked for a penny could be sold for three pounds in London. And the Himalayan tea over which Hardinge enthused seemed to have the potential to match the tea that had hitherto captured British taste and imagination: China tea.

The East India House clerk, a small player in a grand story, closed the bags of tea and sealed them with the wax stamp of the East India Company. Each was sent to one of the esteemed tea brokers of London, the blenders, tasters and traders whose noses and tongues determined the price of a commodity and the fate of nations: Mssrs R. Gibbs & Co., Peek Brothers & Co., Miller & Lowcock, and the revered House of Twinings.

The Court was 'requesting to be favoured with their respective opinion of the quality and value of some specimens of tea grown and manufactured in the District of Kumaon, together with any practical suggestions for its improvement which may occur to them'.

At last messengers arrived to pick up the deliveries.

The Court waited patiently for a response.

When the reports came, they were good. Extremely good.

Twinings, Gibbs, Peek, Miller and Lowcock wrote that the Himalayan tea was as fine in quality as the finest of the China teas. The leaves were perfection, beautiful to look at, picked at the right time, light on the tongue, delicate in the cup, brewing up a rich liquor with a golden hue. The tea would compete admirably at auction, they would stake their reputation on it.

There were caveats, howevers, and exceptions, the experts noted: the Himalayan tea was 'lacking in fragrance', that is, it did not have the floral nose of the finest China teas.

Some of this was a question of stock – the Himalayan teas in the sample were raised from Chinese seed, but not the finest seed from the best regions. These were ordinary seeds smuggled out of Canton, in the south of China, the only place that Englishmen were then allowed. Canton tea was known to be of extremely low quality compared to other Chinese tea regions.

Beyond the quality of the tea stock, none of the Himalayan tea's faults was inherent. Some of the tasters' complaints were instead attributable to poor processing and manufacture. The

Himalayan tea did not have the perfumed notes of China teas which were packed between other materials, such as jasmine, bergamot, lemon or verbena, to scent the brew. The Leadenhall Street tea had besides been poorly packed for shipment, in boxes that were not airtight. The sea air had doubtless tainted the sample, deadening its flavour.

The Company's prototype tea lacked refinement, but if the methods and practices of the world's finest Chinese tea manufacturers could be imported to the plantations in India, if true experts out of China could train the Himalayan natives in the art and recipes of tea manufacture, then the deficiencies of Himalayan tea could be most profitably redressed.

The East India Company had a near match for Chinese tea and the land for cultivating it at the ready – but the precise recipe still eluded them. The process was simple enough, but impossible to decode from dried leaves alone. East India House was making a huge speculation on Indian-produced tea, but there remained a major obstacle on the path to success: the Company had very little knowledge of how to turn the raw plant into a truly sophisticated beverage.

The Company's experimental tea gardens in the Himalayas totalled little more than 600 acres in 1846 (the season in which Hardinge's tea was grown), but the Court had plans for rapid expansion. The Government of India had over 100,000 acres ready for cultivation that very day. From such acreage, the Company could expect to bring in a profit of almost 4 million rupees a year ($100 million today, or £50 million). But to get to that position six years hence – it takes that long for a tea plant to mature to picking stage – the Company needed hundreds of thousands of Chinese seeds from the finest of China's green and black tea regions straight away.

The Company was not just after plants and seeds and a recipe, it was also after an economic formula: from planting to labour to processing, transport and packaging, how much of the per pound price of tea at the London auction was mark-up, and how much was actual materials, manufacturing cost and labour? How much profit would be in British hands once the Himalayan tea was on the market?

China had manipulated the price of tea over the centuries. Secrecy was their way of defending – the Company might have said inflating – the market for their prized Hysons, Oolongs, Congous, Pekoes, and Gunpowders. Controlling scarcity was a simple way for the Chinese tea market to relieve Britain of more cash. The more opaque the market, the higher the cost of tea. China's entire foreign exchange was largely built on the sale of two commodities – silk and tea – and was thus incredibly vulnerable to the loss of either monopoly. To protect tea was to defend the Chinese economy.

For the Himalayan tea experiment, the Company shopping list was short but precise: the Company sought China's materials, her best tea seeds, green and black; and China's tea knowledge, in the form of Chinese tea makers and tea-manufacturing implements.

The Company was well aware therefore that getting tea out of China would be a difficult undertaking and impossible to achieve through normal diplomatic channels. Her Majesty's Consul in Shanghai, Rutherford Alcock, warned Viscount Hardinge as much. 'It will suggest itself no doubt to your Excellency that the Chinese are likely to regard any demand on my part for tea seeds or plants with great jealousy, and that the attempts in conjunction with efforts to obtain seeds, to induce Chinese skilled in the cultivation and manufacture of tea to leave their country and proceed to India for the purpose of instructing people, must inevitably fail.' In other words, if the East India Company wanted tea for India, it would have to steal it.

Tea met all the definitions of intellectual property: it was a product of high commercial value, manufactured using a formula and process unique to China, which China protected fiercely, and which also gave China a vast advantage over its competitors.

The notion of intellectual property and trade secrets was then brand new, only first articulated in the mid-1840s when a Massachusetts judge ruled in an 1845 patent case that 'only in this way can we protect intellectual property, the labours of the mind, productions and interests as much a man's own . . . as the wheat he cultivates, or the flocks he rears'. In the dawn of 1848, the East India Company was planning a project that was nothing short of industrial espionage. If the Company's scheme was successful, the largest multinational corporation in the world, the East India Company, would enact the greatest theft of trade secrets in the history of mankind.

3

Chelsea Physic Garden,
7 May 1848

Robert Fortune returned to England, to a prestigious new job in botany and his family, all snugly united in a verdant stretch of land by the Thames. On a spring day in 1848, he strolled through the Chelsea Physic Garden, admiring some of his own handiwork. The earth was just warming to life: tulips were out in full flower, lily-of-the-valley dipping gracefully towards the ground. The bulb beds planted in the chilly autumn of last year were coming into bloom. Three years earlier, upon his triumphal return from China, Fortune had been appointed Curator of the Chelsea Physic Garden – something of a vindication of the Royal Horticultural Society's assessment of the value of the mission to his future career. A tree peony was bursting into pyrotechnic display too – it was one of Fortune's most treasured finds from his trip to China, further proof if it were needed of the measure of his fame and success.

Now thirty-five, Fortune's trip to China had changed his life very much for the better. He and his family currently enjoyed an enviable position, with a degree of social prominence and comfort to which he could not otherwise have aspired. His book, *Three Years' Wanderings in the Northern Provinces of China*, had been published a year earlier to rave reviews. His position at the Physic Garden paid £100 per annum (roughly $10,000 in today's dollars, or £5,000), no more than he had earned in China, but in addition to his salary he received the use of a charming brick house in the grounds for his family and servants (though this had no indoor plumbing or sanitation), an allocation of coal, and the right to cultivate his own vegetable garden.

The Chelsea Physic Garden, now in its fifth century, is a bucolic oasis of only four acres, situated by the river, not far from the centre of London. Hidden from the street behind high red-brick walls, it serves as a living museum of the exotic and medicinal plants of the world. A leafy repository in miniature of the horticultural mysteries of a large planet, all neatly classified and arranged in ordered beds, the Physic Garden was then, as it is now, an anomaly of calm near an energetic city.

Victorian London was the centre of the Empire, home to the bankers, industrialists and politicians who were busy modernising the world. It was also crowded and dirty. A thick grey smog caused by the smoke from coal and coke tainted the city air and stained its brick and stone. Sanitation was poor, with no working sewers. The city was dangerously crowded and full of the unemployed, many of them displaced from the countryside, with nothing now to claim their attention but crime.

Yet in these testing times, Fortune enjoyed the best of both worlds: access to the dynamic new advances of industrialisation while enjoying his own plot of ground and kitchen garden. Nestled in the posh area near Sloane Square, the Physic Garden was removed from the stench and pestilence of the centre of the city. Fortune was living in London at an exciting time, but with his own patch of *rus in urbe*. Approaching middle age, he could feed and house his family, and enjoy the respect of his colleagues and peers. It was a comfortable position and he should have been justifiably pleased with his accomplishments.

The Curatorship of the Physic Garden provided him with both a showcase for his talents and the opportunity to establish himself as one of the premier horticulturalists in Britain. The Physic Garden was England's second oldest botanic garden, established in 1673 by the Company of Apothecaries. In Fortune's day, it was a living display of the many novelties and mysteries of the Victorian plant world as well as a leafy laboratory for the study of herbal and vegetable remedies, balms, powders, syrups, tinctures, salves, ointments. *Materia medica* as it is known: peppermint for digestion, belladonna for anesthesia, rhubarb for a purgative, and a hundred other botanical solutions. The Garden of Simples, as it was originally named, was instrumental in the development of horticulture, producing *The Gardeners' and Florists Dictionary: or a Complete System of Horticulture*, which served as the definitive manual on gardening technique and cultivation for gardeners around the world for over a century. Alongside Kew Gardens, just a short journey down the Thames, the Physic Garden played a major role in the development of the profitable and strategically important plant-based industries which drove the economy of the British Empire.

In fact the ideas of plant exchange and Empire developed in tandem. Botanists accompanied Captain Cook's first circumnavigation on the *Endeavour* in 1768. Cook went on to discover Australia while onboard scholars mapped the Transit of Venus, collected samples, and painted pictures of the strange-looking plants of the Southern Hemisphere.

Joseph Banks, a millionaire horticulturalist, was among those who sailed with Cook. As a man of influence, Banks campaigned to put a naturalist aboard all future expeditions of England's world-winning naval fleet. Both Banks and

Cook published accounts of their trip; unlike Fortune, their copious notes were not about their subjective impressions but instead contained precise and descriptive catalogues of what they'd found. These Empire-builders translated faraway locations into concrete knowledge, and with the acquisition of that knowledge England gained a growing confidence that she could possess, command, and profit from the entire world.

Plant exchange was a major source of income for the British Empire which then consisted of old colonies, such as the West Indies, and the recently unified colonies of the Indian subcontinent, along with island outposts in the oceans between. Botanists like Fortune were charged with suggesting how newly discovered plants in foreign dominions could meet Western market demands, how cash crops could be improved through selection and hybridisation, where on the globe to cultivate a particular plant to gain maximum effect from cheap colonial labour, and how to process a plant for market distribution.

Plant hunters were highly trained, steely-eyed, uncompromising men who left home and family for the lure of discovery. In the opening years of the industrial era, botanic research would have been the counterpart to today's industrial research laboratories. Botanical imperialism was a way of making colonies pay their way, and plant hunters became the research and development men of the Empire.

Though science was very much at the core of Fortune's work, he was at heart a gardener, and a gardener is an artist: his canvas is land, his medium plants. A gardener works in a three-dimensional world, taking into account the relative heights of trees and depths of borders, the slope of a hillside and the views to be 'borrowed' or enhanced. But they work in a fourth dimension too: time. A gardener plans for seasons; for which trees will bloom in spring – forsythia, magnolia, cherry, lilac and apple – and which will colour and blush in autumn – acer, euonymus and elder. A gardener's art spans years also: which trees mature fast and easily grow tall, delighting viewers in the short term, such as birch and ash and the softwood evergreens like cedar, fir and pine; and which grow slow and hard, to leave a lasting legacy, the oak, beech and maple which stand for generations. Fortune knew that to be a great gardener demanded great patience.

Gardening appealed to the gentler side of his character. He was a spirited man who enjoyed outdoor living, but he also had an innate sense of what a plant needed to thrive: shade or sun, how much water, whether to plant on a sloping hillside for drainage or in a container so as to coddle and warm the roots. He could kneel in the soil and know, from years of practice, exactly where to cut back a bush and how to gently bring on a bud. Plants thrived for him. Among his gentlemen peers, Fortune was often fawning, keenly aware of his social inadequacies, but in the garden he was sovereign.

He could look upon the reawakening Chelsea Physic Garden with a sense of accomplishment. By his account, the place was in disrepair when he took it over, its borders overgrown, its greenhouses in decay, its catalogues worthless. Fortune, with his knack for organisation and desire for accomplishment, seeded a notable transformation. As he wrote to the Garden Committee of the Society of Apothecaries:

> From various causes with which the Committee are doubt-
> less acquainted, the Garden has been allowed to get into a
> most ruinous condition. When I took charge of it . . . I found
> it overrun with weeds, the Botanical arrangements in confu-
> sion, the exotic plants in the Houses in very bad health, and
> generally in a most unfit state for the purpose for which it
> was designed.

Fortune cleared the weeds, bought new tools, built up collections through donations and plant swaps with other gardens, and, importantly, sold off £364-worth of bank and nursery stock (the near equivalent of £22,000 today, or $44,000) to raise money for the erection of new greenhouses and the repair of the standing ones.

His building plans were timely. The year 1845 had seen the repeal of England's 'glass tax' and he seized the opportunity of lower-priced glaziers to order new glass greenhouses to be built abutting the garden's high brick walls. These semi-glazed constructions, warm and protective, were soon home to the most exotic new horticultural imports: delicate orchids and ornamentals, spiky bougainvillaeas and potted palms, prehistoric ferns and brand new begonias, balsa, breadfruit, bananas and bamboos.

The Physic Garden was still arranged in the formal seventeenth-century pattern with plants heavily pruned, and ordered in geometrically aligned beds. Fortune wished to move away from such excessive formality, though. He reorganised the medical garden along the precise and ordered lines of Linnaeus's sexual classification system.

The Victorian age of exploration fed upon an enthusiasm for the natural sciences generated by the work of Swedish naturalist Carl von Linné (1707–78). Writing under the Latin name, Carols Linnaeus, the scientist invented a taxonomy using two names which categorised the world according to the characteristic sexual organs of plants and animals. Linneaus' work divided life on earth into kingdoms, kingdoms into classes, classes into orders, orders into genera, and genera into species. The name alone gives a great deal of information about a species: if something is in the *mamalia* class, it has hair and secretes milk, if two species have the same order, they are more closely related than a third which is merely in the same class. So when a naturalist discovered a new species of beetle on a trip to the Amazon, there were standard questions to answer involving body type and method of reproduction in order to give his discovery a name. Once a two-part Latin name is assigned, it communicates most of that information to everyone. These simple distinctions brought hierarchy and organisation to the natural world in a way that had previously eluded scientists.

But whereas pious Linnaeus hoped that understanding the relationships between living things would bring him closer to an understanding of the Creator, his work instead founded a scientific revolution. Linnaeus fuelled Europe's burgeoning sense that all things on earth could be understood and mastered by the mental application of mankind. It was an Enlightenment moment.

Under Fortune's new scheme for the Physic Garden, medicinal plants were displayed relative to each other in their natural orders. 'What labour is more severe,' wrote Linnaeus, 'what science more wearisome, than botany?' Severe, yes, Fortune would no doubt have agreed; wearisome often; but it was infinitely rewarding to a man with a mind bent towards order and understanding. One could walk through the Physic Garden and see there the march of science and human learning, the relationships between a living organism and its neighbour. To study the beds of the garden was to see Natural History codified in bloom.

It is perhaps no wonder that in such a turbulent time as the Industrial Revolution gardening became a national obsession in Britain. Patience and time was being lost across the country as technology made things more immediate. Where once a length of cloth, a blanket or some bedding, took long evenings by firelight to create, countless yards of fabric were now spun by the day in the mills of Liverpool and

Manchester. Where a trip across counties was once a marathon by several coaches, it was now a single short ride away by train. Candlelight gave way to gaslight, windpower to steam; the world grew ever-more mechanised and reliable. The insecurity of nature and the vicissitudes of weather were becoming things of the past, increasingly marginalised as modern-day concerns – and as natural processes faded from view, they were fetishised. The new middle classes of the industrial Victorian age regretted this separation from nature, mourned its perceived loss, and would soon be willing to pay a premium for it.

Though Natural History was enjoying its moment of glory, it did not always pay its adherents well. As a contemporary of Fortune's wrote. 'People without independence have no business to meddle with science. It should never be linked with lucre.' There were only a few paid positions within the nexus of loosely connected botanic gardens of the Empire: Kew, St Helena, Calcutta. Though there were some rare and wonderful jobs in botany, such as working for the Royal Horticultural Society, or teaching at University College, or running the botanic gardens in Edinburgh and Oxford, on the whole such jobs were few and competition for them stiff. The university positions went to men with university educations, and the posts were seldom well enough endowed to be a person's only means of support. Many of the naturalists who would make names for themselves – such as Charles Darwin – had enormous private incomes with which to fund their studies. Dilettante country pastors and doctors considered themselves naturalists too, treading the local hillsides to pad their collections and often amassing considerable private libraries to advance their scientific inquiries. Some of the prestigious jobs in botany were passed from father to son and often to grandson, such as the Directorship of the Royal

Botanic Garden at Kew, which would be in the hands of the Hooker family for a continuous sixty-four years.

As Curator of the Chelsea Physic Garden, Fortune had ascended to the highest position available to him – and might well have feared it would be his last. Though he enjoyed the success conferred on him by his China trip, he still faced the limitations of his birth and class.

Fortune was not an untroubled man, but had at least the support and companionship of his wife Jane, *née* Penny, a lively Scottish lass. He could not have gone as far as he did without her help. The Curatorship of the Physic Garden brought him a salary, a home and a vegetable garden – Jane managed two of these three, the household and the vegetable garden. While he was attending to his botanical duties and research, she sowed vegetable seeds in March, moving plants in and out with the sun throughout the spring, transplanting seedlings after the final frosts in May. She weeded and tended and grew the food that her family would eat. She mended old clothes and sewed new ones for a man who was all too often in a thicket of thorns, snagging trousers and socks and coats. Fortune would not have been naked and starving without Jane, but there can be little doubt that she made his life better and easier – she made his home.

Jane was not just the gardener and housekeeper for the Fortune family, she was its secretary and accountant too. When Fortune was China plant collecting, his salary was directed to Jane back in London. She paid his debts and put money by, managed expedition accounts and settled his bills. She was also the go-between for Fortune's shipments of trinkets, sent home to auctioneers. It's entirely likely that she would have kept abreast of the newest developments in botany too, forwarding relevant papers and magazines to

Fortune's *poste restante* addresses abroad. Away for years at a time, he could not afford to let scientific developments pass him by. His livelihood depended upon knowledge, and so too on Jane.

Jane Fortune led an existence that was mirrored throughout the country by every woman married to a peripatetic man. A nation of Empire-builders minted women like her, essential economic helpmeets to a husband's career.

The Fortunes had been married nearly ten years by then, but owing to separation and bad luck had hardly been vigorous breeders to date. They had two children, a boy and a girl: John Lindley, named for Fortune's friend and botanical mentor, was four years old; Helen Jane was seven. Helen was already growing into a young lady, her mother's pride and comfort when Fortune was in China, while John Lindley chased after her, pleading for attention. The Fortunes enjoyed a happy home life.

But there had recently been a death in the family: Little Agnes, named for Fortune's mother. She was bright and smiley, an easy baby to love, and was the first child to be born at the Physic Garden. She was not even a year old when she died. The gardener in Fortune recognised that not every seed sown will thrive, but the loss was nevertheless a keen blow to both parents.

His wife was an essential lynchpin in Fortune's life and career, yet there is little information about their private life together. Though there is ample documentation of his time at the Physic Garden, what he built and spent, planted and reaped, no personal records remain from his time in London. It would seem as if he covered his tracks well. In his published work on China, he could present the face he chose to and manufacture the message. At home in England he was exposed to close scrutiny and some censure, and so, in his typically stoic way, gave others as little information as possible by which they could judge him.

It is otherwise unclear why Fortune should have been quite so silent on matters domestic, when he was such a lively character abroad. Perhaps his little garden, his hard-won home and the trivial details of his life seemed too confining compared to the opulence of wild China. Fortune may quite possibly have felt constrained by his walled garden and family life in urban London while the Middle Kingdom at the Centre of the World, the greatest research laboratory he had ever known, still called to him.

It is also possible that his habitual secrecy arose from the shame of his past. For it is not just that Fortune's beginnings were humble, the nurseryman son of a nurseryman, or that he was from Scotland, or that gardening was the only education he had ever known. Professionally, he had overcome many if not all those impediments, with his early apprenticeship at the Edinburgh Botanic Gardens under the famous botanist William McNab, and from there on to a mentorship under John Lindley, London's great Professor of Botany. He could not, however, rise above the common, but telling, discrepancy in the parish records of his birth. Robert Fortune was born on 16 September 1812, while his parents Thomas and Agnes (*née* Ridpath) had only married on 24 June 1812, a mere ten weeks before. His mother, seven months pregnant in a small town in rural Scotland, would hardly have gone unnoticed as she walked to the altar. As Fortune rose to prominence as a public figure, the details of his date of birth would alter – switching from 1812 to 1813, perhaps to preserve a semblance of propriety.

It is also entirely likely, however, that Fortune's reticence in writing about his life in London was merely a matter of gentlemanly deference to the ever-patient Jane. Like so many

women of the Empire, she enjoyed their cottage routine and
blossomed under his continuous attention, and Fortune left
the details unrecorded.

It was on 7 May 1848 that Dr John Forbes Royle made a
momentous visit to Robert Fortune at the Physic Garden.
Royle was then an old man, among the most esteemed in
botany, Professor of *Materia Medica* at Kings College,
London. He was intimately acquainted with Lindley,
Fortune's mentor; a member of the prestigious Royal Society
and the Linnaean Society. Though eminent visitors were not
unheard of, Fortune was nonetheless pleased to receive a man
such as Royle, and the compliment such a visit implied.

An ample and pug-faced man, Royle had come to see
Fortune on behalf of the East India Company, as their horticultural adviser. He had come to talk about tea.

Royle, also a Scot, had grown up with the Company, and
was indeed practically raised in it, having attended the
Company's military academy at Addiscombe. He went out to
India in 1819 and, upon discovering the joys of botany, declined
his military commission to become a surgeon, being eventually placed in charge of the Botanic Gardens at Saharanpur,
in the North West Provinces. Royle's recommendations in
*Illustrations of the Botany and Other Branches of Natural History
of the Himalayan Mountains* and *An Essay on the Productive
Resources of India*, led the Company to establish an entire
department relating to things vegetal. Royle's knowledge of
the growing capacities of the Himalayan range was unmatched
by any other botanist on earth. He believed, along with
Hardinge, that tea could very profitably be grown there.

Royle and Fortune walked together to the far wall of the
garden, to examine one of the new greenhouses. Royle, who
had not been on the subcontinent for many years, admired

the glass gleaming in the sunlight. These warm environs hinted at a skill that the East India Company required. Fortune, on his trip to China, had become an early expert in a new technology then called the Wardian or Ward's case, and known today as the terrarium. Portable glass houses such as these would change the growing patterns of the planet.

Prior to about 1840 plants were terrible travellers, and plant exchange between the colonies of Greater Britain were consequently difficult and often impossible. Seeds and live cuttings from abroad spent months on ship, crossing the equator at least once and often twice on their way back to England or elsewhere. Sailors were not gardeners and plants did not travel well under their surpervision. Fresh water was scarce on a long sea voyage and was not easily surrendered to exotic plants. Often stowed on deck, in direct sunlight, the plants were also subject to corrosive sea-spray. If they were stowed belowdecks, away from the sun, they often died the slow death of deprivation. It was a rare and hardy plant that could travel the ocean and arrive in good condition or even alive.

But one Dr Ward of London had changed all that with a series of papers that set the professional naturalists talking. In the late-1830s, Nathaniel Bagshaw Ward looked into a glass bottle and made a catalysing discovery. In the closed bottle where he kept a hawk-moth chrysalis, he saw seeds germinating on a piece of common mould. The seeds had been sealed in glass since the summer before, warm and protected, and had not been touched. Without opening it, Ward transferred the bottle to a window ledge and took careful note of further developments. Within four years, the seeds had sprouted into a fern and some common grass.

Born in 1791, Ward was the son of a doctor, raised in the docklands of London. The sailors who frequented his father's practice must have awoken in the boy a taste for the faraway and exotic. At his own request, Ward set sail for Jamaica, aged thirteen, to feed his wanderlust. Though the harsh life of a sailor quickly palled for him, the tropics continued to fascinate Ward – he would become a botanist, a herbalist and a man of medicine, following in the footsteps of his father.

Ward was also an obsessive. For years after the chance observation of the seeds in the bottle, he experimented with glass, seeds and mould. He took notes. Nothing died. Indeed, whatever plant he chose thrived in its new glass home. (The songbirds he chose for his experiment under glass did not.) His herbarium grew to 25,000 specimens, and still he kept experimenting. Ward was the first to recognise a fact that was previously unimagined: plants can survive for years kept in a sealed, well-lit environment without water. He had a series of glass boxes made, kept airtight with putty and paint. He was stumbling upon the missing piece of a vexing puzzle – how to keep plants alive during long, arduous ocean transits.

Ward witnessed and documented an operation that was simple and self-sustaining: during sunlight hours, plants use moisture from the soil in combination with carbon dioxide to photosynthesise. At night, they emit oxygen and release water vapour, which condenses in the cool night air against the glass and drips back down to moisten the soil for the next day. The moisture is almost indefinitely retained, so plant life is self-perpetuating when encased in glass and exposed to sunlight.

For professional plant hunters, the implications of Ward's discovery were revolutionary. Previously, the travelling botanist's job had been one continuous gamble. Which seedlings would stay fresh and which become waterlogged in wet sea air? Which were hardy enough to transit the tropics as well as the northern zones? Disappointment and discouragement were part of a travelling botanist's stock in trade.

Now, for the first time in history, naturalists would be able reliably to preserve plant life *ex situ*. Before Ward, there were few ways to show anyone a live foreign plant – no good, reliable method for taking it any great distance for study. A naturalist could study plants by killing them, by digging up a specimen and drying or pressing it. Or, more poetically, he could attempt an artistic rendering.

Before the Wardian case, the foreign plants that grew in Britain were those few hardy varieties whose seeds and seedlings could withstand extremes of temperature. In 1834, when Ward was in the middle of his experiments, a ship docked in England on a return trip from Hobart, Tasmania, with several of the new glass cases on board. Despite the range of climates the ship had traversed – several winters and summers in one crossing, many thousands of miles, with sea spray and salt air buffeting the boxes the entire way – the plants arrived unharmed. Such was the excitement engendered by Ward's discovery that ships were launched to the far corners of the world.

'To sum up all,' Ward wrote of his experiments, 'in every place there is light, even in the centre of the most crowded and smoky cities, plants of almost every family may be grown . . .'

The implications for the Empire were enormous. For instance, the bark of the Peruvian chinchona tree produces the alkaline quinine; this tree could now be transplanted to the subcontinent and locally produced quinine used to cure the malaria that plagued the British soldiers of India and Burma. Brazilian rubber trees, raised by seed at Kew Gardens, could be replanted on the hospitable island of Ceylon (now Sri Lanka) and a new source of revenue procured. Entire industries and economies would germinate in Ward's glass cases. Even hobby gardens were taking on a different look as hardy small specimen trees from abroad, such as the cherry and the flowering crab apple, were liberating the gardener from the tyranny of lavish annual bedding schemes grown from seed. The fashionable horticultural enthusiasts of Britain, including Prince Albert, geared up for an influx of millions of new plants. And the East India Company was ready to bet that the Wardian case could help them transport the finest Chinese tea plants and seeds to India.

Royle and Fortune spent a long afternoon in the garden talking about the Wardian case, the Physic Garden, China, and Fortune's brilliant book. China held a special place in the imagination of plant hunters for it was an entire nation of gardeners. Unlike much of the world undergoing Britain's programme of colonisation, China was, to the British mind, almost civilised. The Chinese had cultivated passions and refinement, poetry, music and philosophy; above all China had a reverence for gardens. Mandarins showed their status by building winding gardens between fish pools, stone bridges and pavilions in which to meditate upon Confucius. Chinese peasants knew how to grow their own food and how to forage for wild edibles. It was a place where everything was for sale, where the fruits of one garden could be bartered for the bounty of another. But beyond the skills and refinements of the Chinese people, there was the plant-hunting bonanza of China's geography. An enormous country with a variety of hardiness zones, from temperate to tropics to tundra, and vast changes in topography, China was a hotspot for genetic variation and natural selection. It was one of the richest places on earth for the aspiring plant hunter and its scientific appeal was enormous.

The grandfather of British botany, Sir Joseph Banks, saw China as the Holy Grail of plant hunting. Banks had arranged for a gardener to attend Britain's very first diplomatic delegation to the Chinese Emperor in Peking, in the late eighteenth century. A gardener could 'never fail of learning something, if he can be brought into contact with his brethren in Pekin', wrote Banks. He sent a blanket request to all Englishmen in China, amateurs and experts, diplomats and sailors, for plants that were 'either useful, curious, or beautiful' and requested they bring these home in any way possible.

Banks's shopping list in China was based on rumour and supposition, there was so little information available from anywhere but the southernmost port of Canton. He nevertheless wrote out specific requests for details of the Chinese method of dwarfing trees – or bonsai as we now know it. Among the plants that Banks hoped would be collected were various azaleas, the Moutan tree peony, the lychee and the longan nut, economic plants such as tea bushes, and hardwoods such as oaks. Britons in China were asked to investigate Chinese methods of turning human waste, or 'night soil', into fortifying garden manure. England, with its rapidly growing population and lack of a working sewerage system, had a surfeit of human excrement. The introduction of this bit of Chinese wisdom could help turn a poorly understood public health nightmare into a productive boon for industrial Britain. So high were the hopes for Chinese gardens.

'To leave behind once scarce and curious plant under the mistaken Idea of its being a common one will be a source of vexation for ever afterwards if the circumstance happens to be discovered,' Banks threatened.

Fortune, on his China trip, had fulfilled Banks's directives nearly sixty years after they were issued. But had he left important plants behind? He most certainly had. Though Fortune travelled far and wide in his first three years, visiting places no Briton had trodden in the history of China, he travelled mainly from treaty port to treaty port. He had done at least as much collecting in the markets of Chinese cities as he had in the fields. Fortune and Royle marvelled at the fact that the Chinese interior, even after three long years of collecting, was still essentially untouched and ripe for exploration.

Now Royle had a proposition to make: would Fortune be willing to go back to China in the employ of the East India Company, as a tea hunter?

The Company's terms would be very generous. In contrast to his present salary of £100 a year, what a starting clerk was paid in the City, Fortune would receive £500 per annum (about $55,000 today, or £27,500), which was equivalent to the wages of a man who had worked in a trusted position for 25 years. His passages out and home would be paid as well as all other travel expenses – including the cost of cargo shipped between China and London. Cargo space was precious to the plant hunter; though the things he would carry home amounted to little more than market produce, it was the single greatest expense incurred in any botanical exploration. Every novel and curious plant had to compete with the profitable teas and silks also vying for the limited space available to hire, and the prices on stowage were raised accordingly.

But the most magnanimous term of the Company's offer was simply that Fortune's remit was so narrow – he was engaged by them only to collect tea. The property rights to all the other things he collected, the ornamental plants, grasses, seeds, seedlings, flowers, fruits, ferns and bulbs, would be Fortune's alone. It would be entirely different from his first trip for the Royal Horticultural Society. With such generous terms, it would be possible for him to start collecting on his own account and to sell samples at auction for potentially vast profits.

Fortune could see the full significance of the opportunity Royle presented him with. As urban centres filled up with people leaving the countryside to work in factories, the gardening obsession of Great Britain was growing. A softer, romanticised 'English landscape' had become fashionable. In country estates, vistas were choreographed, lakes were dug, hills arranged. These new artificial tableaux demanded rare specimen plants to enhance them. While fashions in gardening were trivial to Fortune, he cannily recognised the possibilities for his own personal advancement. The gardens of Britain were changing, and plant hunters were among those effecting the greatest changes of all. The auction rooms were filling up with plants from abroad. Competitive amateurs and experts were bidding up prices on the bright and happy exotics found by the plant prospectors who mined the tropics for flowering gold. If Fortune could go back to China as a collector and actually sell his discoveries, as so many of his contemporaries in other parts of the Empire did, he could become a rich man.

He would give it due consideration, he told Royle.

As the eminent doctor left, Fortune stood at the wall, near the iron gate, looking at the climbing pale pink roses, budding but not quite in bloom. The English rose of legend and lore originated in Persia and had come to the British Isles only a few hundred years before, but China had been cultivating roses for centuries. Only fifty years before Fortune's day, the two strains, Chinese and English, met; an accidental cross-pollination between the two produced what is known as our common garden rose: long-flowering, sweetly scented, hardy and low-growing. There were no deeply coloured roses in England before the introduction of the China rose; the War of the Roses could have had no true red rose for a symbol, only a pale pink one. The pedigree of England's roses was only one example among many in Fortune's Physic

Garden of how flowers from the East had hybridised and changed the plants of the West.

Elsewhere in the garden Asian favourites flourished: the lilac came from Persia, the tulip from Turkey, citrus from South East Asia. And, thanks to Fortune himself, flowering camellias too had come to England from China. There was a fertile cross-pollination between the Orient and the Occident, and Fortune had already played his part in it.

But what the Company had now requested of him was a much bigger undertaking. Fortune must steal samples of one of the world's most valuable economic plants, keep them healthy and arrange for their successful transplanting in another continent. It was the most formidable task a botanist had ever faced.

He would have to speak to Jane.

Barely one week later, a letter arrived from East India House.

To Mr Robert Fortune
Botanic Gardens Chelsea

Sir,
With reference to the communications with Dr Royle on the part of the Court of Directors of the East India Company has held with you upon the subject of your proceeding to China for the purpose of obtaining plants and seeds of the best descriptions of tea from the most desirable localities and of conveying them under your own charge from thence to Calcutta and eventually to the Himalayas . . . I am commanded by the Court to acquaint you that they accept the offer of your services and that they will expect you to be ready to proceed to China not later than the 20th of June next.

The Court will grant you a salary of Five Hundred Pounds

per annum to commence from the date of your embarkation and to cease on your return to this country. They will provide you with a free passage to China and you will be entitled to a free passage on your return to England. The court will also defray all your travelling charges and other expenses which you may incur in India and China in procuring and conveying plants and seeds and in otherwise carrying out the objects contemplated by the Court in view to extend the cultivation of tea in the hill tracts of the North West Provinces of India.

As it is of importance that you should arrive in China as early in the Autumn as possible a passage will be procured for you in one of the Peninsular and Oriental Company's vessels in order that you may proceed in the most expeditious manner.

East India House 17th May 1848

4

Shanghai to Hangzhou,
September 1848

A flat-bottomed boat was moored in a snaking, stinking canal one day's sail out of Shanghai. The boat was small, no more than 40 foot long, a floating home belonging to a seagoing family of brothers and their wives. The family shared the labour and meagre profits of conveying cargo and passengers, illicit or otherwise, through China's coastal network of waterways and canals. It was a creaky junk, unremarkable in the environs of Shanghai except for its passengers.

Fortune's Chinese body servant, 'a large-boned clumsy fellow', was threading a blunt needle with horsehair. He slipped the needle underneath the hairs at the nape of Fortune's head, yanking the stitches taut with every pull. He was sewing a long braid, black and coarse, formerly the pride of some peasant, into Fortune's hair. The queue, as it was called, hung from his neck to his waist as if it were his own.

Fortune sat stiffly, nervously, for though he had been in China several weeks, his true journey was only just beginning. His progress towards the little boat had been efficient and swift: speeding through Hong Kong – which on his last trip he'd dismissed as a 'barren island, with only a few huts upon it,' and now described as a remarkable British outpost of 'palaces, and gardens too' – Fortune moved on by steamer to Shanghai, a city bustling with newfound foreign trade. In the British concession area there, on the banks of Shanghai's Huangapu River, Fortune took up a brief but productive residence in the palatial home of Mr Thomas Beal, of the renowned trading company of Messrs Dent, Beal & Co., an old friend and intellectual benefactor to many British travellers in the East. Beale gave Fortune a free hand with his firm's compradors, the trusted Chinese fixers who in the ports regularly matched the needs of Western merchants to the capacities of China. As the boomtown city opened to Western investment and settlement, these translators and profiteers served as envoys, who could smooth the way towards China's business elite. While in Shanghai, Fortune hired two servants, collected provisions, ordered and directed the assembly of glazed Wardian cases, and planned for a trip that was in reality beyond the scope of precise planning. With little good reliable information on the Chinese interior at hand, Fortune hoped to determine where the best tea was grown and how to get there. He required inside help, and had found that in his choice of servants.

These servants were his entrée into China; they shared the task of collecting the tea – as well as, hopefully, keeping Fortune alive. He'd hired two men from the most celebrated green tea districts in the vicinity of China's famed Yellow Mountain. They acted as his interpreters, cooks, botanical collectors, bodyguards, porters, and, most importantly, guides. The men divided up the travelling jobs roughly between those requiring intellectual skill and those requiring brute force. Fortune's erstwhile hairdresser, 'the Coolie', whom his written account never mentions by any other name, was the human ox hired to move luggage from shore to boat and back or carry the heavy glazed cases on botanical collecting trips.

Wang, an educated man in his early-twenties, was the more refined of the two. He was raised on a tea hill, near China's finest green tea region, Sung Lo Mountain, in Anhui province. For generations, Wang's family had grown and picked tea, sending favoured sons off to the cities of Hangzhou and Shanghai to make their name in trade. China's population had doubled in the previous century and there was too little farmland to support many children. Wang, like many provincial emigrants to Shanghai, was a natural middleman, crafty, seeking a cut from every transaction, making a living in the grey economy of the newly opened foreign concessions. For Fortune, Wang acted as a professional tour manager. He knew all the roads between Shanghai and tea. As a born businessman, he negotiated contracts with porters and boatmen. And, as was common in China, he managed to keep a fraction of each transaction for himself, a practice known to Englishmen in China as 'squeeze'.

Of the two men, Wang had the advantage in Fortune's eyes, in that he could make himself easily understood, while the Coolie could not. Wang spoke a language used in the ports, developed in the hundred or so years of the tea trade, a pidgin composed of English and Chinese, with a smattering of Hindi and Portuguese. Pidgin was at once comical and necessary to the white men who travelled and did business in China. Some words have made their way into our common English lexicon – for instance *Chop! Chop!* Go very fast – but entire sentences sounded ridiculous, a nursery language. *Long time my no have see you. What thing wantchee?* Wang may have said upon entering. With communication sounding so bizarre, it is little wonder that foreigners and the Chinese held each other in such low esteem. Wang spoke pidgin and Fortune understood it, but the Coolie was in effect mute to his master, too ignorant to learn the basic foreign tongue.

Fortune's middling Chinese, learned from wealthy men in port cities, was almost incomprehensible to the low-born and brutish Coolie.

On this mission for the East India Company, Fortune was going deeper into the Great Yellow Country than any Briton had ever dared, beyond the reach of British law and gunboat. While in the foreign concessions of Shanghai, he operated effectively under the protective umbrella of British law, a quirk of the treaty that had ended the First Opium War. All Europeans inside the trade zone enjoyed special status; they obeyed the laws of their home countries, not China. The laws of the Emperor could not touch them there.

On this journey outside the treaty port Fortune needed body servants more than ever, because China was now a more threatening place than it had been during his first trip. The increased European presence on the coasts was fiercely resented by the local Chinese, and in the south angry peasants were attacking foreigners, holding them hostage in factories and hospitals, sometimes killing them without reason. Rebels were taking over the countryside. The weakening court in Peking, humiliated after its defeat in the foreign war, could not control local Mandarins who tyrannised cities and villages with excessive taxes, which rose faster than any peasant could earn a living.

The upheaval created by the Western presence in urban China was very real. As the West moved into Shanghai, the Chinese moved out – taking everyone and everything with them, even their ancestors, Fortune noted, 'Their chief care was to remove, with their other effects, the bodies of their deceased friends which are commonly interred on private property near their houses. Hence it was no uncommon thing to meet several coffins being borne by coolies or friends to the westward. In many instances when the coffins were uncovered they were found totally decayed, and it was impossible to remove them. When this was the case, a Chinese might be seen holding a book in his hand, which contained a list of the bones, and directing others in their search after these last remnants of mortality.'

On the face of it, it seemed entirely foolish to be a lone European in the interior of China. This fact was not lost on Fortune's servants. When Wang tried to negotiate Fortune's passage with the small junk captains in Shanghai, the sailors refused. Boatmen were beaten and tortured for trafficking the waterways with Westerners on board. 'On this account it was impossible to engage a boat as a foreigner and I desired my servant to hire it in his own name, and merely state that two other persons were to accompany him.' It was a shrewd plan, and Wang returned with a contract officially signed, stamped with a 'chop', or character-bearing seal. But as the travelling crew loaded the ship, the Coolie, either from ignorance or malice, let the captain know Fortune's secret identity. Fortune feared the boatmen would no longer consent to having a foreigner on board, especially after being tricked, but Wang assured his master the trip could proceed as planned, 'if only you will consent to add a trifle more to the fare'.

Sitting on a crate, getting a queue sewn into his hair, on only his first day out of Shanghai, Fortune had left the comparative safety of the foreign-trade zones. His status had thereupon shifted dramatically downward and he was now relying on two servants and a new hairdo to protect him. He sought to steal one of China's greatest treasures; angry citizens, merciless officials and opportunistic vendors would face no consequences for molesting, or even killing, him. No one would trouble to report his death.

Fortune was patient as the Coolie attended to his new coif. A small blue and white tea bowl sat nearby on a dusty crate and Fortune reached for it. Sitting still and erect, despite the discomfort of the hairstyling, he swirled the sediment of leaves and spilled the cooling tea out on to the dirty deck. Hair, muck and depleted tea leaves lay at his feet. Floors were for garbage in China it seemed, he was trying to behave in the Chinese manner, in order to fit in. And so, in the Chinese way, he had warmed the porcelain bowl and washed it with the hot water. Green tea was not Fortune's preference, absent the civilised comforts of milk and sugar. He was coming to appreciate the Chinese way of tea, plain and unadulterated. But more, he understood the expedience of doing things the Chinese way.

Fortune was a constant curiosity when travelling as a Westerner; he seemed as peculiar to the Chinese as they did to him. To them the Scotsman looked grotesque; he was so tall, his nose was much longer than a nose need be, and his eyes were too round; round eyes were generally considered a sign of intelligence, but Fortune, with his halting Chinese, would have sounded like a child to them when he spoke. The simple act of eating brought him unwanted attention. 'He eats and drinks like ourselves,' observed one member of a crowd, watching him on his first trip, Fortune recalled. 'Look,' said two or three behind me who had been examining the back part of my head rather attentively, 'look here, the stranger has no tail'; then the whole crowd, women and children included had to come round to me to see if it was really a fact that I had no tail.'

On this trip his servants insisted that they would join him only if he took steps to disguise himself upon leaving Shanghai. 'They were quite willing to accompany me, only stipulating that I should discard my English costume and adopt the dress of the country. I knew this was indispensable if I wished to accomplish the object in view and readily acceded to the terms.'

The style of the day required that all ethnic Chinese men shave the front of their heads as an act of fealty to the Emperor. The tonsure of nearly 200 million people demonstrated the invading Manchurian court's power over the individual. The Qing emperors used tonsure as a way of controlling the mob, of transforming a multi-ethnic, heterodox society into a visually unified one. Refusing to be shaven was an act of sedition whereas agreeing to the ritual was a sign of submission to the status quo.

The Coolie consequently took his rusty razor to the front of Fortune's head and began to create a new, higher hairline for him. 'He did not shave, he actually scraped my poor head until the tears came running down my cheeks and I cried out with pain,' Fortune wrote. 'I suppose I must be the first person upon whom he had ever operated, and I am charitable enough to wish most sincerely I may be the last.'

On that first day of his journey towards tea, Fortune rehearsed the rational for his journey, the hows, the whys and the whens of his planned tea offensive. The job was big, and would require several years in China to complete. To jumpstart production in the East India Company's tea gardens, it was crucial that he bring back several thousand tea plants, many thousand more seeds, plus the highly specialised but previously elusive techniques of Chinese tea-growing and manufacturing practices. He had to recruit tea manufacturers from the finest factories. He was to learn the secrets of growing and processing the world's most popular drink, so that he could pass these secrets on, create a master recipe, and enable large-scale production of tea in India.

It was not just the horticultural challenge of raising tea that excited Fortune; as a man of science he saw no reason why a plant should remain so shrouded in myth and mystery;

why it should not be subjected to the enlightened analysis of Western inquiry. In this he was a man of his time, a British naturalist who believed that simple and rational explanations could be deduced for every living thing under God's sun. He wanted China's secrets.

But before Fortune could formulate the perfect tea recipe, however, he needed to obtain the basic ingredients: the finest classes of tea China had to offer, both green and black. To this end he decided to make at least two separate tea-hunting trips in disguise – one each for green tea and black tea, for the two never grew together in the same regions. Green tea and black tea required different growing conditions, Fortune believed. The best green tea was in the north, whereas the best black came from mountains in Southern China.

Fortune chose to make the first of his trips to the green tea districts of Zhejiang and Anhui Provinces. His second would not take place for at least another season, when he would go to the fabled black tea districts of the Bohea or Wu Yi Mountains in Fujian province, travelling as far as two hundred miles inland.

While black tea was the bigger prize for Fortune and the East India Company, given its popularity in the West, it was also more difficult to obtain. High among the fingerlike mountain karsts, the thin air and chill nights produced the richest Oolongs, Pekoes and Souchongs: the finest black teas in the world. It was at least a three-month trek south from Shanghai to the border areas between Fujian and Shaanxi provinces, without the option of remaining out of public view on a river boat. The misty Wu Yi Shan were remote. No foreigner, save the occasional French missionary, had been there since the days of Marco Polo.

By comparison, the logistics of stealing green tea were relatively uncomplicated because the districts producing the finest greens were easy to get to, requiring only a few weeks' sail on the great Yangtze River and its tributaries. He had made similar, shorter ventures on his previous trip, travelling by boat until he reached a distant hillside, then wandering with Wardian cases until he had harvested his seeds and dug his fill of specimens.

On his first trip to China, Fortune had learned more about tea growing than any Westerner in the world. He had visited accessible green tea gardens near the treaty port of Ning Bo in the company of the British Consul. Two entire chapters of *Three Years' Wanderings* are devoted to what he observed there about the growth, manufacture and processing of the tea plant. Tea was so crucial to the economy of the British Empire that no book on China's flora would be complete without an examination of the subject. Fortune had even brought back tea plant specimens to England's botanical gardens, sad little greenhouse shrubs, useful for study and spectacle but worthless for illustrating just how tea came to be made. Fortune blamed the 'jealousy of the Chinese Government' for his lack of knowledge. The Emperor 'prevented foreigners from visiting any of the districts where tea is cultivated'. Chinese tea merchants had proved an unreliable source for tea-growing knowledge; they were too far down the chain of supply to be of any use to a scientist. His living tea plants in English hothouses could not even settle the ongoing debate as to whether green tea and black were different species or the same. 'We find our English authors contradicting each other, some asserting that the black and green teas are produced by the same variety and that the difference in colour is the result of a different mode of preparation, while others say that black teas are produced from the plant called by botanists *Thea bohea*, and the green from *Thea viridis*,' Fortune had recorded. Preparation or variation? A second trip to China would enable him finally to put the matter to rest.

On the day Fortune sat on his riverboat, under the Coolie's blade, the world had only one source of supply for its tea: China. If Fortune's mission was successful, India would soon be on a path to rival and then surpass China in tea cultivation; the East India Company would save itself; Britain would trumpet its triumph over the Chinese Emperor; Fortune would advance science and gain personal glory. He would be the first man to try planting an entire garden of tea – an entire new industry – from foreign seedlings.

To seed India with inferior tea stock was hardly going to make him a hero – or a fortune. There was no point in sending to India a motely assortment of inferior tea plants, as previous collectors had done. Fortune was only interested in procuring the most celebrated teas in China: 'It was a matter of great importance to procure them from those districts in China where the best teas were produced'. And he was charged with getting them there in good health, ready to transplant in to Indian soil.

Fortune needed to be as sure as he could be about exactly what he was collecting and shipping to India. He considered himself a scientist, though his mission was to conduct espionage. As a scientist, his work was only as good as the data he could collect, so he knew he had to verify, first-hand, the facts about what he was collecting – its location, ecology and cultivation. While it occurred to Fortune that he might manage things much more expeditiously and with less risk if he were to send local operatives to do the collecting and reporting – as the Company had done for generations – Fortune dismissed this option. He had little confidence that Chinese agents would be dependable enough to seek out the best that China had to offer. If India was to rival China in the world market for tea, 'it was a matter of great importance to procure them from

those districts in China where the best teas were produced.'
And if he did not collect them himself, well? Where was the
adventure in that, let alone the science?

But it was not enough to successfully send tea plants to
India: he would also need to be sure whether the tea he was
sending was arriving alive and transplanting successfully. His
envisaged three years of labour in China would be for naught
if his plants did not survive the journey and thrive in their
new locale. So he wanted to ensure that he would receive
word of his results as quickly as possible. For this, he had to
enlist the cooperation of the Government of the North West
Provinces in India, to whom he wrote:

> Having been appointed by the Honourable Court of Direc-
> tors of the East India Company to proceed to China for the
> purpose of transmitting plants and seeds of the best variety
> of tea . . .
>
> It is my intention to send down to Calcutta both seeds
> and plants by variety of opportunities and it will be of great
> importance if they are carefully received and forwarded to
> their destination. [It will] also be very desirable to have a
> report made upon the condition of the plants and seeds when
> they arrive in India which report could be sent to me for my
> guidance with regard to the number which it will be neces-
> sary to collect.
>
> I trust I will be excused in making these suggestions as
> the transmission of plants is always attended with some
> difficulty . . .
>
> I shall be glad to receive any instructions which you may
> think it necessary to give me these [can] be addressed to the
> care of Messrs Dent who will forward them to me.
>
> I have the honour to be yours . . .
> Robert Fortune

'*Hai-yah* – very bad, very bad,' the Coolie muttered in pidgin, razor held aloft in his hand while Fortune winced in pain. 'Very bad' and 'very good' were the only English words the Coolie understood. He took a hot towel and dabbed Fortune's red, bloody scalp. With each scrape of the blunt scalpel and each poke of the needle through his own hair, Fortune was becoming more Chinese.

His boatmen sat nearby the barber's chair, laughing and gambling, the clacking of mahjong tiles animating the otherwise still air. 'The poor Coolie was really doing the best he could,' Fortune noted magnanimously.

His second servant, Wang, had procured for Fortune a pile of folded clothing: a grey silk garment that buttoned down the front, with a high stand-up collar, as alike in status and dignity as the garments any travelling Chinese merchant might wear; wide-legged, flowing trousers so big two men might have walked in them; sleeves that hid his large gardener's hands; and thin slippers, which hardly seemed as if they would stay on a man's feet, let alone protect him from the muck of a city street. Over this he wore a padded coat, sashed and with deep pouch pockets which should prove invaluable once he started collecting specimens.

Fortune had, however, neglected to request an accounting of the copper spent on these garments. Chinese copper money amounted to fractions of pennies and so Wang casually pocketed the change unchallenged. The Coolie, noting this imbalance of accounts, seethed, believing that jobs such as handling money – and skimming it off the top – should rightly go to him, the older of the two, rather than the upstart Wang.

The Coolie, working hard as a barber to please Fortune, tried to complain to his master, who merely laughed off his disgruntlement. His servants' competition for favours made him feel safer; he hoped in this way they would provide a check on each other and would not forge an alliance against him. Fortune was already at risk in China; he did not need a challenge from his closest men.

He was in fact putting his life into the hands of his servants, men with whom he had nothing in common, about whom he knew almost nothing, and who had their own worries, problems and aspirations. Fortune assumed they would be docile, if stupid, but willing servants. He had given very little thought to them as individual human beings: that the Coolie endlessly sought esteem, for instance, or that Wang's impulse to 'squeeze' might grow insatiable throughout the journey. Wang was already playing the game of translation arbitrage: all prices were negotiated on paper, written in Chinese numerals, and Fortune did not read Chinese.

The internecine rivalries and shortcomings of his men were still largely unknown to Fortune at this stage in the journey. But he understood that Wang and the Coolie were putting their lives and reputations in peril, too. He was a thief and they were his accomplices. So he'd obeyed their single request: he was travelling in disguise, dressed as a haughty Mandarin, for the sake of their safety as well as his own. Would it work? Fortune knew that China was both enormous and far removed from the rest of the world. The peasants he travelled amongst could not make sense of the sheer size of their own country, so with no external reference points for comparison, could have no idea just how foreign Fortune really was. A braid and Chinese clothing would signal Fortune's appropriateness. The fact that his facial features were not Chinese, or that he was nearly a foot taller than every man around him, would, he hoped, not be considered too suspicious in a nation already ruled by foreigners. His height could in any case be explained away: it was well known that the people from the other side of the Great Wall were very tall and extremely brutish. To be sure, Fortune looked different from the rural Chinese, but as long as he was wearing the braid he would no longer look obviously European. All Chinese subjects wore queues, Fortune had one too, therefore he must be a subject of the Emperor.

The light turned grey about them as the sun sank from view. From alley doorways and dark shadows, a handful of prostitutes were moving towards the canal to set money on fire. It was hell money, burnt as a way of transferring it from the physical world to the spirit one and offered to appease deities and ancestors before getting down to the night's dirty business. The Coolie cast a wistful eye in their direction.

Fortune felt the braid bounce off his back, dancing lightly between his shoulder blades. He was 'a pretty fair Chinaman', he considered, and reminded himself that, from this moment forward, he would have to speak only in Chinese, rusty as it was after his three year absence; he would have to use chopsticks and remember to kowtow rather than shake the hand of a man of higher rank. He would introduce himself with his Chinese name, Sing Wa, Bright Flower.

With the requisite black braid and bald, if slightly inflamed, forehead, Fortune proceeded to dress in his new clothing. Though Fortune was much larger than the average Chinese, the average Chinese outfit was a great deal roomier than it need be, so his new garments almost fit him, just as Fortune almost fit into China.

The Coolie packed up his razor and scissors and nodded to his foreign master. He then walked aft to the Sea Goddess's altar and lit an incense stick to ask the goddess's blessing on their journey.

Wang, visibly nervous as the boat pulled out into the canal and the journey began in earnest, asked Fortune what would happen if someone asked where they were from? How were they to answer?

Fortune smiled and replied, *Wo hui gaosu tamen, wo shi waishengren cong changcheng geng yuan de yi xie shengdi lai de*. That he was Chinese, from a distant province beyond the Great Wall.

5

Zhejiang Province near Hangzhou, October 1848

For the past 1000 years, the Chinese have loved the city of Hangzhou, about 120 miles inland from Shanghai. Built around a dreamy lake, with green mountains rimming the skyline and a mist working broad strokes across the water, it is a city for poets. It is also a centre of serenity, liberally endowed with temples and gardens. More than simply a picturesque place, however, it is one of the precious few beautiful places remaining in modern China – the city is wealthy and always has been. The people of Hangzhou, from house servants to merchants, wore lush silk robes in bright colours as they thronged the busy streets, feasting on cakes or trading luxuries like pearls and jades. The shops were full and the merchants were fat: no mean feat in a nation that suffered under repeated famines and shortages. Where most Chinese cities were filthy and overrun with vermin, by Fortune's report Hangzhou was hygienic and serene. The surrounding province was then and remains today the wealthiest in all of China. 'Beyond dispute the finest and the noblest [city] in the world,' Marco Polo wrote upon laying eyes on it. The Confucian poets were equally enthralled: 'Above, there is heaven, but on earth there is Hangzhou.'

More than anything else, Hangzhou was a city whose life centred around tea: trading it or sampling the choice blends served in the teahouses. As a city, it was exactly the kind of place Fortune would have enjoyed: an ancient, gardened place, where rich people have the time to not work, but to think, to plan big ideas, to linger over a long hot cup of tea and talk about the magic of nature.

Were Fortune merely a tourist, he might have lingered here. But he planned to avoid the place entirely: Hangzhou was too dangerous for him. It was a bottleneck for trade, situated directly on the main silk and tea routes, a place where merchants from the coastal trading ports might recognise a white man in disguise. Or, at the very least, would notice Fortune as someone who was out of step with everyday Chinese life.

He therefore commanded Wang to arrange sedan chair travel around Hangzhou. Once they were safely beyond the outskirts of the city, Wang was to book them passage on a cargo boat headed up the great Yangtze valley, towards Wang's own home in rural Anhui province, where green tea grew on every sloped hill.

Wang, however, had other plans: the quickest route to the tea country was to cut straight through Hangzhou. The difference in the price of Fortune's passage, the margin between 'around' and 'through', was more than enough to provide some illicit tea and tobacco for Wang, perhaps even a 'flower girl' or two. A little extra squeeze off the top of Fortune's travel budget would buy the Coolie's silence.

Wang negotiated sedan-chair porters to bear Fortune along the long flat road. The 'chair' was little more than a box resting between two bamboo poles, held at either end by coolies. These porters were wide-shouldered men, dark from the sun and with thick-muscled calves. They had no way of knowing Fortune's instructions and so were more than happy when Wang hired them. The more quickly their passenger reached his destination, the sooner they could spend their earnings in a teahouse, inn or opium den.

'No one took the slightest notice of me, a circumstance which gave me a good deal of confidence,' Fortune said of his journey towards Hangzhou.

It might have done Fortune well to be more vigilant.

The road into Hangzhou stretched ahead for miles, surrounded by forests of mulberry trees, the workshops in which China's famed silkworms spun their soft magic. 'I saw little else than mulberry trees,' he wrote. He sat comfortably in his sedan chair and, as the long day of travel drew on, was 'expecting at any moment to get out into the open country'. But it was not to be. With every mile the porters advanced, crossroads became more frequent, buildings sprang up and fields disappeared. 'I was greatly surprised by finding that I was getting more and more into a dense town.' Soon enough, the porters carried Fortune through the gates set in Hangzhou's thick grey walls and straight into the centre of the city, next to the splendid West Lake.

Though Fortune's orders had been heard, they had not been adhered to. Wang had ignored his master's express request for secrecy, and it terrified Fortune. Busy and sophisticated cities were no place for thieves in disguise. 'Had it been known that a foreigner was in the very heart of the city of Hang-chow-foo, a mob would have soon collected and the consequences might have been serious,' he wrote.

Fortune upbraided Wang, using the insults of a low sailor – the only Chinese form of swearing he was likely to know – and the haughty disdain of the gentleman he hoped so fervently to become. He was unaccustomed to being disobeyed and probably feared that if he did not come down on his men like the hand of God among heathens, he would be in for a series of

such misdeeds. With every step inland, the possible consequences could be more grave.

But for all Fortune's recriminations, his words had little
effect. Indeed, a master scolding his servants publicly only
served to build their self-esteem, or 'face', as even a reproach
was a tacit declaration that the servant was important enough
to merit the notice of a wealthy Mandarin. 'Face', or *mianxi*,
was a concept that a Westerner like Fortune did not instinct-
ively understand, describing as it does the prestige and
reputation one gains from every human relationship in China.
Relationships in China were defined by the reciprocal obligations between people, whether of the same or differing
status, and every single person in China existed within a
network of influence, a matrix of duties, pieties and social
connections, or *guanxi*. The family came first, then the
extended social neighbourhood. 'Face' expressed a person's
position within their network and was the mechanism by
which the Chinese assessed their obligations: which orders
to obey, which favours to give, which supplications and apolo-
gies to make. A son might perform humble acts for his father,
an employee bow before his master or a student before his
teacher; but, similarly, the father was responsible to the child,
the master beholden to the slave, the student to the teacher.
You can lose 'face', give 'face', or save 'face'.

However subtly defined, 'face' and *guanxi* were inescapable
facts of life in China, then as now; they forged the social
fabric of the nation. Social connections determined the
measure of justice received and discrimination suffered. While
no Chinese person was free from these relationships, many
peasants had very little 'face' – and therefore little access to
justice, wealth or freedom. When social obligations were met,
someone gained 'face' and an increase in status; when a person
failed those to whom he was socially connected and thereby

obligated, he suffered a loss of 'face' (*diumian*) and a downturn in his social standing. When Wang was shouted at by Fortune for failing to follow orders, it demonstrated to the world that he had responsibilities to an important man. Wang lost 'face' with Fortune, while simultaneously gaining it in the wider neighbourhood of Hangzhou.

'Face' was a very Confucian concept. The great philosopher, who lived during the Han dynasty, 500 years BC, described a world where familial connections and obligations to ancestors were the highest good and greatest aim of an individual – a single person was nothing if he did not bring honour to the world from which he came.

To be a foreigner was to be an alien in China, without any network of prescribed duties, without social capital, lacking obvious 'face'. Many foreigners handled this outsider status well. They engaged in relationships with the Chinese immediately, giving gifts and favours readily to officials and higher-ups; recognising that a servant did not just serve but was owed things other than monetary reward, such as honour and respect. Fortune, however, seems to have bulldozed past the finer points of Chinese social interaction. He treated the Chinese as he would any employee: demanding excellence, refusing excuses, chastising failure. Wang and Fortune would travel together, on and off, for years – their relationship was intimately bound up in the surrounding network of social obligations. But Wang understood *guanxi* where Fortune did not, and, to the degree that he could, the servant tried to negotiate its workings on his master's behalf. Wang gave Fortune his identity as a Mandarin; he forged a fictitious network of prestigious connections for him, elevating his 'face' (and, not incidentally, elevating Wang's own status by association). He also bribed and negotiated on Fortune's behalf, not just for favours but for 'face'.

It might have seemed to Fortune that these obligations only increased Wang's profits and interfered with the efficiency of the expedition. Though Fortune had travelled in China before, he remained an easy mark for those who knew and kept his secrets. Out of necessity, he relied on his servants, making a family of his travel companions: it was a network of consideration, if not care. He did not realise the high 'face' status he conferred upon them by depending on them so heavily. Nor did he foresee how rebellious this would make them.

After the trip through Hangzhou, Wang engaged a cargo boat to take Fortune out of the city towards the tea regions of Anhui province, up the rich Yangtze valley. Fortune's berth would be in the stern, next to a dwarf's; the cost of his passage would include two meals of rice gruel and one meal of rice per day; he would receive a straw mat to sleep on (the servants slept abovedecks) and a basin of hot water with which to wash each morning. (Unlike Europeans, nineteenth-century Chinese bathed daily.) Under Fortune's sleeping mat there were two coffins – presumably occupied. Such was the reverence in China for ancestors and ancestral graves that merchants from the provinces who had the misfortune to die in the coastal cities, away from their clans, were always repatriated to their home ground. It was thought that otherwise their ghosts would be confused when the time came to bestow good fortune on their relatives, and that they would be angry and therefore vengeful to find themselves buried so far from home. Heedless of this, however, Fortune assumed the plinth was simply a bed and slept soundly upon it.

The river towns around Hangzhou were creepy and dilapidated, their crumbling walls overrun with weeds and shrubs. These small towns were dens of robbers and pirates, waiting to prey on the newfound wealth sailing past towards the China Sea. His boatmen regaled Fortune with stories of local terror and brigandry. The tales were affecting and 'almost made me believe myself to be in dangerous company', he recalled. Fortune posted the Coolie to keep watch over his cabin every evening, augmenting the work of the night watchman. 'How long these sentries kept watch I cannot tell, but when I awoke, some time before the morning dawned, the dangers of the place seemed to be completely forgotten, except perhaps in their dreams, for I found them sound asleep . . . No one seemed to have harmed us during our slumbers.'

The boatmen might have enjoyed spinning a good scary yarn, but for the three travellers – Wang, the Coolie and Fortune – their relationship with the crew was an essential lifeline. Boatmen negotiated the way from point A to point B at their own discretion, and were accustomed to doing so, for there were always dark and nefarious forces sailing on the waterways of China: arms and opium, rebels and religious renegades. Above all things and at all times the boatmen were to be kept happy lest they betray their potentially troublesome and thoroughly illegal human cargo. The sailors did not know Fortune's secret – only that every man travelling in China had one.

While the river junk was docked in Hangzhou, waiting for a full roster of passengers before pushing off, Wang conducted some business dealings of an indeterminate nature with the head boatman. Perhaps he was scheming for a larger fraction of the cost of the passage to find its way back to his pocket – with a split for the boatman, naturally. It is possible he had arranged for a false 'chop', the receipt of purchase that acted like a ticket, so that Fortune would never know the full price of his passage. Or maybe Wang had found some cargo down-river that commanded a higher price upriver, and was bartering for a little extra stowage to be added to Fortune's bill. Whatever his game, Wang owed a significant amount of money to the captain.

He paid his debt to the boatman in silver, using a silver dollar, but on shore that night, when the captain was drinking, gambling, and otherwise enjoying himself before resuming the long journey, he put down Wang's dollar coin to pay for his evening's merriment. The inn keeper told him it was counterfeit and unacceptable. Mexican Spanish silver dollar coins were rare inland, though they were the accepted currency of the international settlements on the coast – the very first world currency, in fact. (Mexico received independence from Spain in 1821, but the coins were still considered the 'Principal Money' of the China trade throughout the century.) The foreign trade that came with the end of the Opium Wars increased the number of silver dollars in circulation in China, such that even a simple boatman would have heard of silver's high value against local currency. At a time when the copper currency of China was being radically devalued, the boatman would have jumped at Wang's coin. Yet the relative scarcity of silver inland would have meant the captain might not have known how to spot a true Mexican Spanish dollar.

Settling his debts at the gaming table in Chinese coin, the captain then set off back to his ship, and Wang. He, however, refused to take the dollar back. A dollar's a dollar, he insisted. The captain was resolute: he wanted a refund. It was late at night and Wang was drunk. The two men argued back and forth. How was the captain to be recompensed? How could Wang know that this was even the same dollar he had handed over that morning? The captain threatened him then: he could make trouble for Wang, alerting the Mandarin that his servant was passing false coin.

At last, Wang agreed to pay the captain in Chinese money

instead, mumbling a protest – 'that dollar was good enough' – as he threw down the dollar's equivalent in heavy strings of copper coins, which were the common medium for local exchange.

The boatman was happy with the settlement at first, but when he counted his haul, beaded up on its long thread, he found it was short. Wang was still trying to take advantage of him.

Wang exploded: 'I gave you a dollar, and you said that was bad; I changed it, and gave you copper cash, and you return them; pray what do you want?'

The passengers were gathering round, the cool night air alive with stirrings of interest in their brawl. The boatman left the scene resentfully, clutching the cash necklaces that were, he felt, far too light. Fortune eventually caught wind of Wang's doings. Though he could not follow the angry discussion between the two men, he began to realise the liabilities of travelling with Wang. Fortune was now suspicious of his paid companion. However, he could as yet have no idea how dangerous things would become.

Fortune grew distracted as he travelled inland, reunited with a past love: the scenery of China's rich agricultural regions. The fields were terraced and tawny in their harvest colours. Orchards abounded. The peaches and plums were finished for the season, but apples hung heavy on the boughs, while oranges were just coming into colour. Fortune was beguiled, a farmer's son returning to the rural life he remembered at the same time as he was a frontiersman, setting foot on virgin ground. From the safe distance of the boat, he admired the industry of the Chinese farmers. Tucked into every patchwork display of cereal crops – wheat, rice, and corn – was one evergreen patch of tea. Every farm or household had a postage stamp-sized tea garden of their own, each a sign to Fortune that his travelling band was nearing the intended target. They were sailing straight to the heart of tea.

Apart for the palpable unease that continued to be felt between Wang and the Captain, the river journey was a happy one for Fortune; it took him through the finest scenery and the wildest landscape he had yet seen. There is little to content a naturalist more than watching such an unblemished scene unfurl, like a scroll, as his boat navigates the twisting course of a river. Fortune would see the occasional pagoda or temple nestled in the hills, announcing a nearby town, but mainly he saw craggy mountains, waterfalls, the lush, bamboo-covered vistas of East Asia.

When the rapids were fast or the bed shallow, the boat ran alongside the river bank where a barefoot team of fifteen near-naked coolie trackers slung ropes over their shoulders and manually hauled the vessel along. On other occasions the sailors poled their flat-bottomed boat around dangerous rocks mid-stream. In such instances, it took hours to get anywhere. Where other travellers would take a nap or pull out the tiles and start the evening's gambling until mealtimes interrupted the languor of travel, Fortune used the slow passage to roam the adjacent hillsides and collect plant samples. Early each morning, he and his two men would climb a nearby hill to take a sighting of the curve of the river ahead. If it was a slow day on which the boat would make little headway, Fortune would stay onshore and catch up with the vessel later in the afternoon. One can only wonder what Wang and the Coolie thought of the way their master travelled – complete with his picks and shovels, blotting paper, notebooks, magnifying glass, specimen jars, Ward's cases and wicker baskets. It was Fortune's servants' first exposure to his penchant for note-taking, sample-digging, aimless wandering in order to collect only assorted plants and shrubs, which surely would prove to be more trouble than they were worth.

Fortune lived for these interludes. 'The weather was delightful, the natives quiet and inoffensive, and the scenery picturesque in the highest degree.' These were the days on which he made discoveries. 'My Chinamen and myself, often footsore and weary, used to sit down on the hill-top and survey and enjoy the beautiful scenery around us. The noble river, clear and shining, was seen winding amongst the hills; here it was smooth as glass, deep, and still, and there shallow, and running rapidly over its rocky bed.'

Were the days so pleasant for Wang, when he spent and made no money? Or for the Coolie, struggling behind with armloads of hardware and heavy glazed cases hanging off his shoulders? Perhaps. Rural China is a picturesque place and these wandering days were the rare moments when the attention of all three travellers was fixed on one object: the beauty of China.

Fortune, not unlike his men, had his sights trained on income producers. The hillside jaunts inspired him in no small part because they might well provide the means of his advancement. In his first few days out of Hangzhou, he discovered the hemp palm, *Chamaerops excelsa*, which he would send off to the Royal Botanic Garden at Kew upon his return to Shanghai. The specimen would brave unharmed its first English winter in 1850. On one of the early boating forays, he also found a remote private garden where he spied the very picture of weeping loneliness, the funereal cyprus, *Cypressus funebris*.

'What a fine tree this of yours is!' he told the gardener who stood nearby. 'We have never seen it in the countries near the sea where we come from; pray give us some of its seeds.'

Alas, the funereal cyprus would disappoint: it would transplant to Britain, but it was a tender tree that did not take well to Kew, which is to say it would not make its discoverer's fortune at the Covent Garden auction rooms.

Still, Fortune was hopeful about his finances and content with his recent discoveries. Already China had a reputation for enhancing Britain's gardens – a reputation he himself had played no small part in advancing. China is the very mother of our modern gardens, housing the richest collection of temperate flora in the world. Its ornamental floral descendants announce our springs, with bold yellow forsythias and splashy rhododendrons, azaleas and camellias. China's blooms also colour our summers: roses plus teas and hybrid teas, peonies, gardenia, clematis, apricots and peaches. Mother China then embellishes our autumns with chrysanthemums and enriches our winters with citrus – oranges, grapefruit and lemon. In fact, it would be very hard to find a garden in the northern planting zones that does not owe a debt of gratitude to China's gardens.

The work of a plant collector was colonial by nature. Fortune was working to enrich himself on that hillside, but he also worked on behalf of the gardeners and collectors of Britain. For his herbarium, he collected a catalogue of pressed plants that he dried and maintained for the benefit of his fellow botanists. He trained his servants carefully in this work: constantly changing sheets of blotting paper, looking for mould, insects, and other things that might foul a collection. 'It is possible for an intelligent native to do a certain amount of the changing of the drying paper,' wrote an expert on plant hunting in China, 'but the arranging of the plants in the press on the first occasion may make or mar the beauty of the specimens.' Fortune also collected for the Wardian case, carefully shaking dirt from roots, placing samples in boxed soil, watering them and then sealing the glass, hoping – always hoping – that the tender uprooted plant would take to its new environment and survive long enough to make it to Shanghai, and from thence to England.

Beyond the active work of digging, pressing, replanting and shipping, Fortune had an obligation to history: his notebook. If the plants he catalogued were to be of any use to botanists at home, his observations of them *in situ* must be scrupulously noted and provided to his peers.

The vast treasure trove of Fortune's memoirs from China contain reams of such precise botanical detail. For all but the expert, detail such as this can make heavy reading. Nevertheless, his notes stand as testimony to his skill as a collector, not to mention as a businessman. Of the 15,000 plant species in China, nearly half of which were endemic, Fortune sampled and catalogued so many ornamentals that there was almost nothing left for future plant hunters to exploit. Those who would take up Fortune's mantle in China would have to head west towards Yunnan and up into the Himalayas to find their own *terra incognita*.

Fortune felt content as he journeyed, hopeful even. There was no reason to believe he would not be successful in his mission to source tea plants and seeds. But his day-to-day comfort quickly dissipated.

As the boat continued upstream, the passengers' behaviour to Fortune shifted subtly: his fellow travellers no longer addressed him by his Chinese name, Sing Wah. In fact, Fortune noticed they were no longer addressing him at all. Instead his shipmates stole glances at him, muttering just outside the range of his hearing. They avoided him. He seemed to have become an object of intrigue, even more so than the dwarf.

Their attention made him uncomfortable, where before he had been enjoying his disguise. Fortune had believed he was fast losing his foreignness, that being British was something he could shed like a change of clothing. He'd thought there was nothing innate about his outsider status. Though he was not yet comfortable eating under the watchful eyes of Chinese travellers, he was becoming more so. At mealtimes he sensibly kept his distance from other diners, who drew throughout on long tobacco pipes while drinking distilled grain alcohol, growing louder and more belligerent with every toast. He noticed he was beginning to understand others as they mumbled drunkenly, the rough singsong Chinese shaping itself into words, and words into meaningful sentences. He would not join in general conversation but his ear was starting to tune into the local language. But now, suddenly, it seemed to Fortune that the other passengers were catching on to his ruse.

He called Wang aside to enquire what had brought about this change.

Wang said that the Coolie had once again blown Fortune's cover; that in a flurry of resentment and angling for 'face', the dumb turtle had unmasked his master.

'That coolie, he too much a fool-o; he have talkie that you no belong to this country; you more better sendie he go away, suppose you no wantye too much bobbly.' He's making trouble, Wang insisted in pidgin. He's put you in danger. Get rid of him.

To us, the Coolie's resentment is easy to understand. His life was controlled by someone outside the social code of *mian*. He was kept subservient to Fortune's every whim while his master remained ignorant of the Coolie's reciprocal need for face. The Coolie felt that the only way to right the wrong was to gain 'face' elsewhere, in the public arena of the boat's passengers and crew. He must also have seen an avenue for his own advancement in Fortune's unveiling – though how exactly is a mystery since the illiterate Coolie left no record.

Fortune, ignorant of the way in which 'face' worked, never could work out how the betrayal might have benefited the Coolie. In the end, giving up his master's secret did the Coolie no outward good whatsoever. The crew seemed to consider that he was now in their power, as if the broken confidence were a punishable offence, while Fortune himself was furious with the tittle-tattling servant. The Coolie grew ever more surly and miserable with each day that passed.

When the ship moored at night, its wooden hull creaking as it bobbed gently in the water, there was typically a guard posted to patrol. 'The boatmen informed me that this part of the country abounded in thieves and robbers, and that they must not all go to bed at night, otherwise something would be stolen from the boat before morning,' Fortune recalled. But on the humid and moonless night following Wang's set to with the captain, no one kept watch at all.

'Wake up!' Wang whispered, shaking Fortune awake. *Qichuang!* The boatmen had all gone into town while the passengers slept onboard. Wang believed there was a conspiracy afoot against his master Fortune; the night watchman had been dismissed, the boatmen were planning to kill them all. Wang had heard this from other passengers, or else whispered between the crew. He knew the captain he'd cheated was still angry. Instead of drinking all night in town, he was planning a covert return to the ship with his crew and then they were going to drown the false Mandarin and his servants in the river.

'They have now gone into town to get some of their friends

to assist them,' Wang insisted. 'They are only waiting until they think we are fast asleep.'

Fortune got off his mat to look through the porthole towards the shore and saw a string of lanterns dancing in the distance. It could well be a band of hooligans approaching, paid to avenge the disgruntled boatman.

He was in trouble. No longer seen as a mysterious Chinese Mandarin, Fortune had been identified as a foreigner, disregarding the strictures of the Treaty of Nanking, hundreds of miles from a sanctioned treaty port. If there was violence in the night, the local authorities would never intervene on his behalf. Fortune waited for the imminent attack.

'Get up, get up! Quick, quick!' Wang said. *Chop! Chop!*

Fortune remained in his cabin with 'all the composure I could command', as the lanterns drew near and the crew approached the boat. Fortune stood by the cabin door, anticipating the worst. He makes no mention of where his guns were – or whether he was even armed that night. Wang and the Coolie, ordinarily cool and detached in their attitude towards him, were solicitous. 'My two Chinamen appeared in a state of great alarm and kept as close to me as they possibly could,' he recalled.

The first member of the band poked his head into the cabin and found Fortune and his servants standing to attention. The boatman looked sheepish, as if he had not expected to find his quarry awake, and broke into an ingratiating grin.

The intruder then shrugged and said he wanted nothing. Nothing at all. He turned his back on Fortune and left.

Other passengers were awake by now, chattering and whispering elsewhere on the boat – but Fortune could not understand well enough to make sense of what was happening.

'Now you see that?' Wang insisted. 'You would not believe me when I told you that they intended to seize and drown us, but had we not been awake and fully prepared, it would have been all over with us.'

It was confusing: Fortune had no idea how great the threat was, or even whether he was in any danger at all. What had happened after all? A man opening a door and walking away? Would things have been very different if he had been asleep?

The captain of the vessel returned later that night, acting as if nothing had happened.

Perhaps nothing had.

Fortune could not rest after that, however. He stayed awake, 'cold and sleepy', listening to the nearby clank and squeak of water wheels, the primitive mills powered by the burbling river. For a man who prided himself upon his powers of observation, it was unnerving to have no idea what exactly had transpired, whether or not he had been in mortal danger. Fortune was coming to understand just how much he depended on his companions: he could not trust them, but he had no alternative.

6

A Green Tea Factory,
Yangtze River, October 1848

With Wang walking five paces ahead to announce his arrival, Fortune, dressed as a tall and proud Mandarin, entered the gates of a green tea factory.

Wang began to supplicate furiously. Would the master of the factory allow an inspection from a visitor, an honoured and wise official who had travelled from a far province to see how such glorious tea was made?

The factory superintendent nodded politely before Fortune and led them into a large building with peeling grey stucco walls. Beyond it lay courtyards, open work spaces and store rooms. It was warm and dry, full of workers manufacturing the last of the season's crop, and the woody smell of green tea hung in the air. This factory was a place of scale and ceremony, where tea was prepared for export through the large distributors in Canton and the burgeoning trade in Shanghai. It was here that a diligent observer could steal the secrets of tea-making.

Though the concept of tea is simple – dry leaf and hot water – the manufacture of it is not intuitive at all. Tea is a highly processed product. The tea recipe remained unchanged for 2000 years, and Europe had been positively addicted to tea for at least 200 of them, but few in Britain's dominions had any first- or even second-hand information about the production of tea before it went into the pot. Fortune's horticultural contemporaries in London and the Directors of the East India Company all believed that tea would yield its secrets if it were held up to the clear light and scrutiny of Western observation. Among Fortune's tasks in China, certainly as critical as providing Indian tea gardens with quality nursery stock, was the duty to flesh out a useful recipe for manufacturing tea. From the picking to the brewing there was a great deal of factory work involved. Drying, firing, rolling – and, for black tea, fermenting. Fortune had explicit instructions from the East India Company to discover everything he could: 'Besides the collection of tea plants and seeds from the best localities for transmission to India, it will be your duty to avail yourself of every opportunity of acquiring information as to the cultivation of the tea plant and the manufacture of tea as practised by the Chinese and on all other points with which it may be desirable that those entrusted wish the superintendence of the tea nurseries in India should be made acquainted.' But the recipe for tea was kept a closely guarded state secret, among China's last and greatest.

In the entry to the tea factory, hanging on the wall, were inspiring calligraphical words of praise, a selection from Lu Yu's great work on tea, the classic *Cha Ching*.

> The best quality tea must have
> The creases like the leather boots of Tartar horsemen,
> Curl like the dewlap of a mighty bullock,
> Unfold like a mist rising out of a ravine,
> Gleam like a lake touched by a zephyr,
> And be wet and soft like
> Earth newly swept by rain

Proceeding into the otherwise empty courtyard, Fortune found fresh tea set to dry in large woven rattan plates, each the size of a kitchen table. The sun beat down on the containers, 'cooking' the tea. No one walked past, no one touched or moved the delicate tea leaves as they dried. The scene was completely still, acting like a large outdoor oven for tea toasting. Fortune learned that for green tea, the leaves were left to bake in the sun for one to two hours.

The sun-baked tea leaves were then taken to a furnace room and thrown into an enormous pan – what amounted to a very large iron wok. Men were working before a series of coal furnaces, all in a row, their queues striping down their backs, tossing a giant salad of tea leaves on an open hearth. In the pan, crisp leaves were vigorously stirred, kept constantly in motion, becoming moist as the fierce heat drew their sap towards the surface. Stir frying the leaves in this way breaks down the cell walls of the tea leaf, just as vegetables soften over high heat. The tea leaves went into the pan stiff from the sun, but came out pliable.

The cooked leaves were then dumped on a table where four or five workers moved piles of them back and forth over bamboo rollers. They were rolled and rolled to bring the essential oils to the surface. The leaves were continuously wrung out, as if tightly squeezing a sponge. 'I cannot give a better idea of this operation than by comparing it to a baker, working and rolling his dough,' Fortune recalled. Pressing and rolling, pressing and rolling, until green juice pooled on the wooden table.

Tightly curled by this stage, the tea leaves were not even a quarter the size they had been when picked. A tea picker plucks perhaps a pound a day, and the leaves are constantly reduced through processing so that the fruits of a day's labour, which was once the size of the basket on the tea picker's back, becomes a mere handful of leaves, a few ounces, a few cups. After rolling, the tea was sent again to the drying pans for a second round of firing, losing volume again with every throw and flick against the hot sides of the iron wok.

With leaves plucked, dried, cooked, rolled and cooked again, all that was left was to sort through the processed tea. Workers sat at a long table, separating the choicest, most tightly wound leaves to use in the teas of the highest quality – the flowery Pekoes – and dividing them from the Congou, or lesser quality, and separating that from the dust, the lowest quality of all.

The quality of tea is determined, in part, by how much of the stem and rougher lower leaves are included in the blend. The highest quality teas, which might in China have a name like Dragon Well or in India FTGFOP1 (Finest Tippy Golden Flowery Orange Pekoe First Grade), are made from the top two leaves and the bud at the end of each tea branch. The top shoots taste delicate and mild, only slightly astringent, and threfore the most pleasant and refreshing.

The tea-ness of tea comes from essential oils which leach flavour and caffeine into a hot cup of water. These chemical compounds are not necessary for the primary survival of the tea plant's cells; they are what is known as secondary compounds. Secondary chemicals help plants in all sorts of ways, such as defending them against pests, infections or fungus, and aid the plant in its fight for survival and repro-duction. Dark green plants, such as tea, produce a bitter chemical to protect their leaves from predators. But the taste that repels insects can, after careful processing, be highly agreeable to human beings.

Tea, like other green plants, has several other defence systems against predators: almost all its thick waxy leaves apart from the topmost shoots are bitter and leathery and difficult to bite through. Tea also has hard fibrous stalks to defend it against animal incursion. These harsh chemical and physical characteristics are what makes the distinctive sharp taste of tea. Clumsy pickers can detract from this by including the next leaf down and even some of the stem; once brewed this will taste harsher, more tannic, and in China at least will be qualified by names suggesting crudeness, like dust.

The workers sat at long low tables to pick through the leaves and sort out any pieces of stem. They also looked for any insects that might have tainted the batch, as well as small stones and pieces of grit from the factory floor. Tea was not a clean product in any sense, one of the reasons why Chinese tea drinkers traditionally discard the first cup from any pot. 'The first cup is for your enemies,' the saying goes amongst China's tea connoisseurs. Your enemies can drink insects and dust, but the civilised drinker 'washes' his tea first.

Culinary historians know nothing about the ancient chef who first put leaf to water. But where human knowledge has failed, human imagination has inserted itself and there are a raft of creation myths from China.

Many Chinese say tea was discovered by the mythical Emperor Shennong, inventor of Chinese medicine and of farming. The story goes that the legendary Emperor was reclining in the leafy shade of a camellia bush, when a shiny leaf dropped into his cup of boiled water. As the ripples pooled out from the leaf, a broth began to form, riding out the currents, a light green liquor steeped out of the thin, feathery leaf. Shennong knew all the healing properties of plants and could identify as many as seventy poisonous plants in a day-long hike. Convinced this was not, he took a sip of the stew to find it tasted refreshing: aromatic, slightly bitter, stimulating, restorative.

Ascribing authorship of tea to a revered former leader is a very Confucian thing to do – it puts power in the hands of the ancestors and links the present day to the mythic past. But Buddhists in China have another creation story for tea, concerning a completely different religious and cultural figure: the Gautama Buddha. As a travelling ascetic, legend tells us, the young monk Siddhartha was wandering on a mountain, perfecting his practice, praying without ceasing. The weary supplicant sat down by a tree to meditate, to contemplate the One and the many faces of redemption, and promptly fell asleep. When he awoke he was furious, outraged by his own physical weakness; his body had betrayed him, his eyes were leaden, drowsiness had interfered with his quest for Nirvana.

In a fit of rage he ripped out his eyelashes. Nothing would again impede his path to Truth and Enlightenment. He cast these lashes to the wind, and in all the places where they fell sprang forth a fragrant and flowering bush: the tea plant. Indeed, the fine, silvery fur on the undersides of the highest quality tea leaves resembles delicate eyelashes. Buddha, all-great and compassionate, bequeathed to his followers a draught that would keep them aware and awake, invigorated and focused, an intoxicant in the service of devotion.

It is testimony to the powerful place tea holds in Chinese culture that two such revered figures, Shennong and Buddha, are central to tea's storied creation.

If tea were in fact as simple to make as dropping a camellia leaf in a cup of water then there would have been very little for Fortune to steal. But he was seeking a much more complex body of secret knowledge. Botanists had, to that point, failed miserably in their attempts to decode tea. Fortune's first collecting trip to China in 1843, for the Royal Horticultural

Society, had taken him to the fringes of tea territory as part of his general collecting mandate. At that time, he made an important discovery: green tea and black tea came from the same plant.

The Linnaean Society had hitherto declared unequivocally that green and black tea were siblings, or cousins, closely related but under no circumstances twins. The great Linnaeus, a century before, working off dried samples brought back from China by earlier explorers, said himself that the two were distinct taxa: *Thea viridis* and *Thea bohea*. *Thea viridis*, or green tea, was said to have alternating brown branches and alternating leaves: bright green ovals, short-stalked, convex, serrated, shiny on both sides and downy beneath; with a corolla, or flower, of 5 to 9 white unequally sized petals. *Thea bohea*, black tea, was described as looking nearly the same – only smaller and darker, sort of.

On his first trip, Fortune expected to find identifiable black tea plants in gardens known to produce black tea. Yet he found that the tea plants there looked just like the green tea plants in the green tea gardens. Over the course of that first three-year visit, procuring several tea samples and thoroughly investigating tea, Fortune had concluded that the difference between green tea and black comes from processing alone. The same tea bush can be processed into two very different drinks.

Black tea is fermented, green tea is not. To make black tea, the leaves are allowed to sit in the sun for an entire day, to oxidise and wilt – essentially to spoil a little. Plant chemicals ripen on exposure, the way a banana browns after a few days on display; this is the effect that 'fermenting' has on tea. After the first twelve hours stewing in the sun, black tea is jostled, the liquor is stirred around, and it is left to cure for another twelve hours. This longer process develops black tea's tannins, its strong bitter flavour, as well as its dark colour.

Though it is called 'fermenting', the process of making black tea is technically misnamed. Nothing ferments in a chemical sense; there are no micro-organisms breaking down sugars into alcohol and gas; black tea is cured or ripened. But the language of wine colours the language of all beverages, and so the notion of fermentation has stuck to black tea. (Indeed, if tea does ferment and fungus grows, a carcinogenic substance is produced.)

Most importantly – at least in a practical sense – Fortune's first trip had revealed an elementary piece of the tea puzzle, perhaps the most crucial distinction of all: the difference between green tea and black tea comes from manufacturing alone. Fortune announced these findings to the world.

The Linnaean Society's respected members had mistaken a variation in processing for a biological difference, though as to that point no European botanist had seen tea growing or evaluated it in its living state, perhaps the confusion is understandable. Fortune's documentary evidence ultimately changed tea's Linnaean classification. Tea would soon be known as *Thea sinensis*, literally Tea from China. (Later still it would be reclassified as part of the Camellia family, *Camellia sinensis*.)

In his guise of a Mandarin investigating the green tea factory, Fortune took note of something both peculiar and more than a little alarming on the hands of the tea manufacturers. It was the kind of thing that, once reported, would forever be a boon to the burgeoning Indian tea experiment. It had the power to boost the sales of Indian tea over Chinese forevermore; it would, in fact, be the kind of shorthand for low-quality goods that 'Made in China' is today. While staring at the tea manufacturers busy with the final stages of processing, he noticed their fingers were blue, 'quite blue'.

Amongst the blenders and tasters of the London auction, it was considered gospel fact that the Chinese engaged in all manner of duplicity, inserting twigs and sawdust into their teas to bulk up the loose leaves. It was said the Chinese were brewing their own breakfast tea first, saving the soggy leaves to dry in the sun, then reselling it as fresh tea for the stupid 'white devils'. There was no trust in the trade, no faith in the goodwill of the Chinese manufacturers.

But blue fingers on Chinese workmen heightened Fortune's suspicions further. What could be causing this? He and others had long suspected that the Chinese were chemically dyeing tea for the benefit of the foreign market. Fortune was now in a position to prove or disprove the charge.

He watched each step of the processing carefully, saying nothing, making notes, occasionally asking Wang to put a question to a manager or worker. At one end of the factory the supervisor stood over a white porcelain mortar. In the bowl there was a deep blue powder, made finer and finer with each grind of the pestle. The superintendent was preparing a substance known as Prussian Blue, a pigment used in paints and also known as iron ferrocyanide. That's right – cyanide. When cyanide is ingested, it binds to iron inside cells, interfering with the absorption of certain enzymes and interrupting a cell's ability to produce energy. Cyanide affects the tissues most needed for aerobic respiration, the heart and lungs – in other words, it chokes you from inside. In high doses, cyanide brings on seizures, then coma, then cardiac arrest, killing quickly. At lower doses, cyanide leads to weakness, giddiness, confusion and light-headedness. Exposure to even low levels of cyanide over long periods of time can lead to permanent paralysis.

Elsewhere in the factory, over the charcoal fires where the tea was roasted, Fortune discovered a man cooking a bright yellow powder into a paste. The smell was terrible, like rotten eggs. The yellow substance was gypsum, or calcium sulphate dehydrate, a common component of plaster. Gypsum produces hydrogen sulphide gas as it breaks down. While the gas is produced naturally by the body in low doses, in high doses it acts as a broad-spectrum poison, affecting many systems at once, particularly the nervous system. At lower concentrations, gypsum acts as an irritant; it reddens the eyes, inflames the throat, causes nausea, shortness of breath, fluid in the lungs. Consumed over the long term, it might produce fatigue, memory loss, headaches, irritability and dizziness. It might even induce miscarriage in women, and failure to thrive in infants and children.

On observing the use of gypsum in the tea factory, Fortune estimated there was more than half a pound of plaster and cyanide included in every hundred pounds of tea consumed. The average Londoner was believed to consume as much as two pounds of tea per year.

Between the blue ferrocyanide and the yellow gypsum, Chinese tea was poisoning British consumers, though this was not being done maliciously. The Chinese believed that foreigners wanted their green tea actually to look green.

'No wonder the Chinese consider the natives of the West to be a race of barbarians,' Fortune said.

But why, he asked, were they making green tea so extremely green, since it was so much better without the addition of poison, and since the Chinese themselves would never dream of drinking it coloured?

'Foreigners seemed to prefer having a mixture of Prussian blue and gypsum with their tea, to make it look uniform and pretty, and as these ingredients were cheap enough, the Chinese [have] no objection to supply them as such teas always fetch . . . a higher price!'

Fortune surreptitiously collected some of the poisonous dyes from the factory. He bundled them up in his wax-dipped cloth sacks and stowed them away in the generous folds of his Mandarin's costume.

He wanted specimens, data, samples, to see and touch and analyse. But most of all he wanted to send that dye back to England.

These poisons would go on to be prominently displayed in London's Great Exhibition of 1851. In the glittering Crystal Palace, where Britain displayed to the world all her industrial, scientific and economic might, she also showed off green tea dye. Putting the poisons on public display represented the moment when tea, the national drink of Britain, came out of the shadows of myth and mystery and into the light of Western science and understanding. Fortune unmasked unwitting Chinese criminality and provided an irrefutable argument for British-manufactured tea.

Robert Fortune's personal victory was thus announced on a world stage. He had cracked the tea recipe.

7

House of Wang, Anhui Province, November 1848

Though the day's light was fading, Fortune could see twisted pines poking into a sea of cloud, ornamenting the sharp outlines of the hills beneath. The landscape might have been made for the gestural strokes of a scroll-painter's brush. As Fortune ascended the road to Wang's family home, he made a mental note that he had never before seen the tea-plant so lush, so happy, He took this for reassurance – if any were needed – that he had indeed reached the right place, the Sung Lo Mountains, the area thought to be the birthplace of green tea. It was as if the finest tea plants refused to take root on any but the very ideal of a Chinese mountain. It was no wonder, Fortune thought, that so much of China's appreciation for tea was echoed in its arts, painting, pottery and poetry, for who would not wish to reproduce, savour, and preserve forever such intense beauty?

Wang's childhood home was a mere two miles from the foot of the steep slopes of Sung Lo Shan, a most picturesque mountain range and Fortune's primary destination for this collecting trip. The proximity of the Wang Clan to such famous tea grounds perhaps explains why Wang had remained his principal guide, despite his grasping ways and proclivity for trouble. He came from people for whom tea-growing was a native art. Returning to the tea peaks from the coast was a ritual that Wang's ancestors had performed for centuries.

Wang strode through the heavy wooden doors of his child-hood home steps ahead of Fortune. He waltzed in without carrying any baggage, prince of the palace, happy to be home, eager to announce the arrival of the distinguished foreign Mandarin and, not coincidentally, Wang's own recent stroke of good luck. Given the remoteness and poverty of the area, and the corresponding lack of public inns, Fortune had agreed to make his residence at the Wangs' home. And a guest like Robert Fortune did not come along very often for a farm family like the Wangs.

They embraced their son with joy. Wang's mother doted on him and asked if he had already eaten his rice, while his father beamed with pride. They were also appropriately surprised and impressed by the novelty and stature of the Mandarin to whom their son was attached, protesting earnestly that their home was not worthy of this honour. Looking around, Fortune had to agree, if only silently. The door through which he'd just entered featured hardware so crude and primitive that any blacksmith in England would have been ashamed to call it a latch or hinge. Strips of faded red paper hung limply over the lintel, to bring blessings on the family and protect the house from evil.

At first glance, Fortune could see little grandeur or comfort in the Wang household. The house itself was rickety and almost physically impossible: a dwelling perched on the side of a cliff, as if it were about to drop off, a testament to the persistence of the labourers who had built it there. Fortune had seen many drab dwellings on his travels, but had not as yet dared to enter a peasant's home. The beaten earth walls were thick and white-painted, in contrast to the blackened roof timbers. The roofline was lavishly decorated and ornately carved; upturned corner tiles had the outlines of animals pressed into the clay to scare dangerous spirits away

– it was believed there were demons everywhere. The house had small windows, covered with rough lattice-wood screens to keep out the birds, but not the vermin (and most certainly not the flies).

The Wang home was not so grand as to provide separate quarters for men and women, which Fortune must have come to expect from his visits to the gardens of great men where he had collected some of his finest specimens on his previous trip to China. Only houses of noble rank could afford such luxuries, and the Wang family was poor. Yet, within this house, the respective territory of the sexes was as clearly distinguished as if they had been physically separated. In the 1,000 or so square feet of the Wang household, the different spheres were well defined. The men occupied the public space, a sizeable room with sacks of rice piled in one corner. The occasional chicken wandered through, and a few select pieces of furniture – a wedding chest, a cane kitchen cabinet, a bent-wood chair – bore testament to better days. Off this were other, smaller rooms where the women lived, babies were nursed, food was prepared, cloth was woven, and the old and infirm slept away the end of their life amidst dust and sewage, the detritus of family life.

Yet Fortune was determined not to be outdone in showing the usual courtesies, and almost immediately seemed to be among the best of friends. Wang Senior was a farmer and, like many Chinese, at the mercy of the Yellow Country's growing pains, the boom-and-bust cycle of an agrarian economy undergoing a population explosion. Old Wang had known prosperity, only to be brought low by famine and hard times. Heedless of his poverty, the old man was generous to Fortune, the foreigner. Soon a great dinner was set out for Fortune and the Wang Clan, with the best that the family could offer, and the fattiest cut of pork, the first taste of the stew, was always offered to their distinguished guest. After dinner they retired to their cramped chambers, Fortune harbouring intentions of making an early start to trek up the Sung Lo Shan and commence collecting seeds.

In the morning, however, rain fell in torrents, and there was no way to leave the Wang household. It was then that Fortune first became acutely aware that the home he was staying in held not one but four separate families, various branches of the larger extended clan, each with all of the trappings of Chinese domestic life. Each with its own children, each with its own kitchen and stove, each cooking its own meals. The hours leading up to mealtimes proved especially torturous for Fortune. Each part of the house had a separate kitchen fire – and there were no chimneys at all. The foul smoke and burning smell of pork fat filled the house fourfold, wafting into every nook and cranny, dirtying anything that was clean, seeking escape through cracks in the windows and doors. Fortune's eyes stung and watered perpetually from the stoves' smoke. To his amazement, the other dwellers in the Wang home took this and the myriad other discomforts of cohabiting and collectivism in their stride. They simply, he supposed, knew no different.

Fortune shared more in the way of background with Wang Senior than he might first have thought. Despite being a farmer, and an impoverished one at that, Old Wang was a literate man. China has always enjoyed a high level of peasant literacy – it had a movable type printing press almost 4,000 years before Gutenberg printed his first Bible. Old Wang had been trained to be a scholar and poet, as many young men of the region were despite their meagre circumstances. When families in the neighbourhood became successful merchants, they endowed a local school or Confucian academy in their village. The neighbourhood sons were coached to compete in the national Civil Service exams, so as to join the highest levels of the government and become *jinshi*. Sung Lo was known for producing *jinshi*. Three hundred years before Fortune's arrival, in the sixteenth century, a scholar noted that for every three merchants in the region, there was one poet. At night, after supper, while the dark and downpour kept the full household inside, Old Wang kept alive the ways of his elders by reading Chinese fables to his large extended family while they huddled together to keep warm. That single act in itself was a happy sight to Fortune, who up to that point had found little in his servant's pastoral household to please him.

Though the Wangs were decidedly peasants, they took education seriously; the household bore ample evidence of scholarship, such as the calligraphic poems hanging on scraps of paper on the walls. In China, calligraphy is an art form revered by men of standing and education. Because the Chinese language is pictorial, it lends itself to beautified visual renditions. The brush, the ink stick, paper and ink slabs, known as the Four Treasures of the Scholar's Studio, were all obtained from local forests. Each brush stroke was thought to reflect the character and sentiments of the writer, his psychological state of mind at the time he was contemplating the poetry he performed. To be a good calligrapher required training and respect for tradition, and so complemented the Wang family values of discipline and respect.

Fortune could also see something familiar in the family's existence when he compared it with his own modest roots in the Scottish borders. He noted that, 'The Chinese cottages, amongst the tea hills, are simple and rude in their construction, and remind one of what we used to see in Scotland in former years, when the cow and pig lived and fed in the same house with the peasant. Scottish cottages, however, even in these days, were always better furnished and more comfortable than those of the Chinese are at the present time.' Rustic life was rarely exotic the world over: instead peasants were diligent, stooping over barren fields, tilling hillsides, shouldering baskets up mountain paths, barely getting by. China or Scotland, the workload was heavy. And where Scotland had whisky, in Xiuning county there was tea. Tea like Scotch, was made where other crops would not thrive. And, as with Scotland's finest malts, it was in these poor cottages that the best teas with the most curious names were found.

In the hierarchy of Chinese life, tea was ranked as one of the seven necessities along with firewood, rice, oil, salt, soy sauce and vinegar. For the Wang family to participate in the manufacture of life's basic needs was an honour; they saw themselves as meeting the needs of the broader world order. Though tea was a necessity, it was also considered a luxury. It took time to enjoy tea and money to buy it – if you weren't growing your own. It was the greatest joy of the official classes to sit and drink tea while writing poetry. The Wangs, and millions of families like them, made such civilised pleasures possible.

Conditions on Sung Lo peak were perfect for raising tea, but terrible for raising a family. The steep mountainsides, cloaked in mists, were ideal tea grounds with their well-drained soil and indirect sun, but those same conditions made growing other crops a human chore. 'The district is [set] among 10,000 mountains. Its land is difficult and not flat. Its earth is tough and unchanging . . . Though the people are industrious and use all their strength, the harvest is only enough to provide for half [the population],' wrote a local Mandarin in an 1815 county gazetteer. Tea-growing was a way to supplement the Wang family income on the Sung Lo slopes: '. . . where there is land lacking, those who support [themselves] by tea-growing are seventy to eighty per cent. From this they clothe and feed themselves and pay their land and labour taxes,' records state. The Wangs worked the land both privately and collectively, tilling a public field to pay for taxes and tribute as well as their private field to feed their own kin. This division of responsibility was entirely Confucian: the basic family unit was co-extensive with a wider social world; the men studied, the women worked, and the Mandarins – China's politician-scholars – collected taxes in the name of the Emperor. Sung Lo's topography was a major drawback for an agricultural region, yet the hills were also its greatest asset for it takes a high mountain to grow perfect tea.

Sung Lo's slopes were a masterwork of muscle; the hillsides had been brought to heel and carved into steady, laddered fields for planting grains such as rice and barley; vegetables such as beans, sesame, squash, eggplant, turnip, onions, bamboo shoots, ginger, garlic; fruit and nuts such as peaches, watermelon, papaya, walnuts and peanuts. The terraced slopes were a marvel of human might, testament to what China's giant workforce could accomplish over generations. The Wang family could level a mountain given enough time, but they could not grow enough to eat. Many from their region, over the generations, had left farming for trade. 'Because agriculture is not sufficient to feed the people of the county, most people are engaged in commerce as their constant business . . . They travelled to the south and the north. Some were pedlars and some set up their shops. They consider what is abundant and what is in shortage, and buy or sell out according to the trend of demand and supply,' reported the local gazetteer three hundred years earlier. Thus it was that the younger Wang, like so many sons of Sung Lo peak, had been forced by economic circumstances to leave the tea mountains and try to improve his fortunes in the cities on the coast. 'The bitterness you are eating is what makes a man into a man,' went one local folksong.

Wang's story was repeated throughout China in the nineteenth century. By 1850, it had a population of 400 million; for every person alive in 1650, there were three in 1850. As a result of the population boom, villages and towns grew closer together, farms smaller, woodlands were mown down and converted to farmland. With the population rising, the pressure on land resources increased. Irrigation, fertiliser, and the introduction of New World crops such as corn were used to open up previously marginal farmland. The necessary increase in food supply came from increasingly less valuable sources of calories, labour and land. The local ecology suffered; there were famines, mudslides and floods. There was competition for basic human resources, yet with manpower so abundant wages remained low.

The surfeit of labour meant that young men such as Wang generally left their home villages to work on the coast. But the population boom also led to a dearth of marriageable women as female infanticide swept through China. Girls married away from the family house and needed dowries, so they were considered sources of debt. Male children brought honour to a family as well as wives to manage the house and children to carry on the clan name, but without local women to marry there was little anchoring men to their home village and so they migrated to the cities, to join gangs or become boatmen or sedan chair carriers. Wang's area, in particular, was known for producing pawnbrokers. With the new population boom, the established village order fell away: men became emigrants while women tried to boost the household economy in any way they could, such as spinning and weaving textiles, or, in the Sung Lo Shan, making and selling their own tea.

The Wangs believed in the Confucian tradition in which there was a hierarchy of occupations: the highest, belonging to scholars and poets, preserved beauty and celebrated order; peasants came second, the cogs in the national machine, growing the food and materials necessary to make a complicated country like China work; merchants were rated at the bottom of the collective heap, earning a living off the hard labour of others, producing nothing of note themselves. While there was great honour in being a peasant, especially a literate one, being unable to support your children was a great loss of face – and to have their sons off in the cities reflected badly on the Sung Lo families.

On the evening of that first rainy day, a ludicrous-looking pair, the giant Coolie and the obliging dwarf who had followed Fortune off the boat, arrived bearing the luggage. As they placed the heavy chests and baskets squarely on the stone floor of the entry chamber, a small cloud of dust rose up. The Coolie was anxious to describe how he had nearly met his end at the hands of the boatmen Wang had mistreated, and been forced to take refuge for the night in a temple, the only protection against his ill-wishers he could find. It was a bizarre pantomime, and Wang did not feel compelled to translate. Fortune watched with amusement, calculating that if the Coolie had managed to escape with all the luggage safe and intact then surely things were not quite as bad as the man made them out to be. At any rate, he was glad that the bags had arrived safely, despite the rains.

Although his retinue was back to full strength, there was still nothing for Fortune to do but to wait. For days the weather on the mountain remained dreary as the rains of November became another guest of the Wangs, constraining Fortune and refusing to leave. The Wangs slept late and went to bed early, preferring the warmth of their bedclothes to the damp cold of morning. Rain gave hardworking peasants a chance to rest, and it was more than welcome after a long summer and busy tea harvest. Fortune was encouraged to do the same, but he had come to steal tea, not just to drink it, seemingly without end. The many Wang children were overcome with cabin fever and were curious about the strange man with his round eyes, long nose, tall bearing and exotic possessions. Fortune had seldom been stuck inside with his own children as long as he had with the Wang offspring. For four undifferentiated days, he felt himself a captive of the House of Wang.

And then, at last, the rains eased.

Emerging to a clear day, Fortune was struck by the beauty of the view from the Wangs' house. According to the Chinese principles of Feng Shui, the luckiest location for a house has a mountain at the back and an open view to the front – easy enough to apply in the hilly country of Sung Lo where, whenever there was a mountain behind you, there was a sweeping vista before you. Like the Wangs' house, most Chinese homes followed the general architectural principles of Feng Shui, which literally translates as 'wind and water', the notion that there are physical laws divined along elemental principles to encourage the flow of *qi* (pronounced *chi*), or energy. Houses and rooms faced south; there was a central courtyard to symbolise the centre of the home; the building was symmetrical but with an odd number of bays. A southern outlook was thought to confer an abundance of *yang*, the masculine energy, so the Wang house not only capitalised on the abundance of sunlight and warmth, but bequeathed upon the family the bounty of auspicious, life-seeking energy. Chinese dwellings dating back to the 12th Century B.C. are found to be aligned along the north-south axis, with a primary entrance facing south. Symmetry was revered because it allowed for the central courtyard in which to display shrines to the Wang ancestors. Odd numbers too were considered to be *yang*, whereas an even number of rooms would have introduced too much *yin* – or female energy – into the house.

The Sung Lo Mountains were nearly barren except for the tea plants that clung to their peaks. Though it was famed as the birthplace of green tea and the home of its finest leaves, the region had not been extensively exploited. The production at the time of Fortune's visit was mainly for the use of the growers themselves, and the priests whose temples dotted the rugged hillsides.

From the Wangs' house Fortune headed off towards the Sung Lo slopes to undertake in earnest the collecting of tea seeds. Although they rose in the distance ahead of him, he might well have been guided by his nose as well as his eyes. It was said of the area 'even without seeing [the mountain], you can smell the tea scent a mile away'. Tea is enormously fragrant on the bush; it fills the air and lungs. In a tea garden, the moist and mineral herbal scent is everywhere. It seems obvious that even primitive man would have been compelled to liberate that smell, to release the potent sap and spirit of the odour so as to imbibe or eat it. Tea has been called the 'essence of mountains' in Chinese poetry. The phrase is so apposite: every ounce of the Sung Lo peak, from loam to limestone, is concentrated into tea; soil, water, air and sun combine in the tiniest, newest leaf of the tea plant. Mountains are made manifest and mankind drinks them in.

As always, Fortune found the hillsides welcoming. His chest expanded in the brisk November air. He bent low, picking off the green fruit pods filled with seeds. They looked like little pin cushions, covered in leathery skin. Strange that something so prosaic should contain the prize for which he had journeyed so far from home. The bushes were dormant, no longer growing at the fast clip of summer, pushing out new tea shoots. But this was a good time to collect seeds.

Old Mr Wang followed Fortune every morning, disrupting his meditative walks. However much Fortune wished to pick his seeds and dig his seedlings with a minimum of interference, he could not shake off the old man. Fortune did not seek such friendship, but the elder Wang was his self-appointed shadow.

For a week, Fortune's days settled into a routine of hard work, punctuated by beautiful vistas, new discoveries, and the seemingly continuous negotiations required by the very informal economy of the Wang household. Fortune would rise early, head with Wang and the coolie to the Sung Lo ridge, and pick up all the tea seeds they could find. The work was less exhausting than exhilarating, at least for Fortune, in these magnificent surroundings. In the evening, they returned to the Wang residence and resumed the hard bargaining that seemed to preoccupy, and perhaps entertain, the residents of Sung Lo Shan.

The Coolie was convinced that Wang had badly abused him in the course of the disputes with the boatmen, and had by now marked Wang down as a coward – reasonably enough, Fortune thought. The Coolie therefore demanded that Wang should compensate him for his troubles to the amount of four dollars. Wang, now on his home turf, thought it safe to ignore this. The Coolie then intimated that he would raise an army; would go and collect some of his own countrymen to force Wang to pay the due amount. Wang ignored this. When the Coolie returned later, unaccompanied, Fortune took him aside and told him firmly that the matter was at an end, and that if the Coolie pressed his claim any further, Fortune would withhold his pay. This, and a small loan to the Coolie, which Fortune could never hope to see repaid, seemed to put the matter to rest.

Fortune himself also found it useful to engage in some bargaining, even a little squeeze. A week or so before reaching Sung Lo, he encountered a barberry, or *Berberis*, a woody shrub with large, glossy, spiny leaves the like of which was unknown to him, but which seemed especially handsome as it turned into its bright autumnal colours. It looked like it would be good for borders and generally well suited to the European garden. Unfortunately, the one specimen Fortune saw was too large to transplant, and apparently without progeny nearby. So, having plucked a leaf of it and marked its location, Fortune initially charged Wang with locating a similar shrub in his home district. When Wang took no interest in this task, it occurred to Fortune that some of the vast extended family might be enlisted instead.

He showed his sample leaf to a small assembly of Wang's relatives, and promised a dollar to anyone who could bring him a similar plant of transportable size. Much to his delight, within a few minutes one of the assembly returned bearing an entire branch. Fortune compared it to the specimen leaf, confirmed it was one and the same, and asked that they bring the whole shrub. This provoked a spirited conversation amongst the family members. It seemed that the plant was of medicinal use, they said, and the owner would not will-ingly part with it. Not for any price. 'Sell me this one, and you will be able to buy a dozen others with the money,' Fortune implored.

But the finder was unyielding: 'My uncle, in whose garden it is growing, does not want money; he is rich enough; but he requires a little of the plant now and then when he is unwell, and therefore he will not part with it.' Fortune, sensing the opening here of an attempt to hold out for a better price, changed tack. He asked only if they would show him the plant, and promised not even to touch it. He would then bargain directly with the owner. But this also seemed to be too much to expect. Hands flew up, voices squawked in protest, until Wang himself intervened, vouching for Fortune to his assembled cousins.

The crew eventually led him to the thrilling new plant, giving Fortune the opportunity to negotiate one on one with the uncle. It was no use. He said the plant was rare and the berries were of tremendous medicinal value for curing diarrhoea, fever, weak appetites, upset stomachs, yeast, urinary tract infections, and a whole host of internal agues. He flatly refused to give up the plant – he would not even give Fortune a fresh branch for cloning. Fortune had no idea whether this was just strategy on the uncle's part, or whether the old man really did value the barberry so. And if all the uncle said was true, it made the plant hunter want a sample all the more. Was it all just a sophisticated squeeze? The question was rendered moot when another of Wang's relatives came to him, furtively, the next day, and indicated that he could find Fortune other shrubs of the same sort, for the precious dollar. Fortune took him up on the offer, and the young man promptly returned with three fine, healthy specimens. Buyer and seller were both well satisfied. The barberry, it seemed, was common in Sung Lo. Fortune went on to ship the plants to England, where they became a great favourite for use in hedges and landscape gardens.

In the intimate space of the Wang house, money continued to change hands – Fortune's money, though he had neither consented to nor been informed of the transactions, and frequently had very little idea what was happening. The Coolie, still peeved by Wang's mishandling of the boatmen, kept trying to extort money from the young translator. Old Wang, thinking that no act of hospitality should go unrewarded, argued for hard cash from Fortune's collective purse in exchange for his room and board. Young Wang, busy arranging Fortune's passage back to the coast, finalised arrangements which overcharged him by 2,000 per cent. The squeeze went on and on and on. 'Such is the character of the Chinese,' Fortune muttered.

Yet Fortune the spy had nonetheless managed to get the best of the bargain: the most valuable asset in Sung Lo. His servants and hosts might have scraped a little off the top for their trouble on his behalf, but it was small change by comparison. Once Fortune left the House of Wang, the finest green tea plants in the world would go with him, crossing the seas to become the most prized possessions of the world's only superpower.

Still the Sung Lo region had brighter days ahead of it. Fortune's arrival marked the earliest moment of direct contact between the celebrated green tea region and the Western world. In only a few short years, green tea from Sung Lo, based on the reports from tea connoisseur Fortune, would find its way into export markets in Europe and America. It was branded Green Tun, and was to become a great favourite with fashionable women of taste and society. Though Sung Lo was beset by economic hardship, famine and poverty, and a rebellion by religious zealots was soon to break out, the moment of Fortune's arrival was significant for Wang's family. The young translator who had brought Fortune to the Sung Lo Mountains was leading his province into the future.

8

Shanghai at the Lunar
New Year, January 1849

After a December which had featured a relatively
uneventful return journey from the mountains, the turn
of the New Year found Robert Fortune toiling in a Shanghai
garden occupying the land around some warehouses. This
garden was scientifically oriented, with neat rows of seedlings
and transplants, in an area reclaimed from the rich, silty banks
of the Huangpu River, a tributary at the mouth of the Yangtze.
It was not a garden for walking through, Chinese-style.

To the Chinese, the new garden typified the enormous
changes about to overtake the previously small and sleepy
port. Far beyond the walls of the ancient city, the new garden
was designed to be functional and European: to keep a stock
of *materia medica* ready, and to feed the British merchants
food that was recognisable. It also provided a hospitable home
for the Chinese plants scavenged from the countryside by
Robert Fortune.

Within the walls of old Shanghai there were gardens too,
enormous floral parks with painted red pagodas, temples, and
'stone boats' resting in the middle of cultured carp ponds.
These gardens belonged to rich men. In these places, a scholar
could wander to his libraries, from room to room, between
rough rockery pillars, and demure concubines in flowing
robes could pluck their harps and sing about love. There a

man could contemplate the great texts of Confucius or write a line or two of poetry while observing the changing daylight on different vistas, blossoms and seasons. Such gardens did not resemble European gardens whose viewpoints were static, a vista meant to be enjoyed from a particular point, seated stiffly on a bench under a parasol. The Chinese garden was three-dimensional, enjoyed most when walking, the aspect changing from step to step. Here a rock pillar, there a fish jumping; such gardens were animated. There were no straight lines, for it was thought that demons could not travel in a zig-zag fashion and no trickster spirits should follow important men in contemplation. The Chinese garden was a superstitious remnant of the past, a relic, in a China that was fast losing its battle against modernity.

Upon arrival in Shanghai, Fortune's first order of business was to post word of his success to the Company and the waiting gardeners in India. 'I have much pleasure in informing you that I have procured a large supply of seeds and young plants which I trust will get safely to India. These were procured in different parts of the country some from a celebrated tea farm . . .' Just as quickly, he set to work preparing his living booty for shipment to India.

Fortune took up residence in the foreign quarter, again at the home of the trading company Dent, Beale & Co. The firm was one of the three leading houses in the Far East, and Beale was the oldest of the China hands. Among Fortune's most crucial connections in China was his affiliation with Thomas Dent and his firm. Dent Beale & Co. owned a compound in the British area, north of noisy Old Shanghai and south of the fetid Souzhou creek, on what had been a towing path for trackers moving boats on the Huangpu River. The compound featured a new and largely empty factory, and enough land to provide a garden big enough to accommodate both Fortune's treasures as well as the amateur interests of the British expat gardeners in Dent's circle. The revered senior partner, Thomas Beale, 'merchant prince and opium mogul', had spent fifty years in the China trade, never returning to Britain. He had already made and lost several fortunes in Cathay. 'He was himself one of the old school in its fullest signification: stately in person, somewhat formal, with distinguished manners,' wrote a contemporary.

Dent & Co.'s legacy to the international community was an ongoing interest in and concern with China's horticulture. For his own amusement, Beale kept a garden in Macau, growing the 'choicest and rarest' carnations, chrysanthe-mums, poppies, and all manner of Chinese ornamentals, in addition to keeping peacocks and monkeys. Dent & Co.'s local Shanghai gardeners were plant hunting in places where no white man could ever go – and the firm was happy to share its rare cuttings with other European plant aficionados residing in the East.

Dent and Fortune were cordial and friendly, but the firm's main interest was, naturally, in the success of the China trade, with its crucial opium-for-tea nexus. Fortune's occupation as a tea spy could well be the undoing of all the trading firms in the Far East. If tea manufacture moved to India, all the China merchants would be out of their most profitable commodity. Yet Dent, Beale & Co. provided Fortune with one of his greatest assets in China – a garden. It is unclear who, outside of the consuls in Hong Kong and Shanghai, knew of Fortune's true aims as a botanical spy. Knowingly or not, Dent & Co. was helping sow the seeds of the China trade's destruction. If they took notice of Fortune's tea haul, however, they would have had no reason to expect he was doing anything other than a botanical study of tea for East India House and the tea traders at Mincing Lane.

Fortune had full use of the grounds at Dent's factory in Shanghai, to replant, repack and care for his tea seeds and seedlings. He also had access to Dent's Chinese gardener, a knowledgeable man who was armed with all the answers and reasons for whatever gardening choices he made. Beale once told a visitor to his menagerie that 'the only way to please a Chinese gardener was to let him do as he pleased', especially when it came to methods 'they took much pride in'. To interfere with a Chinese gardener at work, Beale understood, was to make him lose face. Even in a garden, 'face' was the key to success in China.

Nonetheless, Fortune kept his portion of the garden, vast tracts of tea seedlings stretching off into the distance, as an Englishman would. The country beyond the walls of Old Shanghai was still rural and the land beyond the British concession was all mulberry scrub for silkworms and ancestral graves, overhung with the swampy smell of night soil. Dent's Shanghai garden was a bulwark against the vast ocean of China outside the factory walls.

After visiting three other celebrated green tea districts for seed-collecting, Fortune had arrived in Shanghai in the days just leading up to Chinese New Year (being determined by the lunar calendar) in 1849. It was the Year of the Rooster, a flamboyant, feisty, and outrageous year according to the Chinese zodiac. The biggest holiday of the Chinese year, it is a time of celebration, of fireworks, of settling debts, cash gifts and ancestor worship. Expatriates would look forward to it, both for the fireworks and festivities as well as for the chance to pick up some bargains as the locals scrambled to raise cash needed to pay off lingering debts, a New Year's tradition.

Shanghai's gay celebration of the New Year pulsed through the old city's thick walls and eddied out into the foreign concessions. The few Britons, tea and silk traders and Foreign

Office men, were easily tempted into watching the dragon dances and the grave-sweeping in the local cemeteries with bewildered interest. The ancient streets were crowded with hawkers, jugglers and circus performers. Small beggar children with seeping sores tugged at wrists and ankles and wished Happy New Year to allcomers – it was good luck to give alms at New Year. In the temples, Buddhas with engorged bellies sat smugly in clouds of joss smoke, so unlike any of the Chinese themselves who were generally wiry and almost never fat. The Shanghainese had a jolly, cocksure New Year, but Fortune could not join in the merriment.

Under Dent & Co.'s overly generous care, Fortune's collection had survived transplant from the wild, but its next relocation would be the most dangerous. Indeed, no plant had yet survived a trip the likes of which he planned for his specimens, sailing from Shanghai to Hong Kong, and from there to Calcutta and the hill plantations of the Himalayas, contending with heat and sea and salt but also river travel, mountain travel, and monsoon.

Fortune's general disquiet was accompanied by the cold of the Chinese New Year which arrives in the deepest, least hopeful part of winter. Typically, Dent's garden was a drowsy place where the labourers were not made to work too hard, especially in the winter days leading up to New Years' festivities. But with Fortune present the garden was alive with indignant labour – at Chinese New Year, no one is supposed to work. It was essential, however, that the gardeners – and Fortune – get the packing right. He was at his task every morning in gloves and hat, industriously replanting his cuttings and clones, packaging and labelling seeds and seedlings. He was shipping some 13,000 young plants to the Himalayas, the first such shipment the hills would ever see. He had also packed 10,000 tea seeds, about five gallons worth

– not much by volume, or even by weight, but representing weeks of back-breaking fieldwork and hunched-over plucking in Wang's sodden tea gardens. If Fortune's tea were to fail, all his hard work and the East India Company's hopes for overtaking the Chinese would go for naught.

Every day, no matter how cold or bleak, he squatted in the garden, preparing his first shipments of stolen tea for their trip to new ground. He broke up his hoard, meting out separate packages for four separate ships so that if something happened to one load, the rest would be safe.

Fortune knew that the success of his green tea undertaking was still far from assured at this point. No matter how splendid the seedlings appeared in Shanghai, plants prefer to be stationary; they are not generally fond of travel. His precious green tea might not take to the dual stresses of both winter and overseas travel, despite the marvel of the Wardian case. Moreover, winter is a dangerous time for seeds and shrubs; they become dormant and require coddling. A good gardener with a nose for frost can take a breath of the night air and tell whether or not plants will survive the night or, like a baby, require swaddling in rice sacks and rags until the sun melts the frost.

Fortune ordered a local glazier and ironworker to construct for him eleven glazed cases in which to pack his many thousand seedlings. The saplings were perhaps a year old, many much younger, fragile plants with weak and underdeveloped roots. But at least Fortune felt he could rely on his own previous experience shipping plants by this method: his earlier trip to China had relied heavily on such cases, and the results had left no doubt in his mind as to their efficacy.

The tea seeds were a different story. The East India Company had notoriously failed to move seeds successfully from China to India in the preceding ten years. In one early shipment, before the widespread use of the Wardian case and Fortune's day, seeds collected in Canton – where the green tea is in any case of poor quality – all arrived dead in the Himalayas, stymieing the whole tea-planting timetable by an entire season and incurring huge losses for the scheme. The tea gardens of the Himalayas were still too small to be profitable because of the dearth of quality seeds available. The specimen plants alone would not alter this. From seed to shrub takes six years. If Fortune did not prevail in 1849, the whole enterprise would once again be delayed by a year.

The timing of his seed harvest was also not propitious. Typically, the Chinese pick tea seeds in autumn and store them over the winter in baskets of sand until they can be planted in the spring. After a year, the seeds are planted in tea gardens. Fortune had been late by a month or two picking his seeds, though it seemed reasonable to assume they were still viable. However, by the time the seeds arrived in India, the spring planting season would be over and the seeds would be almost an entire season off. They would hit the monsoon weather when torrents of rain washed away a gardener's best efforts.

It was also unclear to Fortune how best to transport them. Standard procedure called for seeds to be wrapped in paper or sent in cloth sacks. He had earlier received the advice of a Dr Jameson, the young Superintendent of the experimental Himalayan plantations. He had suggested Fortune try both systems. Fortune was especially thorough in following this advice: he shipped the seeds from four different regions in two different ways: one a coarse bag containing four paper packages of seeds; the other a box of earth mixed with seeds from each region. A third portion of the four kinds of seeds was kept behind, to be sown and reared in Shanghai then sent out to India once they had germinated into hardier seedlings. Fortune knew tea seeds were very fragile; they spoiled easily, becoming either waterlogged or else drying out in the slightest atmospheric change. He might have noticed that many of the seeds from his early collection had failed to germinate when replanted in the makeshift hothouses of Dent's garden. The best hope, it seemed would be to send such a quantity of seeds that, even if most failed, there would still be more than enough to populate the new tea plantations of India.

Fortune sought out Chinese gardeners to ask how best to store and transport tea seeds. Seeking advice from a native was a daring course for a European in China, not least because the Chinese were reputed to boil or poison tea seeds, 'in order that the floral beauties of China would not find their way into other countries'. But Fortune, ever the scientist, boldly asked an old seed dealer, a celebrated man named Aching, about his procedures for packing, sealing and shipping seeds.

'What is the substance you put in the seeds?' Fortune had asked of the white ashy matter surrounding them, a mixture that seemed to many Europeans as if it might be crematorial remains, charred bones and flesh.

'Burnt lice,' the old gardener replied.

'Burnt what?' Fortune laughed.

Aching, in his faulty pidgin, repeated himself – 'burnt lice' – this time with 'all the gravity of a judge'.

'*S'pose I no mixie this seed. Worms makie chow-chow he.*' The ashes were to prevent maggots; the moist climate of China made packed seeds particularly vulnerable to rot and infestation. Fortune determined that the old gardener was not a rascal, but was doing his best to sell and ship fragile seeds over long distances. And despite Fortune's readiness to pass along a terrible joke about accents in the Orient, if the encounter with Aching happened as written, there can be little doubt that he experimented with packing green tea seeds in the ashes of burnt rice.

Day after day and into the night, until dusk made it too difficult to dig and the falling temperature turned his fingers numb, Fortune worked on his green tea collections. Thoughts of failure dogged him as he toiled in the mud, but he was a thorough man and routine calmed him. He made a catalogue of each plant and seed: where it was collected and in which case it was sent. He requested equal thoroughness from others. 'It will be of great importance if [seeds and saplings] are carefully received and forwarded to their destination,' Fortune wrote to the gardeners on the subcontinent. It will 'also be very desirable to have a report made upon the condition of the plants and seeds when they arrive in India, which report could be sent to me for my guidance with regard to the number which it will be necessary to collect.'

The New Year's celebrations continued. Fireworks exploded with ferocity, lighting up the night sky. The gardeners' children shouted 'Waaahs!' of astonishment with each fizzle and pow.

Fortune planned to escort the tea as far as Hong Kong, to be certain of its care while in China. 'We have no vessel from this place [Shanghai] to Calcutta direct and as any delay or inattention at Hong Kong might prove fatal to the plants I think it much better not to risk committing the [tea] to the care of any person not fully acquainted with such matters.' As easily as weather and the vicissitudes of transplantation, the ignorance of stevedores could destroy Fortune's tea booty.

It would take an entire season for the green tea haul to get to India, and another few months more before a letter would arrive from the botanists there telling Fortune whether or not the shipments had been successful. He could not know where he would be when that important letter arrived. He might be in the middle of his next trip: to the black tea districts. What would happen if his green tea failed entirely? If the first shipments died, if there were adjustments to be made, Fortune would not even know about it until he returned to Shanghai following his black tea foray. He might have to repeat his entire green tea-collecting trip.

In the letter accompanying his first shipment, Fortune added humbly, 'I shall be grateful to receive any instructions which you may think it necessary to give me . . . addressed to the care of Mssrs Dent who will forward them to me.'

It had been nine months since he had received instructions from India's botanic gardeners on what seeds to collect. Fortune communicated frequently with Her Majesty's Consuls in Shanghai and Hong Kong, and they had orders to be helpful to him. But there had been no news out of India House in London and nothing further from the subcontinent: no instructions, no suggestions, no acknowledgement of his task at all. He must have felt he was indeed gardening in the dark.

The letter Fortune sent with his seeds and seedlings detailed his intentions for the next stage of his project.

When this is accomplished I propose returning northward . . . in order to make arrangements for procuring some plants and seeds from the Black tea hills in Fokien.
I have the honour to be, etc.
Robert Fortune

9

Calcutta Botanic Garden, March 1849

Where March in England saw gardeners clearing dead winter undergrowth to make way for bulbs and perennials, March in India was alive with full tropical majesty. Nothing in the exuberant botanic garden of Calcutta would have resembled the timidity of an English spring; the seasons here went from hot to wet, and back again, each year. Calcutta was stewing up in advance of the monsoons of June. March was still 'the cold weather', but as one traveller wrote, 'In India "cold weather" is merely a conventional phrase and has come into use through the necessity of having some way to distinguish between weather which will melt a brass door-knob and weather which will only make it mushy.' The holiday of Holi was upon India, celebrated by marauding gangs of young men who doused strangers with cold water as the year marked its turn towards pitiless summer. Calcutta was another world away from England entirely, and yet India's natural treasures, as housed in the Calcutta garden, would prove essential to the economic future of the tiny, cold and wet island of Great Britain.

Hugh Falconer was reddening in the sun as he walked through Calcutta Botanic Garden in March 1849, surveying rows of tea seedlings that his *malis*, or gardeners, were busy transplanting and pruning. A burly, barrel-chested Scotsman,

Falconer was Director of the garden. He was a Company man in the middle of his career, but Calcutta's tough climate had aged him prematurely. He had already been home to England once on sick leave, though he was only forty-one years old. Worse for Falconer, he knew it was not yet as hot as it would be in April, or in May, or in June – each hot season seemed an eternity to a sickening man. The Monsoon would bring some relief from the heat, but at the cost of continual deluges that would fill the streets of Calcutta as the sewers became rivers to the sea. It was enough to make a man like Falconer wonder whether he had chosen his path well. The Indian *malis* were hardier, squatting flat-footed in the soil and sun, seemingly ageless, tending the roots and pruning back the small white camellia blossoms. Falconer, by contrast, looked ready to wilt.

But he was needed in Calcutta as he awaited a shipment of plants and seeds on which the East India Company was desperately depending. The tea the *malis* were currently culti-vating in the Calcutta garden was of little consequence compared to that which was due to arrive any day. The Calcutta tea was good enough for experiments on planting depth and pollination, but no good for drinking; it came from native Assam stock, tasted bad, and was ill-suited for the high-altitude Company gardens in the Himalayas. The Company and Falconer were awaiting word that a shipment of seeds and plants from China, sent by the Company's young botanist there, had arrived to make good on the long-cherished dream of Indian tea.

Fortune's seeds would be placed under Falconer's care. Falconer, like most naturalists of Greater Britain, was self-reliant and systematic, accustomed to working alone and to being right – much like Fortune. He was a surgeon and a dedicated East India man, and as good a midwife for Fortune's tea seeds as he could wish to have. Falconer believed tea was crucially important to the success of the Company, that the garden at Calcutta was at the crux of India's tea project, and that his lasting legacy as Superintendent was tied in to this scheme. Fortune and Falconer, two gardeners, were of one mind when it came to the need to steal tea from China.

Calcutta was the capital of colonial India, and the garden there was its *de facto* Department of Agriculture. Falconer concentrated on horticultural networking and policy-making, on 'improving' the agriculture of India and fixing the 'unaccountable discrepancy' between the richness of the country's soil and its poor-quality agricultural products. Economically useful plants, such as teak, tobacco, coffee and indigo, came to Calcutta from all over the Empire, for distribution within India. The garden was a magnificent sight: 'Trees of the rarest kinds, from Nepal and the Cape, Brazil and Penang, Java and Sumatra, are gathered together in that spot. The mahogany towers there, and the Cuba palms form an avenue like the aisle of some lofty cathedral. Noble mango trees and tamarinds are dotted about the grassy lawns; and there are stately casuarinas around whose stems are trained climbing plants. There are plantains of vast size and beauty from the Malay Archipelago, and giant creepers from South America. The crimson hibiscus and scarlet passion-flower dazzle the eye, and the odour of the champak and innumerable jessamines [sic] float upon the breeze,' said a visitor.

Calcutta's garden dated from the start of botanical imperialism, around 1786, when a gardening-obsessed infantryman suggested to the Government that a site for the study of India's flora might prove useful – and profitable – to the shareholders of the Company. Initially directed to introduce nutmeg, cinnamon, cloves, peppers and breadfruit into the subcontinent, the gardeners of India discovered that Calcutta was a poor home for equatorial species and a terrible place to grow many valuable trade goods.

Though tropical farming failed there, it was not a total loss as a laboratory. Indeed, the garden became central to the programme of global plant exchange and commerce for the East India Company. The garden 'has fortunately always been a pet with the respective governments of India; and, in consequence, considerable outlays have, from time to time, been made, to keep it in the most perfect order and efficiency. To enable travellers, and others, to avail themselves, as much as possible, of the [benefits] of this establishment, the superintendent has a supply of seeds and roots always ready for those who may apply for them,' wrote Dr Royle, senior botanist of the East India Company, who had originally hired Fortune for the China tea job. On the banks of the Hooghly, exotic specimens were bred, catalogued and numbered, recorded for history and puzzled over for trading purposes. Under Falconer, the Calcutta garden was the crucial nexus for information and plant exchange between the smaller Company gardens in the Indian provinces. Seeds and saplings were shared, native Indian plants were sent to gardeners all over the world, new ideas reported and discussed; India was an extremely collegial place to do science.

The broader aim of the Calcutta garden was to connect the natural glories of Greater Britain to Kew Gardens in England. Kew was the centre of botanical research for the entire world; all seeds, shrubs, specimens and herbaria were forwarded from the Empire's outposts to Kew's gardeners, the ultimate arbiters of horticulture. In science, all roads led to Kew and nothing existed on earth unless it existed *there*. But, practically speaking, Kew's centrality was secondary to botanists in the field, busy improvising their way around the world, cataloguing and describing every living thing, trying to make new plants grow. Developing plant-based industries on foreign soil was the stated aim of Company botanists and they accomplished it with unparalleled skill. The Calcutta gardens introduced teak and mahogany for the timber trade, distributed hardy grains to feed India's famished peasants, conquered malaria with quinine produced from the bark of the South American chinchona tree, and introduced tea crops to the Himalayas. Nineteenth-century Company botanists were studious, independent and intellectually curious, masters of their field.

Among its other ventures and bequests, the East India Company seeded its fiefdoms with botanic gardens – in St Helena and St Vincent as well as Calcutta. The garden in Calcutta remained the most famous, though, and gained renown as a place of great beauty also. Located on the west bank of the Hooghly, it was just opposite and around a bend in the river from Fort William, the high-walled seat of the East India Company administration in India. The fort was impenetrable and imposing, but the garden was relaxed, open and welcoming – as much a park as a laboratory, a place for picnic lunches to keep the hustle and chaos of Calcutta at a civilised distance. 'Every step is a surprise,' acclaimed one visitor. Swore another, 'The Botanic Gardens would perfectly answer to Milton's idea of Paradise, if they were on a hill instead of a dead flat.' Covering 300 acres just below the city, the Company's garden, like other colonial imports to India, was noted for the 'order and neatness of every part, as well as with the great collection of plants from every quarter of the globe'. It was one part of Calcutta to which Kipling's epithet – 'this God-forgotten city' – seemed not to apply.

Falconer had come to the directorship of the gardens following in the footsteps of Dr J. Forbes Royle, the Company's senior botanist, having served as Superintendent at the Saharunpur Botanic Gardens in the Eastern Himalayas. Royle had made the fledgling Falconer his deputy in exploring the Himalayas and, within two years, ceded him the job at Saharunpur.

Falconer was skilled and erudite, a botanist but also an avid if amateur paleontologist. He was the first to articulate the evolutionary theory of 'punctuated equilibrium', which holds that sexually reproducing species will show long periods of stasis for most of their fossil record, but when evolution does occur it appears to happen rapidly and all at once. While working in the Himalayas, Falconer discovered one of the first fossilised monkey skulls – a fact noted by Charles Darwin in his *On the Origin of the Species by Means of Natural Selection*. On home leave to Britain in the middle of his Indian career, Falconer shipped to the British Museum an incredible five tons of fossil bones embedded in their rock matrices.

Falconer and Royle both strode in the footsteps of India's great naturalist Nathaniel Wallich, the man who might properly be called the founder of Indian tea.

For more than thirty years Wallich, a Dane, was the leading botanical authority in India, running the Calcutta garden. Wallich was recognised as a character within Calcutta society and the Company itself. He 'left his country young, and has devoted his life to natural history and botany in the East. His character and conversation are more than usually interesting; the first all frankness, friendliness, and ardent zeal for the service of science; the last enriched by a greater store of curious information,' wrote an acquaintance. Pale, fishy-eyed and beak-nosed, Wallich was the pre-eminent expert on *Flora Indica*. He was also most probably one of the first Europeans to taste Indian-grown tea, though he didn't know it at the time.

There had been ongoing debates in the early half of the

nineteenth century amongst botanists over whether there was any tea naturally existing in India, and if so, what it looked like. Wallich, who joined the Company in 1817, was initially a sceptic, pooh-poohing the possibility. And since he was the leading botanist in India, his word on the existence of tea was the last word, and thus he nearly scuttled the success of Indian tea from the outset.

When the East India Company annexed Assam province, next to Burma, to the rest of its British possessions in 1824, two brothers, Robert Bruce and C.A. Bruce, an ex-Army businessman and a tea merchant respectively, went to the new territory looking for trading opportunities. There they found what they believed were tea plants growing wild on the hillsides. They spoke to natives who steeped a brew from the leaves and chewed them to relax. The brothers transplanted some seedlings to a private garden and sent samples to Wallich.

He steeped some of the dry, fractured leaves, tasted the golden brew, looked again at the accompanying sample of uncrushed leaves of the same, and dismissed the lot as just another unremarkable evergreen. How could it be tea? reasoned Wallich: the area where these leaves came from was at sea level, while everyone knew that Chinese tea grew only in higher, mountainous regions. Seven years later, another set of Assam samples, from an Indian Army lieutenant, were brought to Wallich's attention, and he once again refused to confirm the existence of native Indian tea plants.

But as the Company's position looked increasingly insecure in the Orient, pressure mounted to find a way to grow tea elsewhere. As the East India Company monopoly in China neared its end in 1834, the Governor-General of India created a committee in Calcutta to further investigate the possibility of growing tea in the British dominions there. Wallich was conservative, a follower as much as an ideas man; he was influenced by fashion and the whims of the crowd. With political pressure being applied by the Company to find a viable way to produce tea in India, Wallich was encouraged finally to admit that the leaves he had been sent were actually tea leaves – that, in fact, tea was native to India. With heavy prompting by the Company, and encouraged by the presence of his protégé Falconer, Wallich finally stuck his neck out in favour of scientific discovery. His caution may have delayed the development of the tea industry in India by ten years but his eventual imprimatur, however belated, would allow tea to become the commodity which might save the Company from its growing financial burdens.

From the fiercest of tea sceptics, Wallich went on to become one of Indian tea's most avid champions. Together with his protégé Falconer, he took lengthy trips to explore and map Darjeeling after the Company seized it as a 'gift' from the Rajah of Sikkim and annexed it to India. Wallich dedicated scarce ground in the Calcutta garden to tea seedlings. After collecting land data from the vast network of surgeons employed in the remotest parts of India, he came to believe wholeheartedly in the future profitability and sustainability of a tea economy in India. He conducted a survey among Company surgeons to research the most likely places to establish tea estates, and in the end chose the gardens under the care of his former pupil Falconer: Saharanupur, in the high-altitude Himalayas, would play host to the tea-growing experiment.

Falconer, then a young man, was a keen supporter of the tea project and may have been the first to lay tea seed in the Himalayas. In those experimental trials, the seed was of the most pathetic quality, smuggled out of Canton where even the indigent Chinese peasant resented such a paltry drink.

Falconer persisted, and ultimately produced what looked and tasted to him like a fair facsimile of the Chinese original. The question remained, however, whether Indian tea would catch on back home.

In January 1839 the news that Indian tea from Assam had arrived in London, to be auctioned, set British imaginations on fire. For so long tea had been a drink from China, yet now it seemed there might indeed be such a thing as Indian tea. It was at least an anomaly, and possibly a great prize. If there was a future for British-grown tea on the subcontinent, here was a chance to cut out the Chinese middlemen from Britain's most important drink. British Indian tea would be sold under the normal rules of competition and pricing. Tea prices and tea taxes would come down. Tea quality would go up. An Indian product could be the answer to many tea merchants' and drinkers' prayers.

All the major London tea merchants were in attendance – legendary houses like Twining – as was the press. The Mincing Lane auction reflected a general uneasiness, a low-level panic even, about the stalemate in the Orient, as it took place in the run-up to the First Opium War between Britain and China.

The night before the auction, the Indian tea had been brought before tea inspectors, men whose nose and tongue dictated the blends and tastes of British tea drinkers. Judging tea is every bit as subtle and complicated as tasting wine. The inspectors found the Indian tea leaves were dark and leathery, the brew bitter, the aroma heavy. But the Indian tea was declared 'of reasonable quality'.

First on the block were 'chops' (cases) of the finest quality teas. In heated bidding the first round of tea fetched record prices. The atmosphere was electric. And with each successive lot, the prices escalated as the crowd worked itself into a bidding frenzy.

Finally the hammer went down on the last lot of Indian tea, the chops of the very lowest quality, the filler and twigs of broken, damaged leaves. This last, inferior lot fetched a higher price than the earlier, superior teas, a staggering 34 shillings per pound (roughly £84 or $168).

Those in the room recognised the sale for what it was: tea hysteria. The desire for Indian tea, fuelled by the existence of a previously unknown commodity and fanned by the looming threat of open hostilities in the coming First Opium War, would not be extinguished, though it would take a further twenty years or so to bring about.

In 1847 Nathaniel Wallich decided to retire at the age of sixty-one. This opened up the Calcutta post for a successor and there was no better choice than Falconer, who had been named a fellow of the Royal Society in 1845 and had earned a medal from the Geological Society of London. To add to Falconer's honours, the Company named him Professor of Botany at the Calcutta Medical College. Though the directors of the East India Company thought that Wallich – who had nearly thirty years of service to the Company – was grossly overpaid, the Honourable Board elected to continue the inflated salary for Falconer, so important was the post of horticulturalist to India.

It is likely that the Himalayan tea experiments were on Falconer's mind in March, 1849 as he made his way back from the experimental fields in Calcutta to the caretaker's cottage in the garden: past native orchids in full bloom; past the artificial mound which his mentor had hastily had constructed so as to show off some trees he had collected in the Himalayas; past a great and ancient banyan with almost 200 prop roots spanning nearly an acre. Falconer walked past the peaceful ornamental lakes towards the corpse-strewn banks of the Hooghly beyond. The breeze reeked, as it always did, of sewage.

He knew that this season's tea-planting would hardly be a success. There were not yet enough seeds for it to be truly profitable. Falconer must privately have wondered if Fortune was on a fool's errand; transporting seeds from the finest and most far flung tea provinces of China might well be beyond the capacity of even the most skilled botanist. But it was more than just the travel problems they faced that vexed Falconer, it was also the personnel problem in the Himalayas. He was already having doubts about the man who had taken over from him in Saharunpur, a young botanist named Jameson. Even if the Himalayas received enough imported seeds and seedlings, plus Chinese manufacturers to teach tea-making and packing skills, it seemed increasingly unlikely to Falconer that Jameson would be up to the task of managing them properly.

An Indian servant approached, bowing humbly, to inform the Sahib that afternoon tea was ready. There was a table set for him under an awning. Falconer sat down to a hot cup of the Indian brew – just as refreshing as any he had ever had of China tea, even on such a hot day. Under the tea's soothing effects, Falconer calmed himself. He had spent years in the Himalayas and knew the area well. He firmly believed that tea would prosper there; could indeed someday do better there even than in its native Chinese ground. The world's first multinational company and a Calcutta gardener were resting all their hopes on Robert Fortune, a young Scotsman alone in China.

10

Saharunpur, North West Provinces, June 1849

Calcutta, the seat of British rule in India, was orderly and tame by comparison to India's remoter regions. Whereas Calcutta's Botanic Garden was well-cultivated, manicured and civilised, the Himalayan gardens of Saharunpur were lush and wild, founded on a site that had formerly been an old Rohilla garden. The Rohillas were Pashtun invaders from Afghanistan who had once commanded Northern India and built themselves luxurious pleasure palaces in the hills.

The region was temperate and hilly, with ample rainfall, and every living thing seemed to thrive in the nourishing Himalayan soil. Tigers, panthers and lynxes roamed the rhododendron forests like creatures from fairy tales. Celebrated Rajput warriors, dressed in red silks and wearing handlebar moustaches, bred magnificent horses in the mountains near Saharunpur. Based as it was on the border between the Persian and Asian horticultural zones, plants from either region flourished there. In fact, for everyone but the European settlers, Saharunpur was a happy place. But although it was a horticultural paradise, gardening there was not always easy on a white man. 'A *mens sana in corpore sano* [healthy mind in a healthy body] is absolutely necessary to resist this dreadful climate: the work is very hard, the sun a terrible enemy; there are many comforts wanting, scarcely any society, and in his daily habits a man has to exercise an enormous amount of self-denial and discretion if he wishes to retain good health,' wrote a tea planter barely a generation later. To the Britons engaged to build a tea industry there, Saharunpur was remote, the heat oppressive, the living primitive. 'To these discomforts add one more – an unquenchable thirst that is ever present, but is particularly noticeable after severe exertion, when the desire to drink . . . is painful to a degree. This insatiable thirst is the great curse of the climate, and has accounted for many good men who have gone under the *matti* [earth].' These hardships notwithstanding, the large tracts of land and rainy climate should have made Saharunpur the ideal home for the first transplanted Chinese tea.

But first the plants would have to get there in something like the condition in which Fortune had shipped them. As it turned out, the plants and seeds did not have an easy trip.

Having personally accompanied the seedlings from their home ground in the tea districts to Shanghai and thence to Hong Kong, Fortune sent them seaward. But luck was not on his side. Though the shipment was arranged for Calcutta, for one reason or another it was diverted to Ceylon, modern-day Sri Lanka. Fortune's seeds and plants could not have been the primary cargo of the ship: a haul of 10,000 tea seeds filled only five gallons, and took up at most five crates when packed separately in bags of sand. Fortune's 13,000 seedlings were in glass cases, but the fate of a few vegetables were of little concern to the captain who had other priorities. It's entirely possible the ship was delayed by bad weather, or made an extra stop to offload higher paying cargo. Those were the glory days of shipping under sail, and merchantmen frequently made extra stops for any number of reasons – repair, renegotiation, barter or bad planning. While this kind of shipping delay might have resulted in the first instance of

Ceylon tea, a now prized variety, Fortune's crop did not stay in the small island nation. Ceylon would not develop its own tea industry until another generation had passed.

After completing whatever business took it to Ceylon, the ship reversed its course and made its way east again towards the port of Calcutta. Upon arrival, it fell to Hugh Falconer to assume or delegate responsibility for this precious living cargo, and then to transport it to its ultimate destination in the Himalayas. He collected the shipment, signing for it just after the spring holiday of Holi on 23 March – two full months after the plants had set sail from China. Two months is a long time to spend, getting to India from Hong Kong. In that time, a fully rigged tea clipper could sail halfway from Hong Kong to London around the Horn of Africa. Even so, Ward's technology would guarantee the freshness of living plants as long as the cases were kept in sunlight and sealed from salt spray. The tea stock should have been healthy on arrival in India.

Falconer was careful, upon receiving the shipment, to do nothing to disturb the cases, much as he might have liked to dig into one. He contented himself with peering in, like a child through a sweet shop window, but otherwise left the cases undisturbed for he knew that the plants' best chance of survival was to be left alone. The cases were left outside, shaded from the worst of the sun. As far as Falconer could tell, all looked to be in order; the plants would take care of themselves.

Within a few days of their reaching Calcutta, Falconer ordered the cases to be loaded on to a steamer which was travelling up the Ganges bound for Allahabad, halfway up country from Calcutta to the North West Provinces. Allahabad was a sacred city where the rivers Ganges, Yamuna and Sarswati met as one life-giving force. But it was there, apparently, on 12 April, that things took a considerable turn for the worse. In the highest levels of local government, an official whose name has been forgotten did the very worst thing he could have: he opened the cases. It is certainly a familiar impulse, to receive a package and take a look. Motivated by a desire to see that all was well with the precious cargo, the official, or one of his underlings, broke the seals. So many packages must have come through the outpost on their way to the mountains; that irrepressible someone must have seen that these cases were special, noteworthy, shiny and made of glass, demanding of the highest attention and concern. So he opened them. He even reported to his superiors that the plants inside were doing well.

The trans-shipment in Allahabad took longer than expected. There was a drought that year so the Ganges was low, which meant the seedlings could not be shipped by steamer upriver to the Company gardens in the Himalayas until the rains came with the first summer monsoon, still six weeks away in June. Nonetheless, the tea plants were, according to a report, looked after, tended to, nursed by gardeners even, and in good shape.

The last leg of the long trip up the mountains to the Saharunpur experimental tea gardens was made first by steamer then by ox-cart. In the Himalayas, Fortune's tea would be met by William Jameson of the Company's botanical outpost there.

High in the mountains, Fortune's newly arrived tea was received and inspected. The results were disastrous. Only 1,000 of 13,000 seedlings remained alive. The plants were ailing, full of fungus and mould. The glass cases had the stale reek of rot. The success rate of Fortune's first shipment of tea rested at a pathetic 7 per cent. Gamely, Jameson did what he could to rescue Fortune's tea, picking out and discarding the dead plants, coddling the living and the barely living ones. He ordered the Saharunpur *malis* to replant the robust specimens into the fertile mountain soil. After this had been done, however, the success rate on Fortune's first shipment dropped to a mere 3 per cent.

But what about the sacks of seeds Fortune sent along? 'The result has been an entire failure, not one seed having germinated. I lately removed a number of seeds from the beds to ascertain their condition and invariably found them to be rotten,' wrote Jameson.

In other words, Fortune had failed. Despite an entire year of planning, collecting, packing and hoping, he had done nothing whatsoever to advance the cause of tea in India, save demonstrate how to fall short of the task. He had made no dent in the nursery stock of the Himalayan tea experiment. He might as well have stayed at Chelsea's Physic Garden rather than wasting his time and the Company's money in China. What should have been a triumph for Fortune, the culmination of his first year of tea-hunting, was a catastrophe of wasted energy and worthless tea stock.

Behind the gentlemanly façade of the East India Company there were often hidden rivalries and simmering tensions, and within the Indian network of Company gardeners this friction centred upon the cultivation of tea. The 'smaller' gardens on the subcontinent were only so relatively speaking: by square mileage, the experimental tea gardens in the Himalayas occupied more ground than was available to the Calcutta Botanic Garden. But the Calcutta garden bore the imprimatur of colonial authority, and in the hierarchy of the Company authority must always be respected. As the Superintendent of Calcutta, Falconer issued his orders and the provincial gardeners were expected to follow them. One such gardener was William Jameson, Superintendent at Saharunpur.

Both Falconer and Jameson were Scottish (as was Robert

Fortune); both were surgeons and naturalists; both had studied under the finest scientific minds of Scotland; both were in the employ of the Company on the subcontinent; both took a keen, almost proprietorial, interest in the fate of the tea experiment. But there the similarities ended.

The young Jameson was a great deal less professionally polished than Falconer, more of a bumbler. When other naturalists in the medical corps were mapping uncharted territories and unravelling natural history puzzles, Jameson found himself accidentally imprisoned in Peshawar for trespassing. He did not rise to prominence on the broad sweep of his learning or on his ability to extrapolate from present knowledge to future insight, but through dogged navigation of colonial hierarchy and, most likely, a nepotistic thumb on the scale. Jameson's uncle, Robert Jameson, was a celebrated professor of geology and an expert on India, a peer to Wallich and Falconer and the teacher of Charles Darwin; William Jameson was smart enough to ride his uncle's coat tails, though not perhaps smart enough to nurture Fortune's tea back to health.

Jameson was a good Company man, but not a great mind. He answered every official letter at great, even interminable, length. He issued elaborate protocols and detailed orders for things that had never before needed such fine detail. The skills required to thrive in a bureaucracy were hardly transferable to botany. Jameson wrote pamphlets holding forth on the theory of garden design, the state of the weather, the political situation in China (where he had never been), and the preferred methods for planting each and every species under cultivation. Though exhaustive, Jameson's recommendations were seldom followed by his superiors, and often completely ignored.

Jameson ran the Himalayan tea gardens like a factory,

concerning himself mostly with the management of men and resources. His letters to the Government are intricate as business plans, full of details about size and scale, what the profit per acre could be if he only had the manpower and assets to grow, grow, grow.

The Government chided Jameson, asking him to be more measured in his enthusiasms: 'As it is evidently the wish of the Honourable the Court of Directors that the experiment should be conducted on the most liberal scale the Lieutenant Governor is pleased to sanction your proposal as to the extent of operations to be ultimately reached. It is evident however that some time must elapse before you can employ to advantage so large an establishment as you propose. You will be careful not to extend your establishment till you have the means of fully and profitably employing them.'

Though management and business planning were important skills, they distracted Jameson from his study of pure botany and resulting scientific advancement. Plants grew poorly under his care. Jameson's zeal was continually undermined by his lack of botanical knowledge and failure to investigate thoroughly.

He became an endless source of frustration to his senior, Falconer, who now believed he had filled his old position at Saharunpur with a less able replacement. In most respects, the jobs of the two men did not intersect. They had little to do with each other on a daily or even monthly basis. Falconer ran the Calcutta garden, overseeing the entire botanical and agricultural operations of the Company in India, while Jameson concerned himself only with the Himalayas. But the Himalayas were the botanical prize of India and Falconer did not think the new Superintendent was exploiting them to their fullest. Falconer expected to retire soon and had decided he would not recommend Jameson for the post in Calcutta, though Saharunpur was the traditional proving ground for the top job in Indian botany. Most of the time Falconer could ignore Jameson's shortcomings, but when it came to tea such ineptitude was serious.

In his zealous rush to document everything and gain approval from his superiors, Jameson got his science wrong. His knowledge of gardening was not as deep as his lifelong study of zoology or geology – yet he was employed as a chief gardener. Reading Jameson's ponderous declarations on the anatomy of tea is a little like listening to a parish organist's recital of Beethoven – the notes are in the right place, but it sounds wrong. The natural beauty of the whole is lost.

Jameson's scientific mistakes were many, costly and easily avoidable. For instance, he accepted as holy writ all that he remembered about the tea plant being of two different species, though these studies had been written from the confines of a laboratory in London, by people who had never studied the plant *in situ*. Although there were tea plants to experiment on right under Jameson's nose, in his very own Himalayan garden, he repeated out-of-date hearsay and received opinion without ever investigating further. He designed the vast Company gardens around a single, easily correctable misconception.

It was not simply that Jameson was wrong, but that in the face of a self-evident truth he stubbornly continued to hold the opposite position: the Chinese workers in his gardens told him that green and black tea are the products of the same plant, but Jameson continued to believe otherwise.

Worse, he was actually killing tea plants. In the Himalayan gardens, he set aside flat lands for tea and used flood irrigation on them – as if growing tea were no different from planting a rice paddy. He grew tea like this for years, despite the sickly appearance of the over-watered plants in the swampy fields. Had he used his power of observation, rather than relying on faulty assumptions and habit, Jameson would have seen that tea in fact thrives in rugged, sloping terrain, where there is no easy irrigation. Its roots spoil easily and need a steep hillside with good drainage, otherwise the bushes become waterlogged and mouldy and can't produce the healthy young buds required for plucking and drinking. Despite this, Jameson continued to treat tea like rice. Fortune had already published work on tea in China after his first trip, but Jameson seems to have paid no heed whatsoever to the science of his day.

Jameson failed to read Fortune's first book, the only reliable scholarly work on tea, the crop to which he was now devoting his career and the man on whom his own success depended. It was undoubtedly difficult for Jameson to get *Three Years' Wanderings* in India, but it would not have been impossible, especially as the tea project was so important to his employers at East India House. But, beyond this, he also failed to keep up with even the most basic developments in the botanical sciences of the day. He seems not to have read the publications of the Royal Horticultural Society or the Linnaean Society. For all Jameson was happy to write lengthy letters and hold forth on good botanical practice, one might wonder whether he ever read anything at all.

Most damagingly, Jameson was not aware of the science behind the Wardian case. 'They have received water all the way from Allahabad and had it not been for this circumstance there would not have been so many plants alive,' wrote Jameson to his superiors, knowing – as all Company men did – that his assessment could not help but get back to Falconer at the Calcutta garden. All communications were public unless clearly meant to be off the record, and even then the Revenue Department was notoriously careless with information. Whether Jameson was purposely seeking a fight, or just not particularly deft at Company bureaucracy, his declaration on tea transport found its mark: he made an enemy.

The letter outraged Falconer. It also heralded the demise of Fortune's Chinese tea. Plants in Ward's cases don't need water. It is the genius of Ward's technology that for practical purposes the cases are self-contained and self-sustaining – the only input needed is energy in the form of sunlight. Break the seal on the cases and the ecosystem within breaks down, too. Watering inside the cases once – never mind repeated watering all the way from Allahabad to Saharunpur – was more than enough to make mush of the Wardian miracle. Tea was strangled in its own transitory home.

It was not entirely Jameson's ineptitude – or that of the men who followed his instructions – that had decimated the consignment. 'Many of the panes of glass in the cases, too, were broken,' he recorded in his assessment of the situation. Somewhere between Calcutta, where everything in Fortune's shipment was tightly glazed and shipshape, and Allahabad, where no one understood what the cases were for or how to treat them, Fortune's glass cases were damaged to the point of uselessness. Instead of being sealed and stable self-sustaining environments, they were opened up to noxious air and standing water with predictable results for the delicate seedlings.

Jameson, ever the dutiful Company man, naturally issued a dispatch. 'In future when cases are sent from China, the following instructions ought to be attended to':

A careful Mallee ought to accompany the cases [from Calcutta] and before leaving the Botanical Gardens he ought to be provided with a screwdriver and taught how to unscrew the frames of the cases so as to enable him to water the plants occasionally that in every second day and again rescrew the frames . . .

On arrival of the cases at Allahabad they ought to be dispatched to Saharamfore [sic] in a government wagon appropriated to the purpose and well covered to protect them from the heat of the sun and under charge of a careful person.

If anyone ever followed them, Jameson's instructions for the boxes would forever guarantee dead plants on arrival. He wanted to institutionalise the *opening* of Wardian cases – the very action that had doomed Fortune's first shipment of tea plants. Yet Jameson *recommended* watering, and argued that protecting the cases from the sunlight was crucially important. He wanted *malis* to fuss over plants that were better off left alone.

Confident of his own perfect understanding of what had gone wrong, Jameson played the system, putting the blame on someone else. Clearly Falconer could not have inspected the cases on their arrival in Calcutta, nor had he adequately provided for their safe dispatch to Allahabad. Falconer's poor gardening skills were to blame, according to Jameson, since: 'I may here remark that the arrangements made by the Commissioners of Allahabad for the cases received were of such a nature as to have caused entire success had the plants reached that place in anything like good order.'

Falconer, also a longtime Company man but a better student of current trends in botany, responded simply by forwarding Jameson a scientific article on Wardian cases and how they worked. He copied it to Jameson's bosses in the North West Provinces, to the Revenue Department of India at Calcutta, to Royle at East India House in London. Even

Fortune received forwarded copies of the Jameson/Falconer correspondence. Practically every man in the chain of command bore witness to the conflict between the two rival gardeners in India.

Given the confluence of bad luck and poor decision-making at the highest and lowest levels, it can be no surprise that the fate of Fortune's first Chinese shipment was tragic. It was not just the tea plants in Wardian cases that were dead on arrival, sacksful of seeds did not survive the trip from China to the Himalayas either. Where explanation failed, and fault would not be admitted, Jameson hoped to implement policy; he offered new and eccentric instructions for the care of Fortune's future seed packets:

> With reference to seeds. On receipt of the seeds in Calcutta parcels or boxes ought immediately to be sent to the Botanical Garden to the Superintendent who ought to receive instructions to open them and to inspect them and forward one half in parcels by letter to Saharamfore, the other half might be sown in flower pots or cases and kept at the Garden until they germinate and the growing plants then forwarded under charge of a careful person by the steamer to Allahabad.

Jameson declared there was an historical precedent for this. The only other China tea in India, those bushes grown out of Canton seeds from an earlier shipment, had come to the subcontinent in the same fashion.

> By sowing seeds on receiving them from China, from Doctor Gordon, Dr Wallich was entailed to supply the [Himalayan] plantations with the first tea plants and from these and their produce the plantations now thriving have been formed. By adopting this plan there would be two chances in form of a

successful issue as if the seeds did not germinate in the plantations owing to being so long out of the ground, they might do so in Calcutta.

It seems likely that Fortune's seeds were probably doomed by the time they arrived in India, and that Jameson's suggestions were of no consequence either way. Planting seeds immediately on receipt in Calcutta was an acceptable theory on how to save them, based on past evidence, but probably incorrect. Canton was where Gordon's earliest shipment of seeds were picked, as well as the port of dispatch for all of China, so the time between picking and sailing was negligible – a matter of weeks, or a few months at most. Fortune's seeds, however, were picked on the Wangs' land in Xiuning province, sent slowly over the course of months by river and canal boat to Shanghai, repacked there over several weeks, shipped to Hong Kong, unloaded there then reloaded for India, diverted to Ceylon and thence to Calcutta, over a period of at least six months. Jameson's recommendations would have saved the seeds from travel time within India, but they were probably ruined long before arriving on the subcontinent. If the seeds were to thrive in India, Fortune would need to find a better method of shipment than simply packing them in bags of sand and crossing his fingers. From now on seeds would have to be treated more scientifically.

Doctor Gordon, the man Jameson had mentioned, was hardly a plant hunter worth emulating. Though he was the first East Indiaman to take tea seeds and tea experts out of China in the early-1840s, his experts mutinied and his seeds were of suspect, if not outright inferior, stock. Gordon's seeds came from the markets, purchased through compradors hired to pick in the countryside where no European could travel. Gordon's plant-hunting Chinese surrogates were entirely undiscriminating with respect to quality or kind; their only focus was on volume. Gordon had not used Ward's cases; he had not known about the boxes at all. Gordon's tea experts were even more suspect than his tea: many of the alleged manufacturers had no idea how to grow tea on an industrial scale but had jumped at the chance to leave China, forging qualifications to get a ticket and a contract. Once in India, the experts banded together to make demands of the government, orchestrating sit-downs and even feigning madness to renegotiate their terms. That some of Gordon's tea seeds germinated was more a matter of luck and timing; his seeds got to India before spoilage, where Fortune's were waylaid so many times, by the difficulty of Chinese travel, by bad luck, by the dry Ganges, and by sheer incompetence.

History would remember Jameson not as a great gardener, but as a well-placed man coasting on the tides of his time. He would not be promoted to the top job in Calcutta, he would never gain the scientific honours of Falconer or his uncle. A true botanist would have had better ideas for the management of a garden and plants and would understand how to grow a garden fit for the cultivation of the Company's newest cash crop. Yet Jameson, incompetent as he was, remained the man in charge of tea's fate in India. His lack of foresight and scientific knowledge could cost India its fledgling tea industry, the Company its future, and Fortune his job.

11

Ningbo to Bohea, the Great
Tea Road, May and June 1849

In May the river banks of China were aflame with new growth. Buds ripened on the boughs, apple, cherry and hawthorn blossom signalling in fireworks that the natural world was waking up to the sun. Fortune too had new projects in prospect. He had hired another small junk to sail out of the coastal city of Ningbo, a lesser treaty port, for the black tea hills of Fujian. Now he was nearing his ultimate prize.

He stood at the prow, watching coolies on the quayside, a warm salt breeze blowing his pigtail around his shoulders. He was journeying deep into China again. From the mouth of the Yangtze he would travel south-west, headed for the fabled Wu Yi Mountains and Bohea, birthplace of the finest black teas. There was no reliable report on which route would take him there in time for the second flush of tea picking. It was terra incognita.

'I felt rather low-spirited; I could not conceal from my mind that the journey I had undertaken was a long one, and perhaps full of danger. My road lay through countries almost unknown . . . But the die was cast, and, committing myself to the care of Him who can preserve us alike in all places, I resolved to encounter the difficulties and dangers of the road with a good heart,' he recorded.

Shoeless men, bare-chested and brawny, loaded Fortune's

gear and equipment: glazed cases, baskets, trowels and spades, notebooks and clothing. Everything a gardener spy might need was stowed aboard the snug little craft.

Though black tea and green tea were the same plant, they were never grown in the same place. Fortune sought black tea stock from its most celebrated region.

His fretful winter pondering the fortunes of his green tea consignment was behind him. He still had no news as to the fate of the Ward's cases and would have none for at least another season. As far as he knew, his green tea plants had arrived safe in the Himalayas and all was well.

The trip to the black tea mountains was Fortune's most daring yet. He was going deeper into China than any Westerner had ever gone, travelling over treacherous terrain. He planned to journey for three months, by boat, sedan chair and by foot – a trip of over two hundred miles, most of it by land, all of it uncharted, and almost entirely uphill. In the Bohea mountain range, also known as Wu Yi Shan, he was seeking China's best tea – according to British tastes – the blackest, gentlest Oolongs.

There were no black tea gardens as yet in India, only green – no one there really knew how to manufacture black tea, and besides the transplanted Chinese gardeners did not have access to black tea stock. Black tea in India would be something completely new under the sun. The greatest challenge Fortune faced, was to bring it from Bohea to the Himalayan mountain gardens. If he returned to Europe without introducing black tea plants from the best black tea districts, he would have neglected his full mandate from the East India Company. There was a growing taste for black tea in England, due in no small part to a growing glut of sugar coming out of the West Indies and Caribbean. Black tea takes sugar, green tea does not.

The stevedores were loading Fortune's trunks, but Wang and the Coolie were not directing them. They were not travelling with him at all. At first, Fortune had thought about sending them on the mission to Bohea without him, daunted by the idea of travelling through unmapped parts of rural China when it was known that rebellions were sweeping the countryside. Fortune knew they could deputise for him; Wang and the Coolie were reasonably well trained as plant hunters and knew what Fortune was looking for when he went prospecting. But he had reached the end of his tether on the previous trip, worn down by their constant conniving and scheming. He could not bring himself to stand back from the hunt, nor did he feel he could entirely trust them. He would have to way of knowing whether his servants had indeed gone all the way to the hills of Wu Yi to collect the plants or whether they had stopped short at inferior black tea gardens. He also assumed that when Wang and the Coolie weren't plant hunting, they were likely to be squandering their time – and the Company's money – on a long and loafing inland vacation. Instead Fortune, ever the enterprising traveller, was going himself. 'There may have also been a lingering desire to cross the Bohea mountains and to visit the far famed Woo-e-shan,' he wrote. A Briton ought to lay eyes on the great mystery that was black tea.

Wang, however, was not without his uses. Fortune still counted the trip to Sung Lo and Wang's family land there an unqualified success. For back-up and additional reassurance, though, he had decided that collecting a second batch of green tea seeds, ready for the following year's planting, would assuage the last of his qualms. The cost of doing so was negligible, after all, only the price of Wang's time and travels. He ordered the translator to return home to his father's house and collect more green tea seeds. Perhaps the assignment carried a little sting of revenge, too. In paying Wang to go home, he was returning his haughty manservant to his provincial roots. If the Coolie was similarly dispatched, Fortune makes no mention of it.

Fortune now required a new servant to accompany him on the long journey. As far as he knew, no white man had as yet set foot in the famous Wu Yi hills, and very few of the Chinese he spoke to could confirm what lay in store for him there. After many enquiries through Dent's comprador, he hired a knowledgeable body servant, a portly man named Sing Hoo. With his proud and dignified bearing, Sing Hoo was 'powerful and spirited', like a rooster, and had once been in the service of a high-ranking Mandarin affiliated with the Imperial Family at Peking. His elevated status was clearly visible in his straight shoulders and in the proud stretch of his neck. Hoo came equipped with the insignia of his former office, a small triangular flag that bore the arms of the Imperial Court, which, he said, was a gift from his former master and amounted to a sort of passe-partout or 'get out of jail free' card. To anyone owing fealty to the emperor, this flag signalled that the travellers were under the Court's protection. 'I confess I was rather sceptical as to the power of this flag, but allowed him to have his own way,' Fortune recalled. Sing Hoo carried the flag everywhere, rolled up and at the ready.

He was from Fujian province, where the Wu Yi hills were situated, which meant he spoke Fukienese, the local dialect, an advantage Wang could not offer. Though there was a standard and official court language in China, each province had its own dialect which was almost unintelligible to outsiders. Fortune's halting Chinese would most likely have been a pidgin version of *Shanghaihua* – the formal tongue of Shanghai – for he would have learned it from the men he hired there. He might have spoken a touch of high Cantonese, or *Guandonghua*, also, like so many of the British merchants and government men who laboured in China, but mostly he communicated in pidgin. In the mountainous areas of remote Fujian, he would have been hopelessly lost linguistically. Sing Hoo was his new mouthpiece.

Fortune's previous fear of exposure as an outsider was allayed on this journey. The worrying skirmishes on his earlier green tea trips had been brought about, in large part, by his servants; this time no one recognised him as a loathed foreigner, a *yang guizi*. His Chinese was awkward but by now passable; he was competent with chopsticks; his clothing marked him as a man of the realm. More confident now, Fortune thought it entirely possible that no one would detect him at all – he was going so far from the coast, no one would ever have seen an Occidental face.

Not that this journey was without its danger. Besides the rumours of peasant rebellions, Fortune was as yet uncertain about Sing Hoo: 'The guide I had with me was not fully to be depended upon . . .' But he was at the very least a change from Wang and the Coolie's outright hooliganism. If officials were being slaughtered and the poor were seeking retribution for their suffering, as they were in the hills of Fujian, Fortune's silken costume identifying him as a ranking Mandarin would scarcely provide much protection. Command of the local tongue and the triangular flag of the Imperial Court might well provide all the help he would get.

Sing Hoo spoke imperiously to the men on the junk, instructing them how to stow his master's belongings. This item of luggage would go into the hold, where the master slept. That piece would be stashed on deck. Be careful with the glass, he warned.

Then Sing Hoo addressed Fortune. It was time for the

journey proper to begin; Fortune must become a different 'outward man' and bedeck himself in full Chinese dress. Fortune's braid still hung down his back. He removed his Western clothing, his hard-soled shoes and buttoned-up jacket, donning instead the wide flowing garments of a Chinese official.

'I doubt whether my nearest friends would have known me,' he wrote. 'I scarcely recognised myself.'

'You will do very well,' Sing Hoo told him.

Fortune, Sing Hoo and all their gear floated lazily upriver, their boatmen calling to one another as they poled around the bends. They sailed past walled cities whose ramparts dated back thousands of years to the times of plague and savagery in Middle Europe. In China, those same times saw the rise of highly advanced civilisations, organisation and achievement. They travelled along an ancient network of canals that stretched across China like a spider's web, connecting the vast area of the Centre Country with every-where else worth going.

Within a few days the men came upon a traffic jam in the canal, a bottleneck at a junction point where fifty junks were floating helplessly alongside each other, going nowhere. Fortune's junk queued for its turn on a windlass which would raise it on to a ramp leading to a higher canal. Stevedores on the shore were fixing ropes from the windlass to the lead boat's prow, winching it up inch by inch. Fortune and Hoo were many boats back, biding their time. The delay was not overly long, given the average waiting time in China – only an hour or so. The boatmen – never in a hurry to begin with – were sunbathing and spitting, playing mahjong, enjoying their easy time off and the spring sun.

All except for one fellow, that is, who sailed astern of the queue. He huffed and spat and swore, growing increasingly impatient. The angry boatman manoeuvred his boat towards Fortune's junk, knocking others aside, shouting and threatening any captain who would not get out of the way. With the sun on their faces and diversions at hand, most of the boatmen barely fought back, allowing the interloper to jump the queue and have his way. That is, until the blackguard reached Fortune's boat.

The impatient captain tried to edge past, shouting and gesticulating, insulting Fortune's mother and Sing Hoo's ancestors, trying to bluster his way through. Here was the man in the greatest hurry in all of China.

Fortune was irked by the upset. At times, he possessed moments of true Confucian spirit, prizing order and calm above all.

'You cannot pass this boat,' the junk's captain shouted, perhaps more in an attempt to placate Fortune than actually get into a scrap. He jammed the nose of the junk against the canal wall, closing the gap so that the irate sailor could not pass.

Sing Hoo also stepped into the fray, determined not to let any man outface his master.

'Oh, but I will pass you!' the obstreperous captain rudely insisted.

'Do you know,' Sing Hoo shouted back, 'that there is a Mandarin in this boat? You had better take care what you are about!'

'I don't care for Mandarins,' shouted the angry captain, spitting out a sentiment shared by many, but spoken by few. 'I must get on.'

'Oh, very well,' Sing Hoo replied calmly, 'we shall see.' The servant went down into the cabin and took his yellow talisman from his luggage, unfolding the triangular flag. He walked out again into the sunshine, smiling to himself, and hoisted the banner on to the mast of the boat.

'There,' taunted Hoo, 'will you pass us now?'

Fortune was dumbfounded when the captain stood down. He backed off, got in line, apologised profusely and 'became all at once as meek as a lamb'. From then on, he did nothing but sit quietly on the stern of his boat, eyes cast down, waiting his turn like everyone else in the canal.

Fortune smiled: perhaps he would find safety in this countryside after all, however rebellious and unfathomable it was. Perhaps the path ahead would be strewn with more luck than he had imagined. Sing Hoo's flag had made him an important Mandarin, a *lau ye*, a 'sir'.

Sing Hoo could not even imagine a place like Scotland; he did not need to know where Fortune was from, or what he was doing here, or how great was the deception when his master dressed like a Chinese official. He simply parroted Fortune's script – this was a man of great honour who came from a distant province, a far place beyond the Great Wall – and embellished it with a royal flag.

Fortune penetrated deeper into China, sailing from town to town in Zhejiang, then journeying on by sedan chair and mountain footpath through Jianxi province. As he passed through ruined villages in his sedan chair, beggars reached up to him, their rheumy eyes searching his for signs of sympathy. They held out skeletal hands for a few pieces of copper cash or any throwaway thing that might be useful in barter. Fortune was touched by the supplicants' poverty – and was very afraid, horrified by their scabrous faces and missing limbs.

The trip to black tea country was a slow climb that would take almost three months to complete. It was a beautiful time of year and brought out the poet in Robert Fortune: 'The lowlands were now much broader – the hills appeared to fall back, and a beautiful rich valley was disclosed to view. Groups of pine-trees were observed scattered over the country. They marked the last resting places of the dead, and had a pleasing and pretty effect.' The Chinese would often plant trees over graves, as a sign of respect for their ancestors. Fortune projected on to the landscape all his romantic hopes and fears about this unknown place. As the rich, rolling hills of the Yangtze valley gave way to China's coastal mountains, Fortune's mission took him to areas both beautiful and unnerving.

It did not escape his notice that the peasants of China were suffering blow after blow, season upon season, so many bitter lessons at the hands of their vengeful or unseeing gods. At first glance the view was lovely, dotted with swallows on the wing, but on closer examination China's landscape was uncanny. The luxuriant vegetation swarmed over ancient buildings, forcing its way through dilapidated shacks. The same climate that made roses burst into flower in early-summer was merciless on man-made structures. Each peasant hut looked tenuous and feeble on its patch of land, as if ready to be reclaimed at any minute by the earth. The region was lashed by high winds and was hit hard that year by flooding. What had once been among China's richest areas was now ravaged by natural disasters; famine was forcing entire clans off the land. Extreme weather had always limited the amount of arable land available to the growing Chinese nation, but the relative peace of the Qing reign meant that the population had doubled in size in the previous century. In 1849 there were more Chinese than ever farming fewer fields, while successive rains and droughts bedevilled their efforts.

From his palanquin, Fortune saw tea coolies carrying crates strung off poles across their shoulders as they marched

in line down a snaking mountain path, like colonies of ants
on the move. The tea caravans and the beggars reaching out
to Fortune did not, on the surface, seem to have anything
to do with one another, yet the beggars were there because
the tea route, like the fabled silk route, was one of the most
valuable avenues of trade for imperial China. In marked
contrast to the beggars' poverty, tea was worth almost $26
million a year in revenues to China (equivalent to about $650
million today, or £325 million). Incredible wealth was on the
move down those mountain paths. Each tea crate was filled
with what amounted to botanical gold, but each chest was
shouldered by a man who earned pennies – if that. Yet that
tea coolie, with his muscled legs, ox-like back and leathery
face, was an absolute king compared to the human wreckage
among the starving beggars in Fortune's path.

It was an uneasy time to be so far off the beaten track.
The blow inflicted by the First Opium War upon the people
of China was now being felt inland. The nation's humili-
ation at the hands of the West led to inflation as the
beleaguered peasants paid taxes in a currency radically
devalued by war debts. The foreign powers insisted on
favourable trading terms, chipping away at whatever competitive advantages the working peasantry of China had ever
had for their goods and labours, especially for their tea. There
was palpable anger: against corrupt officials who provided,
at best, perfunctory aid to the suffering agricultural regions,
and against the government in Peking, made up of foreign
Manchus. One of Fortune's boatmen had his sail repossessed
after he could not repay a debt. With no sail, he could not
proceed upriver and had to dispatch all his passengers and
cargo at a loss. The boatman, in despair, threatened to drown
himself in the river to be taken away by the Sea Goddess.

*

If China was ripe for foreign incursion and a fertile hunting ground for foreign botanist spies, it was a nation equally primed for threats from within. Unknown to him, an insurgency was fomenting along Fortune's route. A charismatic rebel leader in the south had seized the imaginations of China's impoverished and bedraggled peasantry. A young provincial man in Canton, Hong Xiuquan, had tried to gain acceptance into the higher ranks of intellectual bureaucrats by training for Imperial service, but like so many rural Chinese had failed to pass the examinations. His impoverished family had sacrificed everything to pay for his education and he had tried three times to qualify for the degree which would give him the social status of wearing scholar's robes and receiving a lifetime stipend from the state. But Hong could not achieve his aim. He piled failure on failure, never joining the ruling elite, nor bringing glory to his family and ancestors. He was a Hakka, a member of an outsider race, one of the hundreds of ethnic minorities in China who did not enjoy the full social standing of the Han Chinese. The Hakka were rural farmers, their women did not follow the approved practice of foot-binding, and centuries after settling in Southern China, they were still viewed by locals as a guest people, foreigners. The magnetic Hong took all the disappointment and rage of his failure and modest beginnings and ploughed them into a creation myth of biblical proportions.

After Hong failed the exams for the third time he grew ill, weak and fevered. For a time he lost his mind and descended into a delirium full of visions of dark and wonderful things. In his hallucinatory state he saw a dragon, a cock and a tiger, all Chinese symbols of power, aggression and luck. He saw demons, too, and the King of Hell.

A woman greeted him in Hell and called him 'son'. She bathed and soothed him, wiping his brow and cradling him to her bosom. An old man with golden hair and beard, who wore a black dragon robe, identified himself as Hong's father and commanded the young scholar to change the world.

'Many of those on earth have lost their original natures. Which of those people on earth did I not give life to, and succour? Which of them did not eat my food and wear my clothing? Which of them has not received my blessing? Have they no scrap of respect or fear of me? It is the demon devils who have led them astray. The people dissipate in offerings to the demon devils things that I have bestowed on them, as if it was the demon devils that had given life to them and nourished them. People have no inkling as to how these demon devils will snare and destroy them, nor can they understand the extent of my anger and my pity.' The old man said. He then gave Hong a sword and a golden seal and instructed him to cast out and destroy all the evil demon devils.

In the vision, Hong saw another man, younger and glowing. This was his older brother. While Hong would gladly have stayed with his family, his older brother was impatient that Hong should return to the world. He could not stay among the dead. Without his help, how would the men of earth be transformed? Hong must return to China.

'Fear not, and act bravely,' his dream-father said. 'In times of trouble I will be your protector, whether they assail you from the left side or the right. What need you fear?'

Hong awoke a changed man: more confident, taller. He did not understand his vision, but he was altered. Soon afterwards, when Hong happened to pick up and read a Chinese translation of the Christian Bible that had been disseminated by missionaries, he was able to make sense of his dream: it had been the Christian God who had spoken to him. The 'older brother' in the dream was none other than Jesus Christ, which meant that he, Hong Xiuquan, a poor Chinese peasant, had to be the younger brother of Christ, and like him a son of the one true God.

Hong spread this revelation to his neighbours and began to preach a fire and brimstone version of Old Testament Christianity. He baptised converts; called for a Christian community, based on faith in God the Father; demanded the destruction of the Confucian state and the demolition of ancestral shrines. He forbade household idols and ordered the elimination of ancestor worship. His followers were called on to shun opium, alcohol, footbinding and prostitution.

Hong declared himself the Heavenly King of the Heavenly Kingdom of Great Peace. He raised a vast Army of the Heavenly Kingdom, the *Taiping Tianguo*, foot soldiers to aid in God's fight against the Qing Emperor's Mandarins. His followers sold their property and earthly possessions and pooled their resources in a common treasury in order to bring the son of the one supreme God to rule over China. The Taiping religion was entirely new to China, a seachange from the passivity of Daoism, the conservatism of Confucianism and the otherworldliness of Buddhist philosophies – the Taiping Heavenly Kingdom was a radical call to arms. In the south, secret societies joined forces with the Taiping in hopes of bringing down Manchu rule. The Taiping wore their hair long, in defiance of the Manchu tonsure. As Fortune travelled on, their army was already 10,000 strong. It would ultimately grow to some 30,000 members and would colonise much of Eastern China, including the countryside in which Fortune was travelling.

The hill country was only months away from falling to the Heavenly Kingdom. The Taiping rebellion, led by Hong

Xiuquan, would wash over sixteen provinces and destroy over 600 cities and 20 million Chinese people within three years. Unaware that he was wading into tide pools of bloodshed, Fortune beat higher into the mountains, crossing the path of the oncoming Taiping Army on his journey towards the heart of the black tea district.

He had not an inkling of what was coming. The small towns seemed so beautiful to him, some 'of the prettiest Chinese towns which I have seen . . . an English place more than a Chinese one'. His descriptions of the scenery became positively florid. The vales were 'even more beautiful . . . surrounded by hills, dotted over with clumps of pine, cypress, and camphor trees, traversed by a branching and winding river, and extremely fertile . . . The whole valley seems, as it were, one vast and beautiful garden, surrounded and apparently hemmed in by hills.' He was at his most effervescent as he described the approach to the Eden of tea.

In his sedan chair, Fortune wound up and around on the narrow gravel mountain tracks, every switchback teetering between the bare rock and the sky. This road was an almost superhuman undertaking, a hand-carved stairway into a mountain face. His bearers carried him straight up the high rock karsts; there seemed to be no downward slope at all, no lulls, no respites on the trail. It was unlike any other place that Fortune had known. 'In some places the height was so great that it made me giddy to look down.' The valleys below were grey pools of mist. Every quarter of a mile or so, the travelling group came upon a teahouse. To give his chair coolies a break, Fortune frequently stopped to sample the wares of the tea merchants, enjoying a cup of 'pure bohea on its native mountains' and feeling all the more Chinese.

We find tea one of the necessaries of life in the strictest sense of the word. A Chinese never drinks cold water, which he abhors, and considers unhealthy. Tea is his favourite beverage from morning until night; not what we call tea, mixed with milk and sugar, but the essence of the herb itself drawn out in pure water. One acquainted with the habits of this people can scarcely conceive the idea of the Chinese Empire existing, were it deprived of the tea plant; and I am sure that the extensive use of this beverage adds much to the health and comfort of the great body of the people.

While Fortune enthused over the Chinese way of drinking tea, he was less willing to acclimatise himself to the dubious comforts of Chinese roadside inns where he took up nightly residence. They were dark and tiny, mere human stables, with walls besmirched with soot and grease from the kitchen fires. Yet the trip was a pleasure to him. His mind was so alive to the possibilities of China that he took even his poor accommodation in good humour: 'I never expected to find my way strewed with luxuries,' he wrote.

As ever, though, Fortune's grand plan was complicated by the personal aims and scheming of his hired help. Despite Sing Hoo's rather elevated background, he too turned out to have an eye for the main chance. Fortune had intentionally tried to keep his luggage to a minimum, just the bare essentials – a few necessary clothes and a mat to sleep on – in order to leave more capacity to cart off the botanic booty of the Bohea. Sing Hoo, on the other hand, had 'a strange propensity of accumulating' unnecessary things.

'Everything good comes from Nanche,' he insisted, while purchasing heaps and bolts of grass cloth. This household staple, used to cover dirt floors in peasants' homes, was a few cents cheaper inland than on the coasts, giving Sing Hoo an unexpected business opportunity – one that outraged Fortune who funded their transport.

'You see,' Sing Hoo explained, while conceding it was necessary to hire a coolie to carry their baggage, 'we have reduced it so much that he will not have half a load. Now the carriage of this cloth will not add anything to the expenses, and the man's load will be properly balanced.'

Fortune remained unmoved.

'Travellers in my country who have a goodly portion of luggage are always considered more respectable than those who have little,' Sing Hoo continued authoritatively.

The continual jockeying for self-advancement made Fortune feel badly used. He would never be at ease with the Chinese eye for personal gain; it ran contrary to his sense of pecuniary propriety. But, worse than that, Sing Hoo's grass cloth threatened to deprive Fortune of space in which to stow the plants he collected along the way, his secondary purpose in Bohea (tea, of course, was the primary objective). Much to the delight of his chair coolies, Fortune could not be contained by it but often insisted on running ahead on the trail, to pick fresh seedlings, take samples of topsoil and explore the mysteries of the ravines and the majesties of the heights. His chair bearers walked an empty sedan chair up the steep hills for the same price as one laden with human cargo.

Bohea was a botanist's dream, foreign and yet familiar, so much newness, so much green: oak and bamboo, thistle and pine. As Fortune wandered, Sing Hoo followed with the cases and trowels, digging up a sample of every undiscovered species and many new varieties of familiar ones. Fortune's empty sedan chair grew laden down with clippings and cuttings from the hillside, but as these were far heavier than grass cloth, the chairmen began to object. They could not make sense of their growing burden of 'what they considered weeds'. From time to time, a coolie would rebel, put down his load and deliver an angry rant about the weight of the sod he carried and how unnecessary it was.

Fortune would have none of it. His sympathy for the burdened men was tempered by his enthusiasm for the hunt. He threatened the coolies and made promises to them, flattered and bullied them, bribed and intimidated, offered bonuses for the increasing weight of his Wardian cases. With carrot and stick, he knew how to get his way in China. He was resolute; the samples and herbaria were to travel with him all the way up into Bohea's mountains, back down to Shanghai and on to Kew. It was only by his 'dint of determination and perseverance' that his plant haul was carried several hundred miles into the tea hills and out again, in complete safety. These would be the first plants ever brought from Wu Yi Shan to Europe. What Fortune's chairmen saw as weeds were a plant hunter's green gold. After an extended journey back to the Western hemisphere, they were to be named, numbered and sold at auction. Fortune was living up to his name, among the black tea hills of China.

After weeks of climbing, they approached the rooftop of the Bohea range, the high mountain pass that separated the interior Jianxi province from that of coastal Fujian. Wu Yi Shan is a peaked and mighty place. Black mountain karsts looked like giant fingers, as if the hand of an enormous beast were reaching through the earth's crust and into the sky. 'Never in my life had I seen such a view as this, so grand, so sublime. High ranges of mountains were towering on my right and on my left . . .'

Fortune was overcome, ascending ever higher into the clouds. There were bamboo forests at the pass, with full, fluffy leaves sprouting from spindle trunks. Fog shrouded the hillsides below him while the mountains reared up to either side. The travelling band had arrived at the 'gates' of Bohea, the limestone pillars to either side of the mountain pass. These karsts were forged by nature then worn down by water over millennia, an enduring struggle between rock and time. Fortune stood at the gateway to the celestial tea country, eye to eye with mountains. It was 'one of the grandest sights' he had ever seen and he allowed himself to muse a while on its beauty.

> For some time past I had been, as it were, amongst a sea of mountains, but now the far famed Bohea ranges lay before me in all their grandeur, with their tops piercing through the lower clouds, and showing themselves far above them. They seemed to be broken up into thousands of fragments, some of which had most remarkable and striking outlines.

Streams trickled down the mountainsides; waterfalls splashed into a main artery, joining below to become the River Min, flowing into the sea at Fuzhou where the pirates made port. China's geography at last made sense to Fortune: like water, tea flowed downhill, from the mountains to the coast, to be collected in Britain's waiting cup.

They were now at the heart of black tea country and it was everywhere. Tea farms striped every mountainside. The weather was fine if chilly, with sunlight gleaming off the eastern faces of the karsts, tinting them gold. Their shaded sides were 'gloomy and frowning'. Fortune's mind began to wander. 'Strange rocks, like gigantic statues of men or various animals, appeared to crown the heights.'

'Look, that is Woo-e-shan!' Sing Hoo exclaimed.

Fortune recalled the sight of those hills with reverence: 'Here I could willingly have remained until night had shut out the scene from my view.'

12

Bohea, July 1849

The day was blue and hot. Fortune's chair coolies spiralled their way into the hills, following the narrow footpath from its low and curling beginnings to its steep, straight terminus in the sky. They were exhausted.

'It is impossible to go any further!' they complained. So Fortune got out of the chair and walked ahead alone, climbing up and over and around for hours.

'Look!' they cried, forgetting their heavy loads and the rough trip, transported for a moment by the beauty of the hills. 'Have you anything in your country to be compared with it?'

Indeed, Fortune did not. No matter how hot, uncomfortable and far from home he was, nor how unending the climb, there was no hill or vale in the British Isles which could stand against the might and grandeur of the flat-topped, cloud-bedecked Wu Yi Mountains, the Bohea of legend and lore. Because Wu Yi's tea leaves look as if they bloom purple and turn red as they ripen, the local dialect called Wu Yi tea *bo he*, meaning red tea, which when anglicised became Bohea.

Fortune was nearly at the heart of black tea production. He said that the plantations looked like 'a little shrubbery of evergreens. As the traveller threads his way amongst the rocky scenery . . . he is continually coming upon these plantations, which are dotted upon the sides of all the hills. The leaves are of a rich dark green, and afford a pleasing contrast to the strange and often barren scenery which is everywhere around.'

There were tea pickers busy on every slope, bringing in the fresh shoots. 'They seemed a happy and contented race; the joke and merry laugh were going round, and some of them were singing as gaily as the birds in the old trees.' The pickers were mostly women, with broad straw hats shielding their faces from the sun and large grass baskets slung across their backs – and perhaps even a child slung in front. The pickers stayed in the fields from early-morning through dusk, from April to October, picking each bush every ten days. A female traveller, who followed Fortune's route in 1870, wrote:

> I am greatly struck by the number of girls whom we meet working as tea-coolies, and by the enormous burdens which they carry slung from a bamboo which rests on their shoulder. Each girl carries two bags thus slung, the weight of a bag being half a picul, which is upwards of 60 lb. Thus heavily burdened, a party of these bright, pleasant-looking young women march a dozen miles or more, chatting and singing as they go . . . The tea-plantations are scattered over the hills, forming little dotted patches of regularly planted bushes. Here the girls and women are busy selecting the young green leaves, which they pick and collect in large basket-work trays of split bamboo.

Tea-picking women, the *caichanu*, were heralded in song and story as dainty, noble and objects of romantic interest. China's long history of politician-poets ensured that, throughout the dynasties, there was always someone commenting on the beauty of these women and the harsh conditions in which they worked. A popular analogy was constructed: the tea-picking girl had all the purity and nobility of the tea she picked, and contained in such beauty was hardship. Tea's purity was personified by the virginal *caichanu*, and her diligence was embodied in the tea mountain's majesty, for tea-plucking was dreary, soul-destroying work.

The tea harvest had some advantages for the women of rural China, however. It relieved them of the solitary sphere of work in the home and brought them into the world. On the one hand a *caichanu* on a hillside was subject to the harsh light of public scrutiny, where her morals could easily be brought into question, but the tea harvest also gave her freedom. Out of the house all day, she walked the hillsides with other women, away from the tyranny of a mother-in-law and the confines of smoke-blackened walls. It was this seasonal liberty – so contrary to Confucian notions of familial right and morality – that invited both attention and serenades from scholars.

Each picking is with toilsome labour, but yet I shun it not,
My maiden curls are all askew, my pearly fingers all
   benumbed;
But I only wish our tea to be of a superfine kind,
To have it equal their 'dragon's pellet', and his 'sparrow's
   tongue'.

For a whole month, where can I catch a single leisure day?
For at earliest dawn I go to pick, and not till dusk return;
Then the deep midnight sees me still before the firing pan –
Will not labour like this my pearly complexion deface?

Today tea plants are kept low, only to waist height, and the bush is 'tabled', as if the entire top half has been lopped off; this makes for a wide, low base for convenient picking, and bushes are kept in neat efficient rows. But in Fortune's time, they were unkempt and allowed to grow at random over a hillside. Fortune was stunned by the sheer labour involved in tea-picking. It was not the bending, nor the hot climate, nor even the high-altitude mountains that made for such hard labour; but instead the sheer volume of tea picked. If the tea bush were a Christmas tree, pickers would only take leaves from the bough where the star is placed, the very tip, and perhaps a few of the branches with orna-ments on them. So from each bush came only a handful of leaves, then on to the next, and so on. Only the two most tender leaves sprouting out of the end of the branch release the gentle and mellow taste that becomes tea – the older leaves on the stem below taste harsh and sooty. A nimble tea picker can pluck up to 30,000 tea shoots per day, which includes the time it takes to examine each shoot and to make sure no stalk enters the mix. It takes about 3,200 shoots to make a pound of picked leaf, so an expert tea picker might pluck ten pounds of green leaf a day. The ratio of picked leaf to dry is a whopping five to one, meaning five pounds of fresh tea leaves are picked for every processed pound for sale. Fortune discovered that tea was a most inefficient and labour-intensive crop.

'The natives are perfectly aware that the practice of plucking the leaves is very prejudicial to the health of the tea-shrubs, and always take care to have the plants in a strong and vigorous condition before they commence gathering,' he noted.

Plucking is terribly hard on the tea plant. A bush is picked every ten days, from late-April once the rains stop, all the way through to October, when the rains begin. It is a repeated insult to the process of growth and a wound to the bush, but continuous plucking also produces the best brew. Cultivated

tea bushes develop a deep network of tap roots to compensate for the constant pruning; the roots then push up a rich
healing sap which fills the leathery leaves with flavour. Pickers
clear the tea bushes of their fruit and flowers as they move
across the mountain. Anything that distracts the efforts of
the bush, such as forming fruit to distribute the seeds, detracts
from the bush's energy to heal itself after plucking and
produce more shoots.

It was not a matter of simple academic interest to Fortune
that he should study tea of fine quality. The price of tea
reflected how careful the picker was at the harvest, and a
failure to pick well, or dutifully, would cost the farmer at
market. If the Company planned to produce a premium
product, they would need to follow this method too.

Along the rocky path, Fortune stopped an old peasant and
asked for directions to the local temple where his retinue
could stay the night.

The peasant laughed at the request. 'There are nearly a
thousand temples in the Wu Yi Mountains,' he replied.

Fortune was among the first of the 'foreign devils' to try
to describe the grandeur of Wu Yi Shan. For centuries, learned
Confucian men carved poems into the base of the hills, testa-
ments to the power of the Eternal, the might of Nature, and
to tea. Wu Yi Shan had good *feng shui*: good wind, good
water. Chinese calligraphy was carved deep into its slate rock
faces. 'At a distance, they seemed as if they were the impress
of some giant hand.' Fortune believed they were initially
created by water 'oozing' out of the porous rocks. 'Emperors
and other great men' then augmented the natural carvings to
make poetry.

He walked on towards a large temple lying at the foot of
the mountains. The outer walls were imposing, but inside
there were lotus ponds, arched bridges and screened prom-

enades. The arrangement of the temple buildings was perfect: its wide courtyards were aligned to the compass and yet maintained perfect sightlines to the lakes and rivers below, to the treetops and the mountains.

Fortune had entered a Buddhist temple, a religion which exalts Nature and the life-force within and the excellence of all living things. The Buddha lived in India at the time of Confucius. He preached that all beings pass through a series of lives, a cycle of endless reincarnation, paying for the sins of one life with a good deed in the next. Attachment to any one world is a cause of suffering, he said, when we are only ever passing through. Buddha practised a series of spiritual exercises to end his attachment to this world and focus instead on the one to come. With discipline, he said, we can escape the prison of the self and the cycle of rebirth to enter Nirvana – non-being.

Buddhism came from afar, but had been eagerly adapted in China for its rigorous regimens and its promises of magic, meditation and ecstasy.

In the view of the Buddha, each tree and every plant was an honour and a gift, to be treated with veneration and tended with care; in that belief, the monks cultivated the temple grounds lovingly. The trees were all pruned and carefully planted in groups; beauty was ritualised, Nature choreographed. There were also, unsurprisingly, tea shrubs to be seen in every direction, for tea was the most contemplative of nature's gifts. Beyond the monastery walls, the forest was entirely untouched, with old trees reaching towards the sky. 'In this respect these priests resemble the enlightened monks and abbots of the olden time, to whose taste and care we owe some of the richest and most beautiful sylvan scenery in Europe,' Fortune noted.

A young boy of six or seven, who had just received his

robes as a novice monk, was sitting under a temple porch, perhaps drawing his name in the sand or studying the movements of some beetle, when he sighted the tall Mandarin, Robert Fortune. Noting the stranger's appearance, perhaps even noticing the strangeness of his bearing, the boy ran across the courtyard into one of the smaller buildings. The pitter-patter of his bare feet echoed against an arched stone bridge.

Fortune was weary from the hot morning's climb, his silk robes heavy with sweat. He wandered into the long reception hall, lined with carved chairs and latticed screens, to sit out of the sun and await his official welcome.

Sing Hoo entered the hall with the high-priest, his head held high. Fortune's stay was easily negotiated: of course he would be received, strangers always were. The Mandarin Fortune was a man of honour so he would be given the finest room, plus the tobacco, rice and tea that the monks had to hand. The priest then dispatched the boy monk with orders to make their esteemed guest comfortable.

He returned with a small iron pot of tea.

Fortune sat down. He had never been so tired. In the past three months he had travelled almost three hundred miles as the crow flies – as many as five hundred by switchback and oxbow – to arrive in tea's heartland. Now he could barely move. The young renunciate in orange robes poured the tea; it was a ripe Oolong, with the aroma of orchids and peach pits. The boy palmed the cup, only slightly bigger than a thimble, and bent low as he handed it to Fortune.

'And now I drank the fragrant herb, pure and unadulterated on its native hills. I had never been half so grateful before, or I had never been so much in need of it; for I was thirsty, and weary.'

The monks prepared a banquet lunch to greet the noble

stranger. In Chinese custom, then as now, there is great honour
when a host overfeeds a guest. This spread was generous and
lavish, with the best of the mountain's summer harvest: lotus
root, mushrooms, pickles, cabbages, beans. They drank liberally, and though Fortune was usually not fond of Chinese
liquor ('rank poison'), for once he found it 'agreeable', much
like 'the lighter French wines'.

The whole monastery was in attendance at the meal: one
monk had a face ravaged by smallpox, which did little to
enhance Fortune's appetite; another had a face beatified by
meekness and prayer, which made him glad to be in faraway
Bohea. Though Fortune could just understand the monks'
Chinese, he chose not to speak in the temple. He did not
engage his hosts in conversation, remaining instead a stranger
in the house of tea. Sing Hoo, Fortune noted waspishly, 'was
quite competent to speak for us both'. And yet, despite the
distance between his world and the monks', and his refusal
to engage in even the slightest pleasantries, he felt warmly
welcomed and generously treated. He felt at home: 'We were
the best of friends.'

Sing Hoo, too, enjoyed a distinguished position amongst
the humble priesthood, for he was a well-travelled man. He
had laid eyes on the Imperial wonders of China: he could
describe the Emperor's yellow robes, the pleasures of the
Forbidden City in Peking, the marvel of the Grand Canal,
and the Great Wall in all its glory. The monks were engaged,
provoked by thoughts of the wider world, despite their remote
life in Bohea. Indeed, Fortune was struck by how little the
supplicants were engaged in prayer and how involved they
were in daily tasks. It seemed to him that his hosts paid 'more
attention to cultivation of tea than to the rites of their peculiar faith'.

Tea was central to monastery life here; far more than

anywhere else in China, certainly. It was served at all times of day, ready at every meal. Within the temple grounds, every vista contained tea bushes: tea was in the hedgerow; tea was at the gate; tea was an ornamental decoration, but most of all tea was useful. Fortune had arrived at the height of tea-picking season, when the second flush had just come on, and picking baskets woven of bamboo were scattered amongst the bushes where the pickers had dropped them in the fields before leaving to eat and rest. In every courtyard there was a wide, flat bamboo withering tray, full of the morning's plucking, drying in the sun. Tea was a religion to these monks. It was a holy charge. Tending tea was a meditation.

Wu Yi's monks were also treasure keepers, much as in the monasteries of Burgundy where for centuries monks took note of which parts of a hillside grew the healthiest vines and faithfully recorded the yield of hundreds of harvests. Fortune too took profuse field notes on latitude, longitude, rainfall, and the consistency and colour of the soil: rocky and well-drained. He was not simply there to gather seeds, he was there to bear witness, to replicate a recipe, for tea plants alone would never make a tea industry.

Did it make Fortune a bad guest to take advantage of the monks' hospitality in such a manner? They offered up their knowledge to him freely, as generously as their wine and food. Would the residents of Wu Yi Shan even miss tea's secrets once Fortune absconded with them?

As much as Fortune believed that the fate of nations rested on his research, his work in Wu Yi Shan would also affect every breakfast in England, in the way a factory worker looked at his morning brew, or a housewife at her evening cuppa, and for every pot of tea in the future. Each man and woman in England had an opinion on how to brew the perfect cup, and as Fortune became the world's leading expert, it was his job to tell them definitively whether or not they were correct. He was the ultimate arbiter of tea.

It was an odd position for a botanist to hold, that of food anthropologist and cultural sleuth: for to make a cup of tea is to enter a realm of ritual and repetition, each step a point of ceremony, a part of some larger social story. While Fortune focused minutely on soil, sites, cultivation and management, the size of plantations, the mode of processing and packing, each piece of data he gathered signalled a broader cultural shift. Britain had been the nation of Newton and Enlightenment, the first people to apply a scientific approach to the natural world with systematised rigour. This quest for knowledge and belief in the capacity of man to master the world had made Britain a capital of industry, and also created an Empire. Tea was far more than Britain's national drink, it was her representative commodity.

At first glance, Fortune's scientific appraisal of the task of preparing tea seems ludicrous: a 'quiet palate' is required to take in tea's subtleties, not the hard light of scientific inquiry. Tea is not so much a thing as a cupful of effects. It does not lend itself to hard-and-fast rules and rigorous testing. Yet Fortune, ever the diligent, shirtsleeves scientist, took notes and analysed the simple steps behind preparing every cup of tea:

Boil water.
Ready cup.
Add dry leaf.
Drink.

Boil Water

The first ingredient – indeed, nearly the entirely – of tea is water. Experts hold that the temperature of water in tea-making matters a great deal: how hot it should be, how long the water has been boiled before it is poured, whether the water is fresh from the source or stale. As much as Fortune paid attention to the taxonomy of tea, he also paid attention to variations in boiled water.

Water cannot be warm; it must be at a boil, he wrote. But it must not be boiling for too long, as that releases the concentration of air suspended in the water. Any tea made with overboiled water will taste flat, just as champagne without the bubbles makes for a very lame white wine. Yet the water must not reach a full rolling boil either, especially for the delicate nose of green tea. Neither overboiled nor underboiled tea will yield a proper extraction.

So how does one measure the ideal tea temperature – if perfection is what one is after? Fortune reported a Chinese rule: 'Do not boil the water too hastily, as first it begins to sparkle like crab's eyes, then like fish's eyes, and lastly it boils up like pearls innumerable, spinning and waving about.'

Ready Cup

In Europe, as in China, there was a preference – smartly chosen – for the pre-warmed cup. To this day, the Chinese warm the cup itself with the first of the tea. An entire cup is poured, brewed, and then discarded unceremoniously. The reason for this is that tea leaves are, like grapes or apples, produce in need of washing, which does not happen at any time during processing. In fact, the finest teas are often processed in a spectacularly dirty fashion. They are left to dry on the ground, in the dust, visited by rodents and insects, then stored on a factory floor in open sacks. So the Chinese will brew a cup of tea and throw the first use leaves away. The first cup is for the demons, or, as is often said, 'for your enemies'.

Either way, pouring out the first brew warms the cup. In Britain, there was a preference for running hot water through an empty teapot to temper the pot, which would otherwise cool the tea too hastily as it brewed. As tea cools past a certain point, it loses its flavour. It is said that this practice developed amongst the lower classes, who did not have servants to clean their teapots properly after each use. Despite the unflattering class assumption – that the lower orders were less than hygienic – pre-warming the cup or teapot keeps tea lively longer: Cooling tea, according to the Chinese, is perfection. Cold tea, however, is a sin.

Add Dry Leaf

So how much tea goes into the perfect cup? In Fortune's day there was so much adulteration in the tea exports to Britain, so much twig and stem padding the weight, that it was nearly impossible to predict how strong a pot would be. Then as now there was a general rule by which most tea was brewed: about one teaspoon per cup. It has a commonsense plainness to it.

Fortune's investigations proved that good tea goes further, less is more. His conclusions smacked of righteous economising: if good tea costs half again as much as poorer quality tea, but brews up twice as strong, buy the finer tea and enjoy your experience more, he concluded.

Fortune, in his travels, found much variety between the teas of different regions: the aroma, the look of the leaves, and the colour of the liquor. Connoisseurs today will in fact enjoy these contrasts and seek them out. Tea, like wine, has *terroir*, a flavour which reflects the characteristics of the ground on which it grows. In some areas, in some pickings, the leaf grows large and flat facing the sun. Some areas grow only small-leafed tea. There is no perfect specimen, nor a grand unified recipe for brewing tea. A large tea leaf must be steeped for a long time, a small leaf for a shorter time: it is a matter of the ratio between surface area and water. The smallest leaves, the so-called 'dust-grade' tea, which is the component of most tea bags today, brews up the quickest. Oversteeping tea makes it 'stewey' in the words of the trade. No self-respecting Chinaman in Wu Yi Shan would dream of letting a hand-picked tea brew longer than it ought.

Drink

When you drink tea, you get high. Tea's gentle buzz has rendered it the second most popular drink on earth, after water. Tea promotes mental alertness, happiness, sharper perception. It is a stimulant, albeit a mild one.

'Tea is of a cooling [*yin*] nature,' Fortune reported. 'And, if drunk too freely, will produce exhaustion and lassitude . . . It is an exceedingly useful plant; cultivate it, and the benefit will be widely spread; drink it, and the animal spirits will be lively and clear. The chief rulers, dukes and nobility esteem it; the lower people, the poor and beggarly, will not be destitute of it; all use it daily, and like it.' He was a faithful observer of the Chinese tea customs. 'Drinking it tends to clear away all impurities, drives off drowsiness, removes or prevents headache, and it is universally in high esteem.'

The taste of tea is an amalgam of several different chemicals, some of which do exactly the things Fortune describes. Tea tastes the way it feels, like a cup full of concentration: it is mildly acid, with a little bit of salt, an astringent. Tea has plant enzymes, known as phenolics, which are produced when the leaves brown and are bruised. Phenolics have a brisk, lively taste, giving the impression of a stimulating but gentle brew. Theanine – a tea-based counterpart to caffeine – is an amino acid which straddles the line between sweet and savoury. We know now what theanine and caffeine do to the body; the effects have made caffeine the most widely consumed behaviour-modifying drug in the world. It stimulates the nervous and cardiovascular systems. Caffeine is a chemical alkaloid, a base, which interferes with the way cells signal the body. It raises mood levels and decreases feelings of fatigue, increasing attention and quickening reactions. It also affects the heart, raising the heart-rate, dilating arteries, increasing blood flow, and raising the respiratory and metabolic rates for hours after it is consumed. Caffeine, in great quantities, results in nervousness, restlessness and sleeplessness.

It is worth considering which drink, tea or coffee, is the most stimulating? The answer is black tea – but with certain caveats. Per pound, black tea has more caffeine than coffee – but where one pound of tea brews some two hundred cups, that same pound of coffee yields barely forty. So, by the cup, black tea contains roughly half as much caffeine as coffee. Green tea, meanwhile, has one-third the caffeine of black, or one-sixth that of a cup of coffee. Medically, it takes about 200mg of caffeine – or about two cups of coffee – to combat drowsiness and fatigue. That amounts to about four cups of black tea and twelve cups of green. Few of us have that amount of time or bladder capacity.

What the world has sought when it sips a cup of tea is a mild effect, a high with neither lift nor letdown, a calming alertness, a drink of moods. What Fortune found in Wu Yi Shan was the heart and source of Britain's reigning temper – the thrill to conquer, but politely.

At the monastery, Fortune was within a day's walk of the Big Red Robe bushes, the Da Hong Pao, the most rarefied – and certainly most expensive – tea in the world. This tea was made from only three bushes situated under the three characters Da Hong Pao carved into a rock face. The bushes were fiercely protected by the monks and were two hundred years old.

Legend held that the bushes had arrived in Wu Yi after nine evil dragons tormented the area, causing havoc, destroying crops, ruining lives. Finally, an ancient and immortal god arrived to fight off the dragons and restore order to the countryside. A great battle ensued, the skies darkened, and the forces of good and evil were pitted against one another. The god destroyed the dragons, one by one, and where each corpse landed, a tall peak formed. It is said that the nine karsts of Wu Yi Shan are these dragons, frozen in a fighting stance.

That victorious immortal, celebrating his success, wished to leave a memorial to the battle so the people of Wu Yi Shan would not forget him or his good deeds on their behalf. High in the ridges of the tall black mountains, deep in the heart of the nine dead dragon corpses, above the river, on a sheer cliff where they were hard to pluck, the god left three tea bushes clinging to the rock face. Being of immortal creation, the tea trees seemed to emit a red light, as if catching the reflected rays of the setting sun.

The memory of the nine dragons dominated the landscape of the Wu Yi hills: the river bent nine times around the nine dragon-like mountain karsts, and the area became known locally as the *Jiulongke*, the Nine Dragon's Nest.

In the time of the immortal's victory over the dragons, an ancient Buddhist abbot, Tie Hua, looked up from his daily meditations and saw the three bright bushes illuminated by the light of the heavens. He was old and frail and could not reach the tea himself. Some say that no human hands could touch the evanescent immortal's tea. But Tie Hua was a man of many resources; he reached into his cassock and brought out a monkey, his favoured pet. The monkey swiftly climbed the precipice, picking his way up the rocks to the overhang where the immortal's bushes sparkled in the breeze. The monkey's small hand plucked the tip of the topmost branches, two leaves and a bud. An animal could not harm the trees' spirit, which was the mixture of heaven and earth.

Tie Hua gathered the tea leaves and returned to his monastery where a revered local Mandarin was suffering great agues and chills. The Mandarin was bloated, wracked with stomach distemper. He could not move, and in consequence would have to miss the Imperial examinations for the Civil Service in Peking, his one chance for greatness, at bringing honour and wealth to his family as well as fame to his village in Wu Yi Shan. The scholar was heartsick at the thought that he might not get to the Emperor's court. But the gentle monk Tie Hua brewed up the tea leaves, the god's triumphant gift to the mountains, and served the drink to the citizen scholar, who was immediately healed. The next day, entirely recovered, the revered Mandarin continued his journey to the North to sit the Imperial tests of knowledge, poetry and character. His mind was alive; his senses were keen; he was more able than he had ever been. The young man took first place amongst every scholar in the land.

Upon meeting the Emperor, the scholar discovered that the Empress too was suffering from a similar illness: fevers, fatigue, nausea. It continued for weeks and neither medicine man nor priest could cure her. The Mandarin carried with him a pouch of tea from the immortal's three red bushes which he offered in tribute to the Emperor. On drinking the tea, the Empress was instantly and permanently cured. The Emperor was the celestial Son of Heaven, the Empress his revered wife, and the tea gave them both a taste of the Eternal.

The Emperor demanded that tea from the first flush in Wu Yi Shan – that is, the first bloom of spring – be sent north to Peking each year to cure the court's illnesses. Grateful and magnanimous, the Emperor also sent the scholar back home with a generous gift of a large red silk blanket to clothe the roots of the immortal's bushes in the coming frost. The tea has been called Da Hong Pao, the Big Red Robe, ever since.

A thousand years later, the last of these tea bushes in the remote mountains of Fujian province is guarded by armed men. They are no less precious now than they were when Fortune was wandering the tea hills. Locals say that the young leaves still glow red through the summer and their dangling fruit still looks like garnets in the sun. The Da Hong Pao bushes are watered directly by the heavens, by pure rain filtered through the hard rock of the mythical dragons' skeletons. Each season, the ancient bush will put out about one pound of tea shoots. The first and second flush of the Da Hong Pao, the most powerful and sweetest crops, sell on the private market as the most expensive tea per pound in the world. At several thousands of dollars per ounce, Da Hong Pao is many times more valuable than gold.

Fortunately, Nature provided tea farmers with a way of minting Da Hong Pao for the masses. Tea is easily cloned. Any branch, cut and replanted, layered under soil and left to sprout, will soon develop a network of roots. The process of cloning plants is called agamogenesis, reproduction without gametes – that is, asexual reproduction. Cloning is not as cheap as sexually reproducing tea – that is, planting seeds – but it will produce direct genetic replicas of the parent plant. The technique has been used for thousands of years in farming to preserve treasured cultivars and rare strains. In this way, genetic clones of the three Da Hong Pao trees have been planted throughout Wu Yi Shan. There was no genetic difference whatsoever between the tea Fortune sought and the mythical tea from heaven. Fortune stole the immortal's tea.

Robert Fortune was tireless in his collecting, bringing home many hundreds of saplings from the hills of Wu Yi Shan, the daughters of the Da Hong Pao. He collected thousands of branches and layered them in soil inside the cases to produce clones. He also hired small children to help him collect tea seeds, finding that a little money 'went a long way with the little urchins'. From the monks he purchased seedlings one or two seasons old to sit beside the cloning branches in the glazed terraria of the Wardian cases.

He was also an avid collector of tea myths: it was said that Da Hong Pao tea, so inaccessible in the crevices of the high mountains, is best when not picked by humans. Fortune heard another tale about monkeys: that at harvest time, peasants threw rocks at the monkeys who careened through the branches of Bohea's cliffs. The monkeys retaliated and returned fire at their assailants with anything they could get their paws on – and in Wu Yi Shan, every other object is a tea plant. The monkeys fired back handfuls of leaves and shoots. Monks would stand at the base of the mountains with baskets spread wide, waiting to catch the tea thrown down by angry monkeys. This tea harvest was literally a battle between monks and monkeys. Monkey paws are, of course, the perfect size for the delicate task of plucking only the top two leaves and a bud. 'Monkey-picked' tea was prized for its purity. So too, Fortune noted, was tea picked by virgins' hands. After a few long slow cups of Wu Yi Shan Oolong, the monks nodded in agreement: 'Virgin tea is best.'

Though Fortune would steal neither Chinese monkeys nor virgins, he purchased over 400 of the finest living specimens of the foremost Bohea tea plants he could find. He enjoyed the bounty of the Wu Yi hills many times over, his successful theft of black tea – favourite of the Emperor, the Gods' own brew – all but assured. If only he could transport it safely to the Indian Himalayas.

Fortune walked out with the monks in the mornings, tracking the rhythms of the gardeners and the priests as they made their tea perambulations. He took note of their small-scale processing and drying, of the regional differences between black tea and green tea. He plucked with them, shadowed them, followed their rituals, his notebook in hand. And then the monks gave him even more.

As Fortune prepared to leave the tea hills, the monk who had served as his host offered him a parting gift – several rare plants and flowers. In the morning sun, on a quiet and balmy mountain day, a senior monk pressed some saplings upon Fortune. The botanist did not record which varieties were given to him, but it seemed to him as if the monk knew exactly what his guest was looking for. The renunciate chose specimens that Fortune had not previously collected or even known about. Delighted and embarrassed, the wordless and mute botanist was happy to accept the plants. Each seedling was in perfect condition for transplanting, an ideal present from the Wu Yi hills. The monk's gift was a lucky haul and 'increased my store [of new plants] very considerably'. Fortune was deeply touched.

However, his double dealing could hardly be sustained for an extended period of time, no matter how skilled a spy he was. The trouble – as so many of the disasters which beset him often were – was Fortune's servant, Sing Hoo. As Fortune grew in confidence during his fruitful stay, so too did Sing Hoo. As the mouthpiece and sole negotiator for his master's comfort, Hoo took some liberties. His explanations of Fortune's origins grew increasingly elaborate. Rather than helping him maintain a low profile, Sing Hoo raised it, then embellished it, in order to bask in the reflected glory of his master's perceived importance. According to Hoo, Fortune was no longer just a Mandarin from a distant province, whose details were shady and indistinct. Now he had become a very great man, a rich man with many wives, a venerated warrior and respected leader, from Tartary in Central Asia. He was a descendant of Ghengis Khan even. Fortune was a man whom all should approach with humility and 'anxiety', since he had the confidence of the Emperor. Fortune's new reputation became more than a little uncomfortable for him. He received the increased admiration of his fellows 'with the utmost politeness', he believed. Until circumstances progressed such that he could not.

Upon hearing that the monastery's honoured guest was a man of such esteemed status and wealth, an ancient monk came to Fortune's quarters. Bent under the weight of his robes, the lines in his face like the characters of some ancient script, the man looked as old as the limestone peaks around him. He moved slowly, randomly, as he lurched through space. Weak and simple, he was 'apparently in his second childhood'.

As the ancient monk hobbled through the doorway to Fortune's room, he kicked off his thin slippers. Immediately the supplicant began the kowtow, the ritual of nine forehead-to-floor bows: a sign of submission and respect in Imperial China. Knees down, hands down, head down, ochre robes splayed on the floor like flower petals. Then up again, each move a symphony of ancient joints and creaking sinews.

'I raised him gently from this humiliating posture, and intimated that I did not wish to be so highly honoured,' Fortune wrote. Yet still he did not give himself away.

It was Robert Fortune's only moment of self-reproach in nearly two years of stealing secrets from China. The monks of Wu Yi Shan held him in the deepest reverence, the highest and best regard – which was why they gave him their most treasured secret: the Da Hong Pao. Steely, hard-nosed Fortune felt, for a moment, a twinge of something that the modern traveller would identify as shame: 'I nearly lost my gravity.'

13

Pucheng, September 1849

After packing seeds and shrubs, Fortune was a wanderer once again, on his way from Wu Yi Shan to the Fujian coast. He had seen the Wu Yi pinnacles, drunk in their beauty and left with their treasure. He 'bade adieu to the far-famed Woo-e-shan, certainly the most wonderful collection of hills I had ever beheld'. He had every reason to believe that he and others would one day return to claim more tea from its majestic homeland. 'In a few years hence, when China shall have been really opened to foreigners, and when the naturalist can roam unmolested amongst these hills, with no fear of fines and imprisonments to haunt his imagination, he will experience a rich treat indeed.'

The return journey towards Shanghai and civilisation would be easier than the trip out. Rather than retracing his route through high ground, Fortune headed in a different direction, directly east towards the Fujian coast, where the mountain passes were lower, the road more certain. A straight line would take him to the seaport of Fuzhou, where he had once deflected the advances of pirates. He was following the traditional tea route, the same path the leaves of Da Hong Pao took to the world market. While the road was easier than his original path into the mountains, it was by no means a simple trip. On the way to the coast, he would encounter for himself the dangers posed by the Chinese opium trade.

In the silence of the night, a loud and terrifying ruckus broke out. Angry voices, shouting and arguing, pierced the stillness of Fortune's room at the inn. Amongst the voices, he could just make out the rasping tones of his chair bearers and the more polished sing-song Chinese of his servant. The voices grew louder, more vehement. Fortune imagined all kinds of terrors invading the night. 'I feared they were seizing my servant with the intention of robbing us, and perhaps of taking our lives.'

The scuffle grew more vituperative and Fortune threw on his clothes and reached for his small pistol. 'Human life is not much valued in some parts of the country . . . and for aught I knew I might be in a den of thieves and robbers.'

Sing Hoo was a man of many stories. For miles on the trail, he bent Fortune's ear with grisly tales of his travels, the scarier and more ornate, the better. He spun yarns about noblemen robbed and murdered in their sleep, of merchants mutilated and travellers beheaded. Fortune tried not to listen, but as the days wore on and the thrills of travel faded, he took a kind of reluctant delight in the intricacies of the horrors and sheer inventiveness of Sing Hoo's imagination. But on that particular night, woken so abruptly from sleep, all Sing Hoo's grim stories came flooding back to haunt him. Fortune could not shake off one particular image of a man who disappeared and was found later stuffed into his own trunk. He imagined himself, headless, all pretzled into a glazed glass Wardian case.

Running down a ladder and entering the inn's central courtyard, Fortune discovered that the source of the disturbance was none other than Sing Hoo himself. There were some eight or ten men surrounding him, including their chair bearers, who were half again Sing Hoo's size and shouting as if all the demons of Hell had been unleashed in that roadside inn. Sing Hoo stood his ground in the middle of the scrum, his back to the wall, defending himself 'like a tiger at bay'. He was determined to fight off the mob alone – and in his hand he held his only weapon, a smoking incense stick. Sing Hoo was thrusting and parrying, every now and again poking the hot scented ember close to the faces of his tormentors. 'The most adventurous sometimes got a poke which sent them back cursing and swearing rather faster than they came.'

Fortune found the scene hilarious, Sing Hoo among the jackals, though Fortune's own safety was in danger too and the scene was 'quite sufficient to alarm a bolder man'. But he had been in China long enough by now to see the comedy of one stout man against ten, of his lone servant defending himself with a joss stick.

Fortune strode into the middle of the throng. The men quickly surrounded him. Reaching into his pocket, he brandished the small pistol for everyone to see. The light of Sing Hoo's joss stick gleamed off the smooth metal of the gun. With a superior weapon before them, the men were immediately chastened and stood down.

Fortune was gambling – the pistol did not work. The moist climate of summer had rusted the loading mechanism shut. The chamber was empty and would remain so for the rest of the trip. He, however, had wagered everyone would recognise the gun as a symbol of his power, while no one would know of its uselessness.

'My chair bearers and coolie, who had always treated me with every respect, immediately fell back in the rear, grumbling at the same time.' He listened to their complaints. It seemed that the crowd was demanding from Hoo some cash they had been promised and had never received. Fortune's servant was at it again, on the take, making a squeeze, raking a little more off the top than the percentage Fortune allowed.

He, as always, was the one who would pay the price for Sing Hoo's sins.

'Had I been an uninterested spectator, I might have enjoyed a hearty laugh at the scene before me; but I was in the midst of a strange country and hostile people, and, being the weaker party, I felt really alarmed.'

Drawing himself up into his haughtiest Mandarin stance, Fortune bellowed at Sing Hoo. Whatever the trouble was, whoever had started the argument, it was Hoo's fault and he should be ashamed. How dare he jeopardise Fortune's trip with petty larceny? In a climate of thieves, why bring down the wrath of the locals upon them too? The aggrieved coolies were all hard-working, honest men, by Fortune's reckoning; they had dealt fairly with him, had carried him for miles on end through the torturous vertical terrain, they were loyal and deserving. Fortune had no qualms about taking their side in this matter and publicly said as much.

The money in question amounted to some 300 Chinese cash, or about one English shilling. Even Fortune, a thrifty Scot, could never have imagined risking his life for such a sum. It felt it was as if he were breaking up a squabble between schoolchildren, but he was in genuine danger. So, with ten local witnesses watching, he flatly ordered Sing Hoo to pay the debt without delay. Fortune cursed at Sing Hoo like a Chinese sailor, calling down the wrath of his ancestors on him for such cruel, hare-brained, insensitive double-dealing with the good men of his retinue. By publicly humiliating Sing Hoo, he placated the eight coolies, and the onlookers, for the time being.

Fortune was staying in a simple travellers' rest house, but he was in the company of thieves. Some 'were evidently opium-smokers, from the sallow colour of their cheeks, probably gamblers, and altogether such characters as one would rather avoid than be on intimate terms with'. Wherever there was opium, criminal interests could not be far away. Users lived on the fringes of society and often had a penchant for skulduggery and crime. Fortune's temporary home was, in fact, a so-called 'flower smoke den', or *huayan guan*, a seedy pleasure palace where men enjoyed poetry, women and opium, in no particular order. Another common name for such inns was 'husband and wife dens', but, a Chinese scholar noted, 'in reality they seduce the sons of good families. They are a place for secret adultery'. The inn was one of many houses of ill repute along the route to the coast, for since the end of the First Opium War, and the resulting institutionalisation of the opium trade, Shanghai had become the centre of drug commerce in the Far East and addicts from throughout the country made pilgrimages to the coast to assemble a fix.

Opium is derived from *Papaver somniferum*, the poppy of slumber, an annual that grows in the mountainous regions of Central Asia, much of which was, at the time, in the hands of the British Empire. The opium poppy has white or purple flowers, it grows three or four foot high, and has a solid cylindrical stem that bends and droops under the weight of a bud, but stands erect when the flower is in full bloom, as if announcing to the world that here is something sinister and lovely. In the centre of the poppy there is a large globe-shaped seed capsule, covered by a papery skin. When this seed pod is sliced open, it exudes a sticky sap which is collected, drained, dried, then kneaded into small balls or cakes. The principal active ingredient in opium is morphine, an alkaloid that deadens pain, produces euphoria, induces sleep and apathy, reduces fever and relaxes muscle spasms. For thousands of years, from the time of Homer even, opium has been used as a recreational and medicinal drug. It can be smoked, drunk, eaten, injected, or rubbed on the skin. In addition to morphine, opium also contains codeine, another pain-killing alkaloid.

By the middle of the nineteenth century, millions of Chinese people, it is estimated one in every three adults, were opium addicts. The affliction was so widespread that the economy of China, once prosperous and wealthy, went bankrupt for nearly twenty years. By Fortune's day, imports of opium were rising 20 per cent a year; 48,000 chests were imported from India in 1845 costing $34 million ($962 million today, or £481 million) but rose to 60,000 chests in 1847 on revenues of $42 million ($1.1 billion today, or £550 million).

China then, as now, was largely made up of peasants whose brute backs and shoulders were the sinew and strength for farming and rough labour. It was these men and women who were most likely to become opium addicts. On its first introduction to China, in the Ming Dynasty, opium was seen as a court luxury that came from abroad. The Dutch began to bring opium to China out of Jakarta about the same time Europe was discovering tea, also via the Dutch. (Then, as now, the Dutch made terrific drug pushers.) Wrote an early scholar of Chinese medicine, opium 'tastes bitter, produces excessive heat and is poisonous. It is mainly used to aid masculinity, strengthen sperm and regain vigour. It enhances the art of alchemists, sex and court ladies. Frequent use helps to cure the chronic diarrhoea that causes the loss of energy . . . its price equals that of gold.' Once opium became popular at court, as an aphrodisiac, it was taken up by the aristocrats, scholars and officials of the middle class. Though opium was introduced as a luxury for the higher ranks, by the mid-nineteenth century, its pleasures were shared with the lower classes. Coolies, chair bearers and boatmen – the people Fortune encountered daily – all benumbed their hard lives with a drug that produced a sense of calm and ease. What started out as a luxury and a signifier of taste had become a country-wide scourge by Fortune's time. As opium use became common, it also became condemnable. China's officials denounced the taverns and brothels where opium was used by the working masses of China.

The consequences of opium smoking, contained as mere personal shortcomings in the upper classes, became vast social ills in the lower orders. Wrote a traveller: 'Smokers while asleep are like corpses, lean and haggard as demons. Opium smoking throws whole families into ruin, dissipates every kind of property, and ruins man himself . . . it wastes flesh and blood until the skin hangs down in bags and their bones are naked as billets of wood. When the smoker has pawned everything in his possession, he will pawn his wife and sell his daughters.'

Opium made for a weak and lethargic workforce, a population which consumed more resources than it produced. In particular, it made a mockery of the Emperor's army. Contemporary reports decry the use of opium in the military: 'Many Cantonese and Fujianese soldiers smoke opium, there are even more among the officers. They are cowards and they have spoiled our operation. They are really despicable.' The Qing emperors were already on shaky ground, the dynasty would end in little over fifty years – indeed, all of Imperial Chinese history would come to a halt in the first years of the twentieth century. With an army in thrall to opium, could there be any wonder at the coming Qing defeat – or that the Taiping rebels would be so victorious? Complained another scholar, 'Although there are more than 10,000 [soldiers], seven out of ten are Guangdong natives. They are cowardly and not used to marching in the mountains. Plus most coastal soldiers are opium smokers.' Writing that as many as seven out of ten soldiers were addicts is another was of saying 7,000 of 10,000 soldiers were too; 70 per cent of the Emperor's forces were rendered completely invalided by opium.

Though disastrous economically, in many ways opium was the perfect drug for China; it was almost Confucian in the way that it took away desire to change the status quo. Whereas caffeine suited the Western need to conquer at very least a hemisphere, the high from opium drove men into a kind of delightful, dreamlike distraction, acquiescent to the established order and the way things were.

Drugs such as opium and tea were the first mass-produced, mass-marketed global commodities; everything and everyone these 'stimulants' touched, from the producers to distributors to consumers, was altered in their wake. The global drug trade, in which England and China were deeply enmeshed, produced new leaders, new governments, new companies, new farming practices, as well as new colonies, new modes of capital accumulation, new modes of transport and communication.

From an economic and imperial standpoint, opium was miraculous. It found new markets and customers almost effortlessly and took up little room on the merchant fleets colonising the world in the first wave of globalisation. From its earliest days, opium was a mode of currency that made the Far East trade run fleet and trim: it was lightweight, easy to pack and fetched a high price.

Opium, like other drugs such as tea, coffee, and sugar, was good for Empire. Where the English had been trading for their breakfast tea with silver and racking up a crushing balance of payments problem, the growing opium trade quickly reversed the imbalance in England's favour. China's silver payments to Great Britain were $75 million between 1801–26 (about $1.3 billion today or £650 million), but the outflow increased to $134 million between 1827–49 (about $2.9 billion now, or £1.45 billion), all on opium's coat tails.

The economies of European nations in the nineteenth century were built on the sale of stimulants and addictive drugs. It was through drug-based commercial enterprises, such as the tea and opium trades, that Britain became the greatest of all hegemonic Empires. The British campaign to sell opium in China was tremendously profitable. It brought in £750,000 in 1840 (about £72 million today or $1.4 billion), and rose to £9.1 million by 1879 (£882 million today, about $1.8 billion). Britain's all-conquering naval fleet might have fought a few more draws had it not been constantly improved with newly minted capital from the sugar, tea and opium trades. Without opium, the India trade would not have flourished, and without India Britain's post-Napoleonic global ascendancy could well have collapsed. Opium out of India paid for tea from China, and the British trade in both put silver bullion into the coffers of the exchequer. Without drugs, the British Empire would not have been possible.

As Fortune's party settled down for the night, he could still hear the resentful clucking and cursing of his labourers. He returned to his bunk but sleep was beyond him. Through the rotting floorboards, opium smoke wafted into the room, thick and heavy, clinging to the floor, swirling over his luggage, mixing with the smells of mould and damp, infusing the space with the sickly sweet scent of burnt sugar. Though overpowering, the smell was oddly seductive. As Graham Greene later said, it 'was like the first sight of a beautiful woman with whom one realises that a relationship is possible'.

In the dining room below, a group of men, including Fortune's chair bearers, reclined on a large bedlike sofa, called a *kang*, with a lit lamp in the centre of the room. Everyone was lying down, everyone was comfortable. One of the bearers leaned over the bed towards the fire to warm a ball of opium, which gurgled and boiled as the flame lapped at the sticky liquid. With a long spoon, he stuffed the marble-sized ball of opium, now a hot, sticky mass, into his pipe, inhaling in deep pulls. There was a loud pop, the sizzle of solids metastising into smoke. 'The stewing and frying of the drug and the gurgling of juices in the stem would well nigh turn the stomach of a statue,' wrote Mark Twain. The user leaned back again on his pillow, holding his breath, and exhaled in a delirium of poppies and painlessness.

'What madmen might do under the circumstances – for madmen they were while under the influence of the drug – I could not possibly foresee,' Fortune wrote. He stayed awake the rest of the night, playing out the possibilities in his head, enumerating all the ways he could die. It was eerie, much like the intricate tales of death and destruction that Hoo wove during their long days on the trail towards tea. 'This kept me awake for several hours.'

After the altercation with the chair bearers, Sing Hoo slept with his clothes on, facing the door, waking at the slightest creak or disturbance in the night silence. Finally the opium smokers' voices died down in the room below. They were seduced by the poppy and robbed of their bile, 'gone off at last into the land of dreams'.

At first light, Fortune was up and his gear packed. He would push on and put all the high drama of the night behind him. He called for Sing Hoo to get a move on, to round up the others and get started. But the inn was entirely empty. There were neither coolies nor innkeepers to help him with the load. Everyone had absconded under cover of night, never to do business again with the likes of Sing Hoo or his master, the strange Mandarin. Fortune had mistaken opium smoking for outright mutiny. He was now without his retinue, in a faraway town, with an angry and shamed servant his only companion.

There was nothing to do but seek help. Fortune ordered Sing Hoo off to the nearest village, to engage more men. He urged his servant not to take advantage of any new bearers, to refrain for once from the squeeze. Sing Hoo set out, as ordered, still stinging from Fortune's rebuke.

The morning passed on, heating up, and Fortune was itching to put some distance between himself and yet another scene of insecurity and danger. He feared that the mob from the previous night were not only complaining to all and sundry about the terrible Mandarin and his awful servant, but were now plotting retribution. Like Wang before him, Sing Hoo made 'enemies' in the small society of the countryside. Fortune was eager to leave before the wounded parties could 'put into execution any scheme of revenge'. And yet he could not go. There were no chair bearers. There was not even Sing Hoo.

Hours ticked by, but neither Sing Hoo nor a new team of coolies appeared. It seemed he could not hire another. His reputation as a cheat and a liar had preceded his entry to the nearest village, and the one beyond that. Though no one was plotting to kill Fortune, they were thwarting his plans and his trip to the coast – it was retribution enough.

Finally, in the late-afternoon, Sing Hoo returned to Fortune, alone and defeated. No one would work for him, not at any price. Sing Hoo's miserably low status sank even further.

Fortune and his plant specimens, Sing Hoo and his bolts of grass cloth, were stranded.

But Fortune was having none of Sing Hoo's self-pity or obsequious apologising. He announced that they would most certainly not be staying another night in the inn while the servant tried to rescue his reputation. They would march on that very day, in whatever daylight they had remaining. And Sing Hoo, who considered himself a high-ranking servant, would have to carry the entire load himself, like a miserable low-class coolie.

Sing Hoo was to strap together the luggage into one piece using rope and bamboo. He would do the heavy lifting alone until they were far enough away for no one to have heard of the evening's fracas with the coolies and the joss stick. They had to walk beyond the reach of Sing Hoo's shoddy reputation.

As the two of them set out from the miserable opium inn it started raining hard, pouring down in torrents. Still, Fortune insisted they walk on through the flooding streets. The two men were soaked instantly, feeling entirely sorry for themselves and completely furious with each other. They plugged on, through the mud, until the inn was behind them, a distant memory on another hill.

When they were a mile beyond the city walls, the bamboo with which Sing Hoo was carrying the luggage slung over his shoulders suddenly snapped in two. Everything Fortune owned, luggage, specimens and every single tea plant, was plunged into ankle-deep mud. Baskets opened up; seeds spilled out. And all of Sing Hoo's grass cloth, which he had bargained so hard for, lay strewn in the filth.

Sing Hoo and Fortune were in the vast Chinese wilderness, surrounded by farmland, alone and very wet. No one could see or hear them; there was no one to bear witness to their frustration. Instead of being angry, Fortune pitied his sodden, exhausted servant. 'I had not the heart to reproach him . . . in the mud and water he looked perfectly miserable.'

14

Shanghai, Autumn 1849

In the relative comfort of Shanghai, a guest in the cosy compound of Mssrs Beale, Dent & Co., Fortune sat down at a writing desk warmly lit by a candle. He had received a package from the Government in Calcutta. All the hard months of travel, his entire sense of success or failure in China, would hinge on the information contained in this communication.

Eagerly, Fortune broke open the seal on the envelope and pulled out page after page of official documents; seemingly a whole book of them. There was a mass of information, reports from Company botanists and officials detailing the fate of his first shipment of green tea out of China. It was all neatly filed in reverse chronological order, clearly and painstakingly copied by hand.

The Company had provided a summary of the information contained in these documents. It was news he was desperate to have, and yet the content beggared belief: nearly all the tea plants had arrived dead in India. Death in every single box. One year of Fortune's work, all the Company's investment, had been most thoroughly and completely wasted. It was as if he had not been in China at all that first year.

He put his head in his hands and tried hard to make sense of the news.

Then he began reading at the beginning of the file.

The plants were sent out the previous winter, but by March there had been a delay, a detour and trans-shipment through Ceylon. Yet his tea had reached Calcutta at the end of March, and all seemed to be going well then.

'Dr Falconer reports receipt of cases of plants containing 13,000 young plants . . . the greater part of the plants were reported to have arrived in Calcutta in a healthy and thriving condition,' a report stated.

Fortune followed the onward fate of his seedlings. Upriver they had gone, on the steamer to Allahabad, the main port for the Himalayan Provinces and the North West Frontier. But they were delayed there, too, for the Ganges was low – they stayed nearly a month in Allahabad. Had the cases been in good condition, delays would not have been such a problem, even after the month's wait in Ceylon. Wardian cases should preserve their contents indefinitely. Only it was clear from the letters that by Allahabad they were not in good order: 'Many of the panes of glass in the cases, too, were broken,' the missive reported. Fortune read on, his stomach turning. Had someone had the foresight to reseal the boxes, the contents might have lived. Or had a competent gardener replanted the seedlings right then and there into pots, and tended the tea like houseplants on their way upriver, they might have made the trip successfully. Alas, his plants had likely been left on the loading dock of a Company godown, or factory, like so much ordinary cargo, ignored until the rains brought the water level up and the boats could pass.

Fortune's jaw drew tighter. He could only shake his head as he ploughed through pages of more material from the Revenue Department: from Allahabad, the cases had been loaded on to an oxcart for the mountain gardens of Saharunpur, the Company's experimental plantation in the Himalaya. They reached it in mid-May.

'The first batch consisting of six boxes of plants reached Seharampore [sic] on the 14th of May in bad condition not more than 30 or 40 plants having leaves on them, but they have begun to show signs of improvement. The second batch of 5 boxes arrived in better condition on the 9th [June] having on the whole 41 plants in good condition in the 5 boxes.'

After sending thousands upon thousands of young plants, Fortune could count only 80 healthy arrivals in the mountains of India. It was statistically meaningless, a failure rate beyond all reckoning, the worst possible outcome. Wardian boxes had failed Fortune. Fortune had failed the Company. Fortune was a failure.

The accounting on his first year looked very grim.

Number Case	Number Plants
6	8 plants in good order
7	All dead
8	1 plant in good order
9	2 plants in good order
10	all dead
11	2 plants in good order and 2 sickly
12	6 plants in good order
13	8 plants in good order and 2 sickly
14	4 plants in good order and have thrown out some strong healthy branches
15	2 plants in good order
Box without number	5 Plants in good order and 1 sickly

But what about the seeds, the other hope for tea in Britain's Indian Empire?

By early-July, some seven packets of seeds had arrived.

'The result has been an entire failure not one seed having germinated. I lately removed a number of seeds from the beds to ascertain their condition and invariably found them to be rotten,' Jameson wrote. Duds, waterlogged, or dried out, they would never grow. No tea in any shape or form from Fortune's first year of tea hunting for the Company in China would grow in British India.

In the pages of correspondence that ensued, Fortune followed what seemed to be bureaucratic blame-shifting. Calcutta officials lobbied accusations against the gardening men in the hinterlands. The men in the provinces insisted that no one knew tea the way they knew tea – certainly not other botanists in Calcutta – and that their word was final on all subjects pertaining to tea. In the end, Fortune's first plants may have been doomed by collective corporate incompetence.

In his own notes, he eschewed the self-aggrandising revisionism that characterised official communication in British India. Fortune noted dryly and simply that he had not succeeded, and that attempting to move plants to a new home and develop an entire industry out of transplants was a very difficult thing indeed.

In the autumn of 1848 I sent large quantities of tea seeds to India. Some were packed in loose canvas bags, others were mixed with dry earth and put into boxes, and others again were put up in very small packages in order to be quickly forwarded by post; but none of these methods were [sic] attended with much success. Tea-seeds retain their vitality for a very short period if they are out of the ground. It is

the same with oaks and chestnuts, and hence the great difficulty of introducing these valuable seeds into distant countries
by seeds.

The time had come for further botanical experimentation.

Though Fortune's entire green tea haul had been rendered
useless, it seems that he had no fear that the Company would
recall him from China. Instead he remained sanguine, focused
and not the least bit apologetic. There was no self-reproach
at all, Fortune dwelt purely on solutions, possibilities. He was
confident enough of his basic gardening skills to know he
could obtain better results.

He had in mind a new method of seed transportation, one
that would force seeds to germinate inside the Wardian case.
He decided the problem of the previous trip was that he had
exceptionalised the seeds, dividing the lifecycle of the plant
into two distinct moments, the living seedlings and the inert
seeds, and shipped them to India as entirely separate cargo.
But the Wardian case was the safest place for all manner of
plant life, no matter what its stage of development. Fortune
remembered that when Ward had made his original discovery,
he'd looked into a sealed glass jar and seen seeds sprouting
on a piece of mould several years after the jar had been shut.
Plants weren't frozen in time in a Wardian case, they *lived*.
Seeds should not be isolated from a living environment,
shipped in hemp sacks like so many grains of rice; they too
would thrive in a terrarium.

Fortune immediately instigated a Wardian case experiment:
packed into the soil of the potted plants he was sending to
the Calcutta Botanic Garden, he planned to stow many
hundreds of black tea seeds. This experiment was not so
different from the conditions in which Ward had made his

first discovery. Fortune simply recreated those conditions on a mass scale.

He was sending mulberry plants to India, from the district where China's best silks were spun. He had travelled through the silk district on the Yangtze as he made his way in and out of tea country and believed that India too, with its thriving cotton industry, might benefit from experiments in softer silk. He planted the mulberry bush in the 'usual way', as he did any other shrub of economic and scientific note, carefully, with enough space, soil, and light to be comfortably sustained on the long journey out. Fortune watered the transplant, left the mulberry bush in the sun, and a few days later, after the soil had absorbed the water and the plant had adjusted to its confined new home, he scattered handfuls of black tea seeds – each the size of a marble – over the surface of the soil. He then added another layer of soil, about half an inch deep, over the tea seeds. Fortune had his boxmakers fashion cross-bars for this case, so that the earth would stay in place, whatever turbulence the sea swell or ox-cart travel might bring.

Fortune, like all Victorians, would have known a British dessert called a trifle, which has layers of fruit, custard and sponge cake topped with whipped cream. It is served in a glass dish to display the contrast between the sticky cream, sugary fruit and absorbent cake, like striations in a rock face. Fortune's idea was essentially a Wardian case parfait: loam, seeds, soil, topped with a plant. But unlike the British dessert, the appeal of Fortune's layering would become global. 'This method will apply to all short-lived seeds, as well as to those of the tea plant, it is important that it should be generally known.'

Fortune's first mulberry 'trifle', planted with seeds from the Da Hong Pao, was opened in Calcutta and hailed as a complete success. Not only did the seeds survive, they had fully germinated on the voyage out, arriving healthier than in their fragile seed state.

Falconer, the senior botanist in Calcutta, was delighted. A scientist's inventiveness in China had circumvented a Company gardener's incompetence in Saharunpur. Nature had triumphed over human inaction and bungling. But not only that: Fortune had made a great leap forward in the global imperial project of plant transfer – which was, essentially, the transfer of technology. If not only living plants but fragile seeds as well could travel overseas, then entire industries could be transplanted – not one plant at a time, but one entire profitable species at a time. Whole crops could travel; whole economies could transplant. Fortune expanded the global exportation of knowledge and technology in a four foot by six foot plant trifle. For an imperial power such as Britain, with a planet full of subject colonies just waiting to be tilled and planted for profit, Fortune's discovery was nothing short of revolutionary.

'The young tea-plants were sprouting around the mulberries as thick as they could come up,' Falconer wrote to the Company and Fortune, erupting with enthusiasm.

Fortune, buoyed by his success, made up another fourteen Wardian cases using his new method. Knowing that the principle at work was generally successful, he grew decidedly less meticulous about the layering for his next experiment. With a bushel of seeds on hand, he made a mixture of one part earth to two parts seeds and tossed them all in together, like so many raisins in a pudding, then spread the soil in the bottom of cases planted with rows and rows of tiny young tea plants only a season or two old. He was daring and careless because he now had every faith in the incubator of the Wardian case. He believed his black tea seeds would survive the trip to India, and so he sent hordes.

On a ship, protected from rats and seawater by glass, the seed/soil mixture produced thousands upon thousands of germinating black tea seeds, all of which sprouted abundantly and gloriously on their way to India. There were too many healthy plants for Falconer to count, it seemed. Out of a single season's devastation, Fortune secured immortality – for himself, for Britain, and for Indian tea.

The delicate black teas of the Himalayas might not have thrived in the same way had Fortune not come upon this method. Most, if not all, of the existing tea in India was green, and came from inferior tea stock. Fortune shipped the first viable black tea to the Indian Himalayas. In a single season he provided India with an entire crop of China's finest, cloned from the Da Hong Pao, the immortal's own brew.

'The success attending their introduction in Ward cases has been so great, that I would recommend the attention of Government to be confined to procuring seeds and sowing them as recommended,' wrote Jameson. There was no longer any need to hunt for living plants, the tender yearlings small enough to travel but hearty enough to survive transplant; seeds could do the trick. The new method was better, 'proved by the admirable condition in which Mr Fortune's seedling cases reached us. The plants so reared reached the plantation in full vigour of growth and were but little injured on being transplanted into beds.'

Fortune's new seed-shipping method increased the yield over shipping live seedlings tenfold – 'for every young plant there will be, on the arrival of the cases at their destination in the [Himalaya] ten available seedlings'. Every tea garden in the Himalayas from that season forward would bear the daughters of Fortune's tea plants, enriching the Indian tea industry for generations. He had radically changed the job of a plant hunter, which henceforward might more accurately be called a seed hunter; so too would he change the world's agrarian economies.

Seed selection and breeding is a large part of the cultivation of finer-quality teas. The difference in quality between what Fortune provided for the Himalayas and what had been growing there already, the teas in the first shipments sent to the London tasters, was vast. Processed tea is subject to the vagaries of climate and rainfall, harvesting and shipping. But the raw material matters enormously, and Fortune improved the Himalayan teas beyond all measure. His tea seedlings would breed and crossbreed with the stock already in the Himalayas, the inferior seeds out of Canton as well as the native Assam variety. Through the next several generations of selection and breeding, Fortune's stock – bred for the highest Chinese tastes over generations (called the China *jat*) – would mix with the best qualities of the native brews, the heartiness and maltiness of Assam tea (called the India *jat*). The new hybrids would produce unique flavours, flowery, mellow, rich and supple, the finest teas in the world.

The Himalayas provide perfect *terroir* for tea, as if God had always intended it to grow there and only needed Fortune's help to kickstart the industry. The tea plant has a natural affinity with the Himalayas, like a budding flower takes to sunlight. Good tea requires seasoning with frost, which the highest of the world's mountains provide. Tea needs sunlight – but not too much – and a mountain mist that burns off during the day will protect the leaves from singeing in too much light. Tea needs the rich loamy soil that comes from geologic lifetimes of mountains breaking down into minerals. Tea flourishes on a steep hillside, where the roots won't puddle in too much water. The Himalayas, in short, provided the perfect canvas on which to paint tea.

Fortune provided the ink. His seeds, seedlings, and clones brought world-class tea varietals to the Himalayan range.

As the Company gardens expanded using Fortune's tea haul, and the Company opened up other mountain territories to production, the tea grew finer still, year upon year. Out of Fortune's theft and ingenuity, Indian tea went from a common table drink to a beverage of distinction.

15

Shanghai, February 1851

On the quayside in Shanghai there was a scene of pathos and heartache as eight Chinese tea experts said goodbye to the land they knew and loved, to their every extended family member, to China and, perhaps, to tea itself. For though the Mandarin from beyond the Great Wall promised there was tea where they were going, each of the departing men believed only one place could grow tea – China, the centre of the world.

Mothers pressed packages of food upon their sons. The men bowed their heads in respect to their fathers who had seen lifetimes of hardship and looked upon the loss of a son as simply one more in an endless chain. Wives, where the men were lucky enough to have them, wept openly. Children clung to the legs of departing fathers. The young tea makers bent down to kiss babies in arms whom they would not see for many long years to come. Finally the men pulled themselves away and walked up the gangway to the tender which would bring them to H.M.S. *Island Queen*, a wooden side-wheeled steamer bound for Hong Kong.

Fortune was unmoved by the tears and tragedy of his travel companions. He found it instead 'an amusing scene'. The tea makers were so unsophisticated, 'inland Chinamen', afraid of the new and the different, very much less worldly than the Chinese in the ports who were fully conversant with foreigners and their surprising ways. These men were miserable to be 'taking leave of their friends and their native country' and yet Fortune could not see anything to pity.

At the mouth of the Huangapu River, in the deep-water port, *Island Queen* lay at anchor waiting for the manufacturers, the tea-making equipment and Wardian cases, and Robert Fortune. The ship would depart for Hong Kong the following morning.

Fortune walked up the gangway after his new workforce, leaving the mainland for what might, so far as he knew, be the last time. He had completed his last task for the East India Company: finding and engaging Chinese experts willing to follow him to India. He had amply stocked the tea gardens of the Himalayas with new plants and seed stock. He had sent glazed cases full of plants he had collected home to the English salerooms and Kew, and had packed up a further consignment of porcelain, silk, trinkets and other curiosities to sell at auction when he arrived.

It was a great deal more difficult dealing with people than with plants. Fortune had hired true experts, from the deep tea country to instruct the Indian *malis* in the proper planting and processing of the new crop. Finding willing employees had not been easy in the atmosphere of danger and distrust following the outcome of the brutal First Opium War. Men from the Chinese interior were particularly wary of foreigners, unfamiliar with them as they were and having heard chilling tales of their barbarism. Fortune made the task even harder for himself by refusing to hire anybody but the sons of tea growers, men who carried with them the knowledge of generations. 'Had I wanted men from any of the towns on the coast, they might have been procured with the greatest of ease . . . But I wanted men from districts far inland, who were well acquainted with the process of preparing the teas.'

Absconding with plants was one thing; absconding with Chinese men another altogether. 'The Chinese authorities have always watched with the most jealous eye any attempts made to export the tea plant; and any endeavour to procure good tea makers would assuredly be foiled or greatly delayed by specious difficulties,' advised an official in Calcutta. Fortune, heeding the warning, did not recruit the men himself. If he were caught soliciting Chinese natives away from their homeland, he would most certainly be put to death for kidnapping and probably spark an international incident. At the same time as he was seeking tea experts, a rash of abductions and forced immigrations – impressments really – swept through southern and eastern China. Emigration out of China was picking up speed as foreign nations in need of cheap labour began hunting for men to do the heavy lifting in colonies such as Australia or to build railways in the North American West. Fortune himself noted that 'a shipload of emigrants had been induced to embark for California only a short time before, and emigration was carried on most extensively'. By his day, the 'incurable corruption' of the Mandarins was draining the country. Peasants were pouring out of China in search of better homes and lives. Many native Chinese, however, had been killed in the villages for seeking to recruit emigrants. Fear of the 'pig sellers', as these employment agents were called, ran rampant in rural areas.

In Imperial China's millennia-long history, the country had never officially recognised emigration. Every Chinese person was considered both the subject and the property of the Emperor in Peking, and consequently going abroad was considered in the same light as a theft from the Son of

Heaven. For centuries China had forbidden her citizens access to the ocean, even to fish. It was among the most important duties of local officials to stop emigration. The ban on foreign travel was both a functional and a foundational part of Chinese culture. The Qing court feared invasion and so prohibited any contact with foreigners. Laws prevented political contacts with outsiders; there would be no free marketplace of ideas. The law in fact reflected traditional Confucian values. To abandon parents, connections and ancestors was considered a shameful act: how could a son sweep graves at the Qing Ming Festival when he was in California mining for gold?

Fortune himself had met the tea experts he would be bringing to India only days before their departure. He took no direct part in their recruitment and his notes on how this was achieved remain vague. He simply dispatched agents, hired through Beale's compradors, to the Chinese countryside, and let them do their work. How these agents collected tea experts from China is a matter for guesswork, based on details of other efforts to recruit Chinese emigrants for other overseas work.

Fortune relied, as always, on Dent & Beale's compradors, the men who worked for the European trading firms as purchasers, negotiating with the Emperor's trade Mandarins. These compradors were known quantities to Fortune; he'd used them for the past three years of his Company plant hunting and in his previous three years for the Royal Horticultural Society. He felt he could depend on them to find suitable experts and negotiate a fair price.

Despite the Chinese Government's prohibition on emigration, a vast and thriving trade in sending Chinese workers abroad had developed during the late Qing Empire. As the African slave trade wound down in the latter half of the nineteenth century, the coolie trade replaced it on the global exchange in cheap labour. For Britain, the traffic in African slaves officially ended in 1833 and the Empire was then unable to find workers for her sugar colonies. The cost of abolition was high for Britain and showed up on the balance sheets of her merchant ships. Simply put, bodies were needed to fill a production gap. By the mid-century, gold discoveries in Australia and California had lured overseas thousands of Chinese who could no longer eke out a living on the land while famines and floods devastated China. In the first few years of the American gold rush, some 25,000 Chinese coolies would emigrate across the Pacific to California. By 1870, 2 million Chinese had found their way across the globe, exporting their culture and heritage with them. All too often, though, the only difference between an African slave and a Chinese coolie was that the Chinese possessed a contract.

'*For Sale: A Chinese girl with two daughters, one of 12–13 years and the other of 5–6, useful for whatever you may desire. Also one mule,*' read a typical handbill at the time.

Coolies were enticed into coolie-ticket contracts by brokers using all manner of duplicity. Some were seduced by fantastic stories of the promised land to which they were heading, embellished with promises of free clothing, food, lodging, travel and a fortune to be made. Some coolies signed on to repay their gambling debts. Others were sold by their families in the aftermath of clan wars, abducted as pirate bounty, or kidnapped in the middle of the night by crimps – thieves who dealt in human flesh. The term 'shanghaied' comes from the fact that many coolies were drugged, stolen and shipped off to the fleshmarkets of Shanghai to be traded as chattels. All coolie immigrants were put into holding pens called 'barracoons'; they would wait there, locked up for months, until a full shipload was ready for dispatch to the New World.

Coolie-ship quarters were nearly as cramped as those on the African slave ships. A coolie's queue was cut off as a sign of his obedience to his new master, symbolically severing the ties of fealty to the Emperor. A coolie's clothing was burned on arrival in Shanghai – he was charged for the cost of replacements – and he was then scrubbed with straw brooms to eradicate any lice and vermin he might have brought with him from his home. Once aboard ship the men stayed below decks and were seldom allowed, or capable of coming, topside to breathe fresh air for the many months of travel required to reach the New World. The coolie ships were consequently hotbeds of dysentery, disease and death.

Coolie mutinies were routine. In 1852, the *Robert Browne* sailed from Amoy for San Francisco with as many as 475 coolies on board. Once at sea and confined to the hold, the men were forced to sign contracts of labour; those who refused to cooperate were flogged. In the name of hygiene, the 'barbarian' crew cut off their queues. The group's health began to deteriorate and the crew simply threw the sick and dying overboard. Nine days out of port, a mutiny erupted. The captain, two officers, four crew, and ten Chinese died in the fracas. Days later, the ship put in at the Yaeyama Islands of Okinawa. The coolies were put ashore or escaped – there are several versions of the story, some of which were recounted under torture – and the *Robert Browne* returned to China, empty, ready for another load of wretched human cargo. The coolies stranded in Okinawa later found their way to Canton, where they would tell their stories to moralising missionaries and sympathetic diplomats.

Both the Americans and British in Canton as well as the Chinese investigated the circumstances of the mutiny for two years. Should the mutineers be hanged? Did the crew members deserve such terrible deaths? There was never any resolution. The Chinese were sympathetic to the mutineers; some suggested seeking out the remaining crew who had 'kidnapped' them, and beheading them. Locals agitated for a revolt, to send the foreigners a signal that impressments such as this would not be tolerated. Popular sentiment was stirred up against the coolie trade in China. It was clear that no matter how much gold was found in the Sacramento River, it had exacted a high price on the men of China.

The British were naturally incensed that their citizens, the captain and crew of the *Robert Browne*, had met such a horrible fate at the hands of the Chinese. Britain wanted justice for the crew, but the Chinese bureaucrats could not allow an official investigation that would pronounce judgment on the coolie trade, for to regulate the trade would be to recognise it. And so, as with prostitution, neither the Chinese nor the British could publicly acknowledge that such a trade existed at all. With this head-in-the-sand logic, the practice proceeded entirely unlegislated for twenty-five years. Officially, there was no such thing as a trade in coolies, therefore it could not be a problem.

It was in this brutal and tumultuous context that Dent & Beale's compradors went hunting for tea experts. These well-heeled middlemen of the coast spoke in pidgin, were loyal to the Westerners, and had been affiliated to the big merchant houses since their apprentice days. More importantly, the compradors maintained a rich network of contacts in the countryside. They could go where foreign men such as Fortune dare not. They could purchase people, tea, porcelain, silk – all at a good price. The compradors were the essential middlemen who made the China trade run smoothly, and they had been making a good living at it for centuries. Exporting coolies or tea experts made little difference to them.

Fortune was nervous about the way the business would be

conducted, though. It would be improper for the Company to be openly associated with anything as gruesome as the coolie trade, so all the contracts and dealings had to be conducted with the utmost formality and protocol. Using a comprador was a necessary risk; it kept the dealings one level removed from the British Government, which worried about how such espionage would be received by the Chinese. 'Being too, a private individual, anything done by him to procure good men and tea seeds for exportation to India, would not attract the attention of the Chinese authorities,' wrote the government in Calcutta. Working on Fortune's behalf, the comprador was instructed he could not cajole, caress, lie, trade for pirate booty, or buy a tea expert indentured in a clan war. He could not conjure a story about a better life in a distant place to peasants already cast off their lands. The comprador had to be honest in all his dealings. He must also be secretive, holding his cards close to his chest, lest factory owners catch wind of his plan and report him to local Mandarins. The comprador would then be sure to die, and as a well-known employee of Dent & Beale's trading house, would tarnish by association the name of one of the greatest firms in the Far East.

But Fortune was even more worried about importing 'experts' to India who were really no experts at all. The comprador's recruitment mission was doubly delicate.

To entice him away from family and friends in China, the sums offered to a tea manufacturer had to be very great. Fortune's tea experts were offered a salary upwards of 33 rupees, or about $15 a month ($415 per month in today's money, or £208) for a three-year term in India. Fortune's men were to be of a 'better class' than the previously imported manufacturers, and would be paid better, 'for it cannot be supposed that men thoroughly skilled in the cultivation and manufacture of an article to which so much importance is attached as tea and also of which the Chinese to a man believe themselves to be the exclusive possessors can be procured to live abroad for the small consideration of [less than] 33 rupees *per mensem*'. The first two months' wages were paid to each man in advance as well as a stipend for 'diet money' for the three months of travel to the Indian gardens.

The comprador convinced his potential experts that the bad press given to 'buyers and sellers of pigs' did not extend to the tea trade. He said that the Company men would be treated well, as professionals. An entire industry depended upon their knowledge and they would gain a tremendous amount of 'face'. The tea experts would also have their autonomy and power over others: over brown people, over white people, over entire hillsides and mountains of tea. In the new land, the experts could grow tea the way they thought it ought to be grown. They would be assigned to different plantations and encouraged to compete against each other, to produce higher yields and better quality products for which they would receive bonuses from the Government, 'to encourage the Chinese to exert . . . the full development of their skill and knowledge'. Each season, the manufacturer of the best tea of each description, green and black, would be publicly and monetarily rewarded.

Each man was presented with two copies of the standard contract, one in Chinese, one in English:

I [Name Here], a Chinese Tea maker, hereby engage to proceed to [the Himalayan Gardens] to manufacture tea in the Government Tea plantations on a monthly salary of 15 dollars or Rs 33–2 commencing from [date] and I bind myself to serve for a period of 3 years. I further engage that I will [work] diligently as a tea cultivator or in any other

manner in which I can be useful and failing any part of the
engagement I shall be liable to pay a fine of one hundred
dollars to my employers. I acknowledge having received from
[Mr Fortune] on the part of Government an advance of two
months' wages or 30 dollars, etc, etc.

    Witness Signed in Chinese

The terms of the contract between the East India Company
and the Chinese manufacturers it sought to hire for the
Himalayan plantations seemed to be generous enough for
the time and the place, except for one of the clauses: that a
man who earned $15 a month would pay a penalty of more
than six months' salary should he fail to perform his duties
for any reason, including illness. As generous as the Company
might have felt the contract was, the tea maker's employment
was unmistakably a form of indentured servitude. Whether
or not the Chinese under contract to the Company understood this aspect of their employment is not documented, but
the record does show that at least some of the early Chinese
experts were displeased with the terms.

While Fortune was tea hunting in China, the Himalayan
gardens already had a handful of Chinese tea experts on the
job, working for Jameson, the incompetent overseer of
the Government's tea plantations. Many of these men had
come from the disbanded Assam Company; others had been
imported direct from China by Government consuls on
the mainland. 'I myself well remember the arrival of the
Chinamen ... in June 1843,' wrote a Government functionary in his diary. 'Ten Chinese Tea-bakers amuse the
puharree [turban-wearing] population by their strange figures
and stranger propensities.' He notes that among the tea manufacturers' peculiarities, at least in the eyes of the locals, was

the Chinese love of pork. The population of the Western Himalayas was, by and large, Muslim, and pork was forbidden them. However charming the locals found the Chinese, however, the Company was greatly discouraged by their performance. Of the ten Chinese tea experts originally signed on, two had died by the time Fortune was in China. The rest were all from Canton, a low-lying green tea region that produced a poor product by international standards. The tea makers were also, by Jameson's estimate, disagreeable and stupid. 'And so ignorant are they as to be unable to make the common Black Tea exported to Europe,' he reported in a dispatch.

When the Company wanted to split up the Chinese group and disperse individuals to the many experimental gardens in the Himalayas, the manufacturers staged a coup, refusing to be separated. The Chinese tea makers also used this as leverage to demand higher wages.

Jameson, at his wit's end, refused: 'I communicated to them the orders of Government but all have refused to go unless their wages are increased and state that if Government insists on them going that they beg to tender their resignations.' This was characteristic of dealings with the Chinese: they seemed simply to have forgotten that there was no way for them to resign or alter their contracts in any way without also sacrificing six months' wages. The remaining Chinese manufacturers sought an increase of 7 rupees per month (about $50 in today's money, or £25). 'And with this increase they offer to enter on another engagement for three years.'

Rarely in Company documents is there any record of the voice of the powerless or colonised people with whom the Company interacted. Yet the dispatches from the North West Provinces of India include a copy of this rather fantastic communication from the Chinese tea manufacturers to Jameson listing their demands.

1. We were ordered to remain at Almorah [a plantation] on a salary of Rs 33–2 annas *per mensem*, which we always have obeyed. To remove to any other stations we beg to say that if we get our pay increase of Rs 7 each in addition to that we now get we will go.

2. As we have been about 7 years in Government employment as no hope held out to us of an increase of pay, we object to go to Dehra and to Porree [other plantations in the Western Himalaya]. We have no objection to go any where the Government like to send us, but in the event of our leaving this station, we request for more pay than we at present enjoy.

3. If on the other hand Government want to send us to any new station without giving us an increase we beg to resign our situation and hope that it will be considered and accepted.

4. If Government increase our pay Rs 7 *per mensem* we are working to enter into an agreement of three years to the effect that three of us will serve at [satellite plantations] Dehra, three at Porree, and four at Hawalbaugh and to remain stationary for that period at the above mentioned places.

Patiently, Jameson reiterated to the Chinese tea makers that they were already under contract and that this could not be renegotiated mid-way; he showed each of the men the original contract marked with his very own chop, the stamp which stood for their signature. Though they could see their names on paper next to the unintelligible English writing, the tea makers flatly refused to be reassigned to other gardens.

Perhaps sensing that Jameson was not the brightest light or the most forceful of authorities, they repeated they would not be separated from their countrymen and sent alone into the wilds of India. Their position was that they had been hired to work together at a single plantation, and that employing them individually on different estates constituted a renegotiation of the previous terms. If the Government could unilaterally change a deal, so could the manufacturers. And their argument that seven years of service without a raise was too long, was a valid one to which the Government ought to have been sympathetic. Finally, after much to-ing and fro-ing in the absence of a translator, Jameson arrived at a compromise and agreed to vary the contract. He agreed to most of the tea experts' new terms: the men would be assigned in pairs rather than singly, and at higher wages; in exchange they would stay for an extra three years beyond their original contract. The Chinese were indeed hard nego-tiators, as Fortune had already learned.

Grudgingly, the Government paid up. The Company could not compel a Chinese man to work alone in the remote Himalayas. Jameson, however, was rebuked for the increased expense to the enterprise. 'The Lt Governor considers it necessary to urge upon you the importance of observing the strictest economy in all your proceedings. You must be aware that the success of the experiment will be in a considerable degree tested by its economical results,' wrote the bigwigs in Calcutta, displeased with the idea that stealing secrets from a sovereign nation also meant overpaying the Chinese minions who implemented them. In reality, the Chinese tea manufac-turers' wages were never so high as to be unduly burdensome to the Company. It was more the case that the Chinese were paid higher than market wages and this offended the British sense of fair play (though it remained curiously undisturbed by the fact that the British in India were paid substantially better than the Chinese). However much it bothered the Company at the time, though, the Chinese tea makers in the Himalayas would be among the very last Chinese middlemen to squeeze the British tea traders.

It wasn't as if the original tea manufacturers had been overly useful to Jameson's experimental gardens. By everyone's assessment, they were lazy and poor workmen. Jameson wasn't even certain they knew anything at all about the finer points of tea manufacture. He lobbied hard for the tea makers' replacement – a tough argument to make, given how much they had already cost the government: 'The Chinese manufacturers who were obtained some years since . . . are, in my opinion, far from being first-rate workmen; indeed, I doubt much if any of them learned their trade in China. They ought to be gradually got rid of and their places supplied by better men, for it is a great pity to teach the natives an inferior method of manipulation.' The Government heartily agreed, noting that none of the original Chinese tea makers were 'first rate'.

The original Chinese manufacturers did little to teach the natives and *malis* the proper cultivation of tea, processing, packing or scenting it, Jameson complained. 'If the Chinese Tea Manufacturers are left to themselves . . . they would never be particularly interested in instructing natives in the art of making good tea (though they would willingly and readily show the process) nor would they, themselves, pay such attention to its manufacture and packing as is necessary to ensure its good quality.' He cajoled, he insisted, he threw tantrums, but he could not get what he needed from the Chinese under his employ. It seemed to him that the Chinese were weaselling out of part of the bargain – a tactic that seemed to him frustratingly typical. They were happy to take

British money and make tea, yet remained oblivious to all demands for them to *teach* the making of it. Similarly, they were deaf to Jameson's requests, however aggressive and impolitic, for teas of higher quality. He needed to address the 'deficiency of fragrance' cited by the tea tasters of London if Indian tea was ever to be of top quality. Maintaining a consistent standard seemed unimportant to the original manufacturers, however: 'Nor would they, themselves, pay such attention to its manufacture and packing as is necessary to ensure its good quality,' Jameson complained. The first crop of tea makers were as obdurate and unfathomable as the country they came from – making, but not sharing; practising their skill but not promoting it.

Yet they were essential to the British plan. Finally, Jameson conceded that a Western overseer was necessary to keep the Chinese experts and Indian gardeners up to the mark. An overseer would increase the cost of the operations, but Jameson could not be everywhere at all times. 'To superintend the plucking of leaves, or rather to order the leaves to be pulled when ready, the presence of an European is very necessary as if they are allowed to remain too long on the bushes they become hard and are only fitted for making the coarser kind of tea and finally, in transplanting on a large scale the presence of an European overseer is of importance in order to see that it is properly done and also that the plants are regularly watered.'

Of course, Jameson's constant watering of the plants was more of a problem than a boon. Fortune's plants would have been better off left to the regular rains of the monsoons, as the Chinese experts had suggested. But Jameson was by this time so frustrated with his Chinese experts that he would not listen to their recommendations – even when those recommendations were right.

His poor decisions did not, however, go entirely unchecked. He would have liked all of Fortune's men to submit to medical examination in China. 'Before engagement they ought to be examined as to their constitution, and none but strong and healthy men employed, and any with organic disease of any kind rejected,' he wrote, obviously tired of his Chinese experts dying. Falconer showed his usual good sense in retaliating swiftly: 'I have only further to submit that . . . the appearing before a medical man would to be startling to most Chinese and very likely to throw an insuperable and unnecessary obstacle to the management of a good man's services.'

Within a few months of setting out from Shanghai, Dent's compradors had come through with true experts for Robert Fortune, masters of their art who would also be prepared to teach it. The compradors collected six tea men from the same districts in which Fortune had been tea hunting over the previous three years. The men were young, obedient and willing, and each had signed on for a three-year term in India. The men 'looked up to me with the most perfect confidence as their director and friend. While I had always treated them kindly myself, I had taken measures to have them kindly treated by others,' Fortune wrote.

He had also acquired equipment: the ovens, woks, and wide spatulas to fire the tea with as well as the farm equipment specially developed to cultivate it. But for this task, too, Fortune dispatched his servants – Wang and Sing Hoo – to the various mountain districts to hunt down 'a large assortment of implements for the manufacture of tea'. He had known what he was looking for: firing pans, drying pans, rolling tables, furnaces, spatulas. He did not need to collect them himself, only send his servants – reliable, if not trustworthy – to do the bargaining for him. They would, naturally, keep more of the budget than Fortune would wish, but the last squeeze could be considered a parting bonus.

The compradors had also secured Fortune two men who were expert in the making of tightly sealed lead boxes for the shipment of tea. Proper packing and shipment would help preserve quality, and remedy what was becoming a rather dismal 'Deficiency of Fragrance' problem in Indian tea. 'By the London Brokers the black teas sent home have all been declared to belong, as stated, to the class of fancy teas, and to be more or less faulty in aroma,' reminded one dispatch, 'this could scarcely be otherwise expected.'

In addition to the carefully packed tea plants and seeds, all meticulously labelled, Fortune secured a collection of the perfumed plants that Chinese manufacturers used for scenting teas when they were packed, such as jasmine and bergamot. Samples of these scenting agents too were packed and shipped with him and the tea makers to India, with the names labelled in Latin as well as in Chinese, with a loose Chinese transliteration beside them. Fortune felt satisfied that he had done his job well. 'Everything had succeeded beyond my most sanguine expectations.'

Fortune then said his goodbyes. He made the rounds of the international community in Shanghai, collecting good wishes and returning borrowed items. There was no sadness in these farewells; the diplomats and traders of the Far East were accustomed to parting from friends. 'Nothing therefore remained for me to do except . . . proceed on my voyage to India.'

In the chilly February air, the emigrating tea experts stood on deck and faced the Chinese mainland for the last time, watching it slip farther and farther away.

'The boat was immediately pushed out into the stream. Now the emigrants on board, and their friends on shore, with clasped hands, bowed to each other many, many times and the good wishes for each other's health and happiness were not new, nor apparently insincere. Next morning the *Island Queen*, Captain McFarlane, got under way, and we bade adieu to the North of China.'

By Fortune's count, 12,838 tea seeds germinated en route to the Himalayas.

16

Himalayan Mountains, May 1851

Behind a bungalow in mountainous Darjeeling, rosy-faced children were playing on a hillside, their laughter echoing off the steep slopes. White magnolias flourished their cupped blooms towards the sky, rhododendrons glowed scarlet on every rockface; there is nowhere on earth with more floral fireworks to herald the spring. The children's father, a Scottish Surgeon-Major by the name of Archibald Campbell, bent down, trowel in hand, beside his *malis*, to dig a new home for some seeds and seedlings recently sent to the Eastern Himalayas from the Company's gardens at Saharunpur. In keeping with the ad hoc administrative style of the Government in India, Campbell was the one man given the task of administering, planning, overseeing, building, policing, planting and dreaming up the newest addition to the Indian Empire: the mountain town of Darjeeling and all twenty British families who resided there. Campbell worked knee-deep in the dirt, in the service of Fortune's tea. If Robert Fortune can be said to be the father of Himalayan tea, then Archibald Campbell was its guardian. He reared Fortune's plants in Darjeeling and raised them to maturity as if they were his own offspring.

The Darjeeling hill station was a real life Shangri-La, charming and green, picturesque and pleasant. The Himalayas do not resemble Chinese mountains: there are no elegant karsts there, shrouded in wispy cloud. The Himalayas are instead rough-hewn craggy monsters, enormous and furious, like a set of giant's teeth ripping at the sky. Darjeeling is an island of beauty set in a sea of fierce peaks, remarkable for the sheer diversity of its landscape. The rugged crests, streaked with snow and crowned with firs, have lush tropical valleys just below. Orchids grow on palms just under the snowline, while temperate hardwoods such as oak and birch mingle with jungle fruits like bananas and figs. Drier than the Western Himalayas, at nearly 7,000 feet above sea level, shaded from the afternoon heat by mountains and mist, Darjeeling was a welcoming new home for Fortune's black tea.

It was bordered by other small mountainous kingdoms – Tibet, Nepal, Bhutan and Sikkim – and the isolated mountain paradise had been only recently added to the growing mass of British India. Darjeeling's warring neighbours had passed the little district back and forth for generations until, in 1836, the Rajah of Sikkim gifted it to the British Government as a token of friendship and fealty. Darjeeling was a concession, or more accurately a bribe, to the Company: the Rajah believed that if Britain ruled quaint Darjeeling, it would not try to annexe the greater kingdom of Sikkim in its quest to conquer China from the West. (Sikkim did in fact remain a semi-independent state until it joined India in 1975.) The Company paid rent, or tribute, on the territory of Darjeeling for some years, until Campbell accidentally and providentially ended the arrangement.

He was among the world's leading experts on all things Himalayan. In his service to the Company Campbell learned the mountain people's language, publishing articles on their customs and peculiarities. His head was full of statistics on the region: its geography, zoology, ethnography and, of course, local agriculture. He was as avid a hunter and herbalist as he was a student of Ghurka and Lepcha rituals. Educated in Scotland, like so many in the Indian Medical Service, Campbell's own health laid him low several times and so he was put in charge of the Company's Government in Darjeeling. He was among the many Government enthusiasts who helped catalogue, collect, detail and describe the opulence of the Himalayas for the professional botanists at Calcutta and Kew.

'Quiet, unobtrusive' is how people remembered Campbell. He was a perfect functionary, a good solid Company man. But he had the distinction of being among the first Imperialists arrested for botanical theft. Although Robert Fortune was in genuine danger in China, he survived his spying trips largely unmolested by those from whom he stole. Campbell, on the other hand, had only recently been released from a Himalayan prison for his botanical crimes.

While prospecting in the mountains for plants with the botanical eminence Joseph Hooker, son of the Director of Kew and close friend to the great Charles Darwin, Campbell was arrested by the Rajah of Sikkim in 1849. On an impulse, he had followed Hooker to reach 'the Snows' of the Tibetan plateau on a botanising trip. Campbell had stayed behind at first, nervous that plant prospecting in Sikkim would jeopardise his dearly desired promotion to Resident to the Court of Nepal, but ultimately decided he could not miss an expedition that was 'the kind of opportunity for which you would give gold.' He caught up with Hooker five months into his journey and surprised him one night in camp. His was the first 'white face' Hooker had seen in months and they reunited with 'unspeakable joy.' Campbell was a mine of information for the charming young naturalist, providing him with coolies, guides and supplies, and sharing a wealth of local botanical and geographical knowledge with him. Mrs Campbell sent along plum puddings, mince pies and English sherry to remind the men of home's comforts. But at the Chola Pass, in the Eastern Himalayas, they were taken hostage. Campbell was 'seized, bound, treated with brutal violence, and called upon, at the risk of his life, to put his signature to whatever might be dictated to him.' There were rumours that their murder was discussed at the Durbar, the Sikkimese Court. Even their Lepcha porters were harassed and 'barbarously treated'. When news of their capture reached Calcutta, European 'outrage' was tempered by Government anxiety. The Company was stretched to breaking point with border wars in the Punjab and Afghanistan, and so warned against taking 'extreme measures' to secure their release. Troops were dispatched to Darjeeling in a display of Company force, though the Government had no intention of acting upon it.

After six weeks Campbell and Hooker were released. Sikkim was rebuked – the Rajah's allowance for the annexation of Darjeeling was cancelled, and he forfeited a chunk of Sikkim's southern territory. Hooker thought the punishment did not fit the crime; he wanted a further show of strength from the Company – total annexation of Sikkim – but the more retiring Campbell was happy to be restored to his family and fresh-faced children.

The two men remained friends for the rest of their lives. Campbell used the botanical trip to the high Himalayan plateau to his own advantage, saying he 'had gained that knowledge of its resources which the British Government should all along have possessed as the protector of the Rajah and his territories'. In a characteristic display of administrative perversity, Campbell was then made British

Resident of the territory in which he had been all too recently imprisoned.

Comfortable and protected from the dust of the high Gangetic plain, Fortune travelled by carriage to the Government plantations in the Western Himalayas. At the Saharunpur gardens, he met Jameson and was able to inspect the small tea settlements scattered around the hills and valleys. Most of these gardens were not yet two years old, and all had been planted with Fortune's seeds and seedlings.

The meeting with Jameson was frosty, for though the Superintendent was overjoyed at the eventual success of Fortune's tea, the tea hunter himself surveyed Jameson's gardens and found them wanting. The plants looked mangy, mismanaged, showing poorly per acre.

The two men sat down in Jameson's bungalow and discussed Fortune's views. He was forthright about them, saying to Jameson in person what he would write in his report to the Company and to the Government in Calcutta. He praised the scheme of leasing the tea lands to the local zemindars, which translates roughly to 'caretaker' but refers instead to a kind of sharecropper. As rich as the mountain soil was, it was mostly not under the plough and would otherwise have been left fallow had Jameson not been so dedicated to promoting the zemindar scheme. It pleased Fortune to see that the Indian natives took readily to tea growing. I am happy to add that amongst these hills there are no foolish prejudices in the minds of the natives against the cultivation of tea,' he told Jameson and the Company, and related a story about a zemindar approaching him directly, to beg 2,000 tea plants off him, so that the man could begin growing tea right away. Fortune was overjoyed, and shared his enthusiasm in his report.

It is of great importance that the authorities of a district and persons of influence should show an interest in a subject of this kind. At present the natives do not know its value but they are as docile as children and will enter willingly upon tea cultivation providing the 'sahib' shows that he is interested in it. In a few years the profits received will be a sufficient inducement.

It was not a popularly held opinion. Many of the Company men in the Himalayas balked at the zemindar arrangements and any attempts to make the natives into practised horticulturalists. 'I regret that it should have been deemed necessary to make stupid pedants of Hindu *malees* by providing them with a classical nomenclature for plants. Hindostanee names would have answered the purpose just as well . . . If these names are unpronounceable even by Europeans, what would the poor Hindu *malee* make of them? The pedantry of some of our scientific Botanists is something marvellous. One would think that a love of flowers must produce or imply a taste for simplicity and nature in all things,' wrote a contemporary with scorn.

But beyond the zemindar scheme, Fortune had some severe words for the gardening decisions of Superintendent Jameson – whose bad advice had so recently contributed to the ruin of Fortune's first shipment of tea seeds and seedlings out of Sung Lo Shan. In particular, Fortune took him to task for irrigating tea. Fortune had never once, in three years' travelling in China, seen tea under flood irrigation. Though tea cultivation was practised with slight variations from region to region in China, no farmer would dream of such a thing. Fortune even asked the Chinese tea manufacturers whom he had brought over from China if they had ever seen such a thing. 'No,' they replied. 'That is the way we grow rice, we never irrigate tea.' The heavy rains that come with India's monsoons and the runoff from the annual glacial melt are enough to water mountain tea. In every experimental garden Fortune visited where there was tea growing in a valley, it was rotting on the stalk. At least a third, and as much as half, of his early crops were lost to failed experiments in irrigation.

As the world's leading expert on tea, his main concern was to ensure its ultimate success in India and he held forth on this aim, at length. Whether or not Fortune liked the Company gardener is lost to history, but his report to the Company was emphatic.

> I have already observed that good tea-land is naturally moist, although not stagnant; and we must bear in mind that the tea shrub is NOT A WATER PLANT, but is found in a wild state on the sides of hills. In confirmation of these views, it is only necessary to observe further, that all the BEST HIMALAYAN PLANTATIONS ARE THOSE TO WHICH IRRIGATION HAS BEEN MOST SPARINGLY APPLIED.
>
> Indeed I have no hesitation in saying that in nine cases out of ten, the effects of irrigation are most injurious. When tea will not grow without irrigation, it is a sure sign that the land employed is not suitable for such a crop.

Fortune's last shipment of Wardian cases had made it to Saharunpur in stupendous shape. No fewer than 12,838 living plants were counted in his cases when he pried them open, and many more seeds were germinating – too many to count. Tea was thriving, despite the long trip out of China, and the frequent trans-shipments. To Fortune, the plants seemed as 'green and vigorous' as if they had never left home ground.

It was crucial that his last shipment, the crowning achievement of his time in China, not be squandered to bad gardening and Jameson's feeble decision-making.

Though Jameson was less than competent and Fortune's first year of tea prospecting appeared to be a failure, tea was so suited to the Himalayas that even the 80 surviving plants from Fortune's earliest shipment were now thriving. As Jameson and Fortune sat down to discuss the evaluation, those precious plants imported in the first season were about four foot high, and 'profusely covered with blossoms'. They had taken well to their new ground and were yielding a good return of seeds, if not a high volume of tea shoots. They had produced several thousand offspring, Jameson reported.

Fortune was the crucial lynchpin in the chain of events that had brought Chinese tea to its adopted homeland. He felt deservedly proud of himself and his accomplishments and tacitly acknowledged that Jameson in India had at least played some role in tea's success. 'The flourishing condition of many of the plantations is, after all, the best proof and puts the matter beyond all doubt,' wrote Fortune to his superiors.

And his Chinese manufacturers? Were they feeling green and vigorous, flourishing in their new climate?

They had 'nice cottages and gardens' given to them. They were told they would be separated, divided up between the plantations, and eventually were – though this caused consternation amongst the new recruits. The Chinese all wanted a fellow countryman to talk to, but the Government required one expert per plantation. Still, Fortune felt that the Company was serving the tea manufacturers as best it could, as 'everything was done which could add to their comfort in a strange land'.

On the morning of Fortune's last day in the Himalayas, the tea experts rose early and bathed. They dressed in their finest linen robes, their celebration clothes saved for special occasions like New Year's Day and the Full Moon Festival. In the dawn hours the appointed leader of the manufacturers, slightly older than the rest, a man of about Fortune's own age, stepped forward and presented him with a small token of their appreciation. Fortune makes no mention of what the gift was and the tea makers possessed little other than what they had carried on their backs.

He felt he could not accept it, though he thanked them profusely, extolling their virtues and generosity. 'I told them how much I was pleased with the motives by which they were actuated.' A more sensitive man would have known that to refuse a gift would injure everyone and there would be tremendous loss of face. Fortune had become as good a scholar of tea as the world had ever known, but his understanding of human nature and Chinese social interaction was never as sharp.

He was still eager to help the tea makers in any way he could and readily agreed to take along a packet of letters from the men. There were notes to wives, parents and children. He promised to take the letters with him to Calcutta and direct them towards a steamer on its way to China. He would do anything for the men, but not take anything from them. 'Never, from the time of their engagement until I left them in their new mountain home, had they given me the slightest cause for anger.'

Fortune left the Chinese manufacturers in India with a heavy heart. 'I confess I felt sorry to leave them.' It was as though he were saying goodbye to all traces of China, leaving his last three years of endeavour behind in India.

There is no hard evidence in Company documents of the exact date of the first arrival of tea in Darjeeling. By Government accounts it would appear that the first tea seeds to hit the famous Darjeeling Mountains arrived sometime in the early-1850s, or maybe as early as 1849. In other words, the first tea in Darjeeling arrived during the first years of Fortune's travels on behalf of the Company. But because his first tea haul was an utter failure, it is unlikely that the very first seeds to migrate to Darjeeling were divided from Fortune's first lots of seeds. The very first tea plants in Darjeeling were green tea and likely came out of the Canton stock – all that was available to the experimental Saharunpur gardens in the 1840s. However, the very first black tea in Darjeeling could not have been from anything other than those plants and seeds sent by Fortune in his Wardian case 'trifles'.

Plant exchange between Calcutta, Saharunpur and Darjeeling was commonplace. Campbell's mentor, Brian Houghton Hodgson, former Resident to the Court of Nepal, had stayed on in the subcontinent and retired to the hill country of Darjeeling. Hodgson too was an avid collector and amateur naturalist. He kept an eye on the development of national industries throughout the Himalayas and maintained a lively correspondence with Company botanists. Within the first year of Fortune's seeds and seedlings arriving successfully in India, it is very likely that the two lay naturalists cultivating Darjeeling, Hodgson and Campbell, campaigned hard to have the new seed haul subdivided and sent to the territory. If Fortune's seeds were not represented in the very first season's planting, they were most surely sown by the completion of his travels.

Campbell had Fortune's tea neatly planted in rows on the face of a hill, a large tract of land that could expand as needed. There were many such experiments under cultivation in Darjeeling; Campbell was also concerned with cotton, even opium and other crops that might be economically viable in the region. When Fortune's teas began arriving in the North West Provinces, shipment after shipment, for the next two years, some portion was always set aside and sent onwards to Campbell, along with other potential nursery stocks. Though his gardens were not producing teas of any great quantity when Fortune arrived in India, and though Campbell would not have the manpower to make much of his stock in those early days, a happy collaboration was formed. Tea seeds took to Darjeeling at the rooftop of the world. In the shadow of Mount Everest, black tea found its pinnacle.

'Dr Campbell raised British Sikkim in ten years from its pristine condition of an impenetrable jungle, tenanted by half savage and mutually hostile races, never previously brought into contact with Europeans, to that of a flourishing European Sanatria and Hill Settlement, an international tribal mart of the first importance and a rich agricultural province,' read an homage to Campbell.

In 1860, Campbell would be just as welcoming to chinchona, the South American tree bark from which quinine was made – the only known chemical which cured malaria. By cultivating tea and quinine, he introduced two products to India that would make further European colonisation of the globe possible. Quinine would kill the deadly mosquito virus, and when water was boiled to make tea, it reduced the transmission of water-borne parasites.

Today, Darjeeling is considered the champagne of teas. It has the finest brew, the most delicate floral nose, the richest liquor, the most opulent amber colour. At auction, Darjeeling teas fetch some of the highest prices in the world. It is almost impossible to buy a lot from the first flush of the Darjeeling estates; they are snapped up as soon as they hit the market. Tea is, as the Chinese say, the essence of mountains; and the mountains that produce Darjeeling tea are the most magnificent on God's green earth.

Within a generation, India's nascent Himalayan tea industry would outstrip China's in both quality, volume and price. India, meanwhile, was to become an ever-more important asset to Britain, if only she could hold on to it.

17

Royal Small Arms Factory, Enfield Lock, 1852

Behind the gates of the Royal Small Arms Factory (RSAF Enfield), Enfield Lock, north of London, engineers and gunsmiths were experimenting on a new weapon, to be used wherever Englishmen ventured on the subcontinent. Just as science and technology could revolutionise agriculture by moving plants around the world, advances in weaponry would change the nature of soldiering – and perversely dissolve the Company's hold on India.

Guns had played only a small part in Fortune's success and survival in China. A combination of inventiveness, stealth, subterfuge, and an understanding of his environment and the people he encountered, kept him alive. He argued for guns on his first trip, and he resorted to them to fend off the pirates on the Min, but the arms themselves were more or less symbolic, their threat magnified by deception and cunning to overcome superior forces.

By contrast, the Company's fortunes depended on keeping a tight grip on the people and resources of India. The Company possessed an overwhelming superiority in arms and a monopoly on violence over the Indians. The East India Company was potentate over the subcontinent, backed by the force of the Indian Army. Ruled by Englishmen, the army was manned by Indians, with 26,000 Europeans commanding

200,000 sepoys. From *sipahi*, Hindi for soldier, sepoys were
Muslim, Hindu, Sikh and Christian, and mostly recruited from
the upper echelons of Indian society. They were proud men
and every one of them was given a gun.

The Enfield experiments gave birth to a rifle that came to
be known as the Pattern 1853, or P53 Enfield Rifle. Based on
this pattern, the designs of subsequent years were manufactured according to a single standardised design, used
throughout the British Empire. In particular, the P53 would
be sent out to India for use by the Indian Army in regiments
throughout the Indian states.

The Honourable Company would ultimately perish by the
barrel of that gun.

The Indian Army commanded a territory as large as the
United States, containing a population of about 285 million.
Without a private militia on the ground, the Company could
never have dominated India as it did, nor envisage using it
as Britain's larder.

Although gunpowder was invented in China about 850 AD,
it had long been used to propel rockets and mortars and bullets
everywhere on the planet. But the technology behind the
weapons Fortune carried with him to China had not advanced
substantially for hundreds of years. The weapon used by the
British in the defeat of Napoleon at the turn of the nineteenth
century was still the most common gun in the Indian Army
in the 1840s and early-50s. It was called the Brown Bess, a
'smooth bore' flintlock musket.

From the seventeenth through to the early-nineteenth
century, shooting a gun involved connecting a fire or spark
with gunpowder in a confined space, creating an explosive
pressure that would send a spherical projectile in the only
direction it could go – out of the muzzle of a pipe barrel.

The main limitation of these weapons was the amount of time it would take to load one. Each reloading was a multi-step process, which required a soldier to pour and ram-rod a measure of powder, a lead ball and some wadding in through the muzzle end of the gun, down to the end near the trigger. Ignition was provided by a flint striking steel behind the gunpowder charge, producing a spark near a hole leading to the powder chamber. A sprinkling of primer powder conveyed this fire to the internal gunpowder. Preparing a shot in this way took a seasoned and well-drilled soldier a minimum of 15–20 seconds per shot.

Even in its day, the Brown Bess was regarded as relatively inaccurate and sometimes unreliable. The problems with accuracy stemmed from the generous fit between the barrel and ammunition. Since Bess tended to become fouled by gunpowder residue after a use or two, making it harder and harder to load, the barrel was designed to be somewhat larger than the projectile inside, which was a simple round lead ball. But this also meant that a musket ball had a lot of space around it on the way out of the gun, bouncing and bobbing through the barrel on its way to the exit. Gases from the explosion would also escape around the ball, slowing down the force of its propulsion. Being a 'smooth bore' gun, Bess lacked rifling in the barrel, which also affected its accuracy. Rifling – a groove cut in a spiral inside the barrel – helps impart a spin to the projectile so that it flies straighter and flatter. The flint-on-steel ignition mechanism was also of some concern, since it worked under fair conditions, but tended to fail when things got damp. (The monsoon season lasts from June to November in India.)

Nonetheless, Bess worked well enough for the military techniques of the day. Indian soldiers were trained to stand in lines perhaps two or three deep and fire four rounds a minute at targets 50–65 yards away. When a phalanx of soldiers standing in a row fires volley after volley in the same general direction, the fact that such weapons are not very accurate, or not certain to fire, is less important than the speed of their reloading. Someone is bound to hit something in the field of fire. And when their opponent was in retreat, or ammunition was low, the Brown Bess's 17-inch bayonet provided a more certain means of attack during a direct charge. For one hundred and fifty years, almost the whole of the Company's glory years on the Continent, the Indian Army used this single method of warfare, backed up with cannons.

The longevity of the Brown Bess is not surprising: armies have good reason to be conservative about replacing a known, tested technology with something experimental. Since armies are most efficient when equipment is standardised, with as little variation as possible, there's no simple way to phase in new and improved weaponry. But improvements were in the offing. Advances in personal weapons such as pistols and hunting guns were about to transform the standard soldier's firearm, making it more accurate, reliable and deadly than it had ever been before.

The trick to improving on Brown Bess was to make a bullet that could both grab on to the grooves of a rifled barrel, while at the same time being quick and easy to load. An inventor at Enfield named Pritchett thought a French bullet might offer help in mastering Bess's shortcomings, and achieve these dual aims.

The French Minié bullet was more like the bullets of today. It was roughly cylindrical, but rounded on the leading end and hollowed out at its base. When discharged, the pressure of the expanding gases inside the base of the bullet would force its base to expand to fill the width of the barrel, and thus to grip the rifling grooves.

The early days of the Pritchett experiment were greeted with enthusiasm at the Enfield Arms Factory. Where Bess could hit a target at 60 yards handled by an experienced soldier, the new rifled weapons were accurate up to 600 yards. But the Pritchett bullet still required the marksman to go through myriad steps to load the gun before firing, as the bullet did not come with its own casing, gunpowder or priming charge. Moreover, because of the tight fit between bullet and barrel, the barrel needed to be kept greased so the bullet could be shoved smoothly into the chamber and pushed up tightly against the powder. To simplify loading, the bullet was packed in a paper 'cartridge' that also included the necessary gunpowder and was greased on the exterior to ease its way into the barrel. Soldiers followed a precise standard routine for loading their weapons based on a standardised design for these cartridges. The newly designed weapon and ammunition together made the bullet a better missile, and the weapon a better missile-launcher.

The P53 Enfield Rifle may have been a superior weapon in almost all regards and may even have been adaptable to India's circumstances, had the Company been more sensitive to the population over which it ruled. Unfortunately it was not.

The East India Company's Platoon Exercise Manual stipulated the correct way to load the P53 – it was no different from the way Indian sepoys, or soldiers, loaded the Brown Bess.

Upon hearing the first command – 'Prepare to load' – a soldier placed his rifle butt on the ground, six inches in front of him. Upon receiving the command 'Load', the drill went thus: '1st – bring the cartridge to the mouth, holding it between the forefinger and the thumb with the ball in the hand, and bite off the top; elbow close to the body . . .'

This standard procedure of 'biting the bullet' was so much

a part of the routine that the phrase survives long after the procedure itself has been forgotten. With the cartridge and bullet still in his mouth, the soldier tore open the cartridge to gain access to the powder. He poured this into the muzzle and then shoved the bullet and greased cartridge paper (as wadding) after it, ram-rodding it down to meet the powder.

Grease on the paper cartridge was needed to keep the barrel slippery over repeated firings. It also protected the gunpowder in the cartridge from the wet, variable weather of India, since ammunition might be kept in storage for up to three years. A good, reliable grease became an integral part of the operation of the new P53.

The grease of choice for the Company, both cheap to manufacture and reliably available, was a mixture of beef tallow and pork fat.

Had the Englishmen in charge tried to be less sensitive to the needs of an Indian sepoy, they could hardly have been more successful. Pigs are *haram*, outlawed, to the Muslim soldiers of Northern India, while no high-caste Hindu will touch a dead cow, let alone bring one to his mouth. Either impure or holy, the animal fats in the P53's cartridges would defile and debase, in one way or another, every religious Indian who was commanded to use them.

It took very little time before the new cartridges became explosive – and not in the way intended. The Enfield rifle was adopted and rolled out to the Indian troops as a general issue weapon in 1856. The Company trained its infantry and musketry divisions first. Regiments and detachments were sent to the various arsenals and depots to receive instruction in the new weapons.

As soldiers were exposed to the new cartridges, rumours spread. It was said that the Enfield Rifle was part of a mass plan on the part of the East India Company to convert Indian troops to Christianity by rendering them impure, and thus forcing them to give up their caste status. 'Bring the cartridge to your mouth and bite down, tearing the end off with your *teeth*,' the instructions said. But what the sepoys heard was altogether different: 'Pollute the troops, expose every man to religious poison, then save his soul with the teachings of the Christian God.' It seemed all too likely to the angry Indian troops, seething after centuries of British domination in India.

As the story goes, one January day a low born *khalasi* or labourer at the Dum-Dum arsenal near Calcutta would say to a high-caste Brahmin sepoy who refused to sip water out of the same water pot, owing to his loftier ritual status, 'The *Saheb-logue* [Europeans] will make you bite cartridges soaked in cow and pork fat, and then where will your caste be?'

Throughout the winter and spring of 1857, news of the pig-and-cow tainted cartridges spread. On 9 May 85 sepoys of the Third Bengal Light Calvary flatly refused the order to bring the cartridges to their mouths and load their weapons. The religious rebels were court-martialled on the spot and sentenced to ten years imprisonment under hard labour. The punishment was severe. For two hours the rest of the regiment stood watch in the afternoon sun as officers stripped the mutineers of their uniforms and paraded them naked, shackled in leg irons, through the army town of Meerut. Even the local prostitutes were disgusted, afterwards refusing their favours to anyone in the regiment. 'We have no kisses for cowards,' the women said.

That night, several other sepoy regiments, from both the infantry and the cavalry, broke ranks and turned on their officers. The sepoys liberated the 85 rebels from jail, hailing them as heroes to their race. Then they burnt the Company's buildings, bungalows and offices. Every European was massacred on sight.

The cavalry retreated to Delhi, and for the next six months India would catch fire.

The Company had expanded too aggressively, annexed too much land, disgraced the local people and their rulers. Pig tallow and beef fat – a simple cartridge in a simple gun – unleashed a vast, wholesale slaughter that consumed the subcontinent. The P53 Enfield Rifle ignited a holocaust of murder, siege, brutality and repression; women and children, Indians and British, were butchered, cities were sacked, civilians murdered by soldiers. The British refer to the summer of 1857 as the Indian Mutiny; Pakistanis and Indians refer to it as the First War for Independence. Whatever name is used, it was bloody beyond all precedent and it threatened the very existence of the East India Company.

The mutiny continued throughout the heat of spring, before the monsoon arrived to dampen down the country and its conflict. In the town of Kanpur (known as Cawnpore before 1947), in the north of India, a deposed former ruler named Nana Sahib brought the mutiny to its gruesome pinnacle. The Company had recently deposed Nana Sahib according to the 'doctrine of lapse' – a policy by which a native Indian ruler was induced to 'sacrifice' his territory to the Company if he could not provide a legitimate heir.

When 300 British troops, along with their wives and children, were holed up in the barracks of Cawnpore, with no food and little water, surrounded by a trench, awaiting relief, Nana Sahib stepped in and offered the British safe passage downriver to a city still in Company hands.

Starved, dehydrated, diseased, some 200 of them already dead, the British accepted Nana Sahib's offer. But as they boarded the boats for safety, the native crew members set fire to the boats' thatched canopies and suddenly jumped overboard.

At the same time, a volley of rifle fire started from the banks. Only four British men survived the escape downriver by swimming to safety.

The Indians gathered together those who had avoided the boat massacre and herded them into an open courtyard. They shot all the men. Some women and children survived, for a time. Some were carried away and raped.

The British sent a relief column, but it came a day too late. The sepoys butchered the remaining women and children in the courtyard. The 'floor of the yard and the verandah and some of the rooms were bespattered with blood and the bloodmarks of children's hands and feet, women's dresses, hats, Bibles, marriage certificates, etc, lay scattered about,' wrote one eyewitness.

Nana Sahib, the Butcher of Cawnpore, was said 'to read Balzac, play Chopin on the piano and, lolling on a divan and fanned by gorgeous Kashmiri girls, to have a roasted English child brought in occasionally on a pike for him to examine with his pince-nez,' a newspaper would report.

When the British arrived, they ordered every mutineer to clean up the blood by hand, or lick it up, under threat of the lash. If touching a holy or forbidden animal was degrading to the men of India, touching the blood of humans was beyond defilement.

'I wish to show the Natives of India that the punishment inflicted by us for such deeds will be the heaviest, the most revolting to their feelings . . .' wrote the officer in charge. After the 'culprit' had cleaned up his share of the bodies and carnage, he was immediately hanged.

The British could be just as cold-blooded as the mutineers. In September, Company forces attacked Delhi and massacred every man on sight – not just the combatants fighting British rule. The British slaughtered defenceless citizens in

cold blood, striking down some 1,400 men in one neighbourhood alone.

'It was literally murder,' wrote one officer witnessing the
massacre of Indians in Delhi. 'I have seen many bloody and
awful sights lately, but such as I witnessed yesterday I pray
I never see again. The women were spared, but their screams,
on seeing their husbands and sons butchered, were most
painful.'

The Company oversaw a civil war full of as much cruelty
and bile as mankind has ever known. It brought to ruin the
reign of Mughal Emperors who had colluded with the
Company as proxy rulers. Wrote the last Emperor, Bahadur
Shah, from exile:

> My life now gives no ray of light,
> I bring no solace to heart or eye;
> Out of dust to dust again,
> Of no use to anyone am I.
> Delhi was once a paradise,
> Where Love held sway and reigned;
> But its charm lies ravished now
> And only ruins remain.

When the dust from the uprising cleared, Parliament in
London rescinded the privileges of the East India Company
in ruling India and revoked its charter at the stroke of a pen.
The East India Company ceased to exist. Henceforth, the
British Crown would be the Government of the subcontinent;
Victoria would become Empress of India.

In half a millennium of existence the Company had
amassed possessions to rival Charlemagne's and created an
Empire on which the sun never set; it was the first global

multinational and the largest corporation history has ever known. Yet it failed spectacularly at one significant task: to govern India in peace. However ingenious the idea and profitable the industry, growing tea in India could not save the 'Honourable' Company from extinction.

18

Tea for the Victorians

By the time the Chinese realised the treasure Fortune had stolen from them it was many years too late to recoup their loss. His theft helped spread the gospel of tea to a wider world at lower prices. He democratised a luxury and the world has been drinking it ever since.

Like sugar, coffee, tobacco and opium, tea was among the first mass-produced, mass-marketed global commodities. Though tea would not cause the Industrial Revolution, its popularity in Britain and the increasingly easy access to it brought about by the advent of Indian tea spurred British industrialisation along.

These global commodities were kinetic economic energy – picked for a penny, sold for a pound, transported around the world. They rearranged the axes of power all along their supply chain, each step of the way from mountain farm to British homesteads. Through a simple drug, tea, coolies in rural China were connected to American and Parsee traders in Canton, to peasant farmers in India, to merchant bankers in London, to mothers and children in Manchester enjoying their breakfast.

Tea revolutionised Britain's capital and banking systems and influenced the rapid growth of trade networks in the Far East. It was instrumental in moving the British Empire east. Colonisation spread throughout places such as Burma, Ceylon (present-day Sri Lanka), East Africa, and other regions where tea could be grown, creating economies in places that were previously considered blighted jungles full of warring tribes. Tea also influenced efforts to colonise the Caribbean and the South Pacific, to meet Britain's demand for sugar. The Oriental trade catapulted Britain and the pound sterling to nearly two centuries of global prominence, a feat that no sparsely populated agrarian island nation could otherwise have achieved.

Tea changed the role of China on the world stage. It gave birth to the colonial territory of Hong Kong, a thriving city – now once again a Chinese city – and the capital of the Orient. Some say Hong Kong demonstrates the role China might have taken on the world stage had a series of tea-trade inspired revolutions not halted progress on the mainland for much of a century. The British Empire's demand for tea (and by extension the opium trade) destabilised the Qing Dynasty. The foreign presence in China and the havoc wrought by the tea/opium exchange jointly undermined Imperial leadership and debased the common Chinese people. The fall of the Qings gave way to the Nationalist Kuomintang and eventually the Chinese Communist Party, a turn of events which would later spark the modern-day division between Taiwan and China. No one can reasonably lay the blame for this on tea alone, but neither can one ignore the role that foreign desire for this quintessentially Chinese commodity played in opening China up to the West, and in the country's subsequent fall from Imperial self-sufficiency.

In fact, tea altered nearly every single thing it touched.

Transportation

By the 1850s, the passage to London from China lasted one month less than it had previously, spurred on by the race to bring tea to market. Tea gave rise to the fastest ships under sail; their speeds have never been matched.

For the first two hundred years of the tea trade, the only ships making the trip to China out of Britain belonged to the East India Company, the one business chartered to trade in the Far East. These boats were slow floating warehouses – East Indiamen, they were called. Like their corporate name-sake, they moved at a languid pace. The 'tea wagons' sailed from the Thames to Canton, and back, in their own time. Tea reached the Mincing Lane auction in London nine months after picking; sometimes it took an entire year. East Indiamen idled in the Pearl River delta until they were chock full of tea, then slowly rolled outwards for London.

The lackadaisical voyage out of China meant even the finest grades of tea, the flowery Pekoes and Souchongs, lost their edge. Tea could be as much as two years old by the time it was brewed in the pot. There was no such thing as the 'new season' tea, though travellers' and merchants' reports suggested the 'first cut' off the first blush was the most pungent and choice brew. However impossible it might have been for all but a few of London's tea drinkers to notice a degradation in quality, those in the tea trade imagined there was vast room for improvement, that a premium might well be paid on higher quality, newer teas. But without competition, with no lean challenger to bring tea from hillside to table in the same season, there was no innovation and no improvement for many years.

The nineteenth century saw tremendous technological advances in shipbuilding. After Britain defeated Napoleon in 1815, there was no longer a pressing need for the old British warships, heavily gunned and self-sufficient enough to stay at sea for long stretches, avoiding land. In the peace that followed, ships became longer, sleeker and faster.

When the East India Company monopoly over China ended in 1834, new trading companies sprung up in the China Trade – names still revered in the Orient: Swire, Jardine and Matheson. These new companies fought for a cut of the lucrative tea profits, squeezing the mighty East India Company which, like their ships, was bloated and inefficient. This competition created new incentives for faster boats, and the tall-masted sailing ships grew sleeker yet and more refined.

Ultimately, when the 1849 repeal of British Navigation Laws allowed American shipbuilders to ship to and from China, the Americans could finally offload Chinese tea right on to British docks – and did so weeks ahead of British-built ships. International competition drove the tea ships harder still. American ships, modelled after the finer hull lines of the swift privateers from the War of 1812, could make the run between New York and Canton in under a hundred days. With speed at a premium, British shipbuilders went back to their drawing boards; they shaved the bows, narrowed the hulls, and raked the masts to compete with the best of Boston's designers.

In a matter of twenty years, these three factors – the end of Napoleon, the end of the East India Company monopoly, and the entrance of Americans into China shipping – accelerated the delivery of tea and revolutionised navigation under sail. Ships grew increasingly lean and efficient with each development. The new ships were called tea clippers. They sliced through the water.

Clippers are immediately recognisable by their long, low hulls with a 'fish head' stern hanging sharply over the water. They are square-rigged and triple-masted, 'a perfect beauty to every nautical man', as one captain remarked.

With the advent of the clippers, the tea trade became a hugely popular spectator sport. Once the first raking masts of the Oriental fleet were sighted in the English Channel, the City of London turned out on the banks of the Thames to watch the annual Tea Race, when the China clippers landed the new season's picking: the finest, freshest and newest tea in the Western world. Tugs were engaged, signals were flashed from every headland all the way up to London, wagering began, and fortunes were made or lost on which ship would be the first to throw a box of tea over its gunwales and on to the wharf. There was as much interest in this race as there was in the Derby. England's enthusiasm for tea was, to a small degree, like an average Frenchman's fancy for the new season's Beaujolais.

The tea clippers remain the fastest sailing ships in the world, in part because they were marvels of engineering and enterprise, and in part because there was never again a need for a big fast sailing boat. Trade with the Far East became so valuable to Britain and France that together they built the Suez Canal. Clippers couldn't sail in the canal; the Red Sea's winds were too challenging, whereas a steamship could, and get to China in half the time of a clipper. With well-placed fuelling stations the run out to China and India grew ever easier. By 1869, when Suez was complete, all the improvements in navigation brought on by tea would become a thing of the past. The ambitions of the British merchant fleet could be fuelled by reliable and steady coal, not fickle wind. And so the risk and romance of tea under a cloud of canvas came to an end.

Manufacturing

Tea's light weight meant that a merchant ship needed ballast to stay trim, and for much of tea's early years that ballast was blue and white Chinese porcelain. This was dead weight and was undervalued by the traders who could make better profits on the more highly desired tea and silk. Still, it was worth trading; it was a necessary filler and offset tea's light weight while taking up less than half the room. Luxury items such as tea were high-risk: they were vulnerable to water damage and a ship was always in jeopardy of being lost at sea so porcelain helped spread the risk around. It was used to trim the ship as 'kentledge', the ballast padding between layers of tea crates, and it had the added benefit of insuring against leaks, lining the hull and keel. Porcelain also protected the more valuable cargo from dirty bilge water, the run off that collects in the hull, contaminated with oil, soil and every liquid nastiness on the ship.

Porcelain originally got its name from Marco Polo, the first Westerner in China. In Italian, *porcellana* means a 'little pig', which is the same name give to the Mediterranean cowrie shells that share the same translucent, smooth, white surface and transparent glaze as a tea cup.

Tea's growing following encouraged the development of the porcelain industry in Britain – among the very first industries to take advantage of the nineteenth century's mechanical innovations. Prior to the eighteenth century, no European factories could make a ceramic teapot capable of holding boiling water. The teapot was an entirely foreign notion to the Chinese who drink their leaves in the cup, at something close to body temperature. Some clever English entrepreneur asked his Cantonese supplier if he could make such a thing as a pot to brew tea, and soon afterwards they were produced in Chinese factories.

Sometimes, however, Chinese ideas were improved upon on British home ground. British tea drinkers decided they preferred handles on their tea cups, while the teaware from the Far East was handle-free. Chinese drink their tea cool enough for a handle not to be necessary; Europeans boiled tea and drank it hot off the hob. In part this difference in taste reflected a difference in quality – the finest grades of tea stayed in China, and there was little sense in drinking prize tea at boiling temperatures; it lost its nuance and delicacy. Tea sold to the foreign markets was of a lower quality, though, it could bear higher temperatures and the addition of sugar and milk. So boiled tea took hold in Britain, and Britons demanded handles to hold on to.

European clay could not meet the service demands of tea the way Chinese clay could, for in Europe clay lacked an essential ingredient: kaolin, or China clay. Chinese porcelain was fired at a high temperature, so it was cheap and durable with a strong, transparent glaze. European clays were fired at a lower temperature; they were likely to break and were burdened with porous glazes.

The difference in quality stimulated an industrial race in England. Could British manufacturers make kitchenware harder and cheaper? English factories worked with stoneware; it was heavy, coarse and fragile, but by virtue of its lower transportation costs it could compete with Chinese porcelain on price. Ultimately, by about 1750, European factories discovered the secret of porcelain production and a new industry was born, using the machines then taking hold of British industry. England could now compete on price *and* on quality. An industrial revolution followed. (Entirely coincidentally, one of the earliest potters to make these technological advances in the areas of mass machinery was Josiah Wedgwood, who could count among his great-grandchildren the naturalist and contemporary of Robert Fortune, Charles Darwin.)

The tea trade, through the porcelain trade, also stimulated the *idea* of China and the exotic East. Images of *Chinoiserie*, of weeping willows and towering pagodas, of demure women clothed in flowing robes, all came stamped or painted on the side of an imported tea cup. Inherent in England's favourite beverage was the idea of travel and Empire. This romanticisation of the Orient was highly useful for advancing the Imperial project; it made a pretty thing of an unknown place; it lent an image of beauty to what was otherwise a fearsome, treacherous journey abroad. If an Empire required travel to defend the Crown and stimulate the economy, then it made sense to maintain the myth of a picturesque destination. Great poverty was devastating England, along with disease and dislocation. Cities encroached on the countryside and its former inhabitants were now working in factories, breathing smog, and living in crowded tenements; but the images visible everywhere on porcelain represented a link to a wider, bigger and better world. It was a world of trade and possibility; a world that England could conquer.

Life in England

As predicted by the Honourable East India Company, Indian-grown tea would lead to an overall decrease in tea prices. Fortune's success, combined with repeals of tea taxes and the advances in shipping, spurred first by the clippers and then by the Suez Canal, led to an overall drop in the price of tea.

The end of the Company also lowered prices as new merchant importers and tea dealers rushed to India to fill the void left by the Company monopoly. Cheaper tea meant that shady dealers felt less need to pad their tea with other plants and dangerous chemicals, and so its quality improved. Although England had been a nation of tea drinkers for over a century, as well as a growing nation, cheaper tea became an outright boon to the rapidly urbanising country.

Demographers and doctors had long noticed a drop in the mortality rate as the taste for tea took over the nation. The growth of cities in the eighteenth and nineteenth centuries also saw a growth in pollution and disease. Cholera, which had long plagued the Indian subcontinent, made its first appearance in England in the 1830s when infected sailors, drinking water from ships' barrels filled in India, returned to their home port and polluted the local sewers with deadly bacteria. By mid-century, plagues of cholera were repeatedly wiping out Londoners in their tens of thousands; the outbreak of 1848–9 claimed 50,000 lives – all from drinking water.

Countries such as Britain where boiled tea was drunk in preference to coffee, which is steeped in hot but not boiling water, reaped immediate health benefits: boiling water killed the micro-organisms that spread contagion at close quarters. Even when not plague-ridden, London's drinking water was far from sanitary, owing to the density of the city's population and lack of proper waste removal. A nation of tea drinkers was more likely than one of coffee drinkers to survive the repeated infestations seeping in from the global economy of the Victorian era.

Tea was a boon to the imperial project as well. It became a standard part of rations for the British Army. Native troops were likewise encouraged to take up the tea habit. As Englishmen were slogging through the marshes and muck of the tropics, tracking the boundaries of Empire in the name of Victoria and Great Britain, they comforted themselves with a nice cuppa and water-borne illnesses were kept at bay.

Tea answered a series of modern problems. As previously noted, sugar was another imperial commodity, an essential part of the intricate gear work of the British Empire; it came from the Queen's remaining colonies in the New World: Barbados, Jamaica, St Thomas. Britain had a glut of imperial sugar, and tea gave Britain somewhere to dump it. Tea created a market where previously Britain had exhausted its sweet tooth.

But more so, tea with sugar provided Britons with an easy source of calories. The urbanisation of Britain meant that the poor no longer had access to farm products – tea, though not inherently nutritious, could be drunk with milk, a protein, and sugar, a cheap and dense source of energy.

Prior to widespread tea drinking, factory workers obtained much of their calorie intake from beer and ale which made for a slovenly, disoriented, and frequently rowdy workforce. Beer could be tolerated by workers doing lots of heavy lifting and manual labour – as they would in pre-industrialised economies – but it was no use in conjunction with the fine motor skills required in the industrialised sectors of Britain's economy. A drunken worker was a danger around the fast-moving shuttles and looms of Manchester's textile industry, for instance. But by drinking sugared tea and eating bread, plus meat on Sunday, Britons could get all the calories they needed without the risk of intoxication. Indeed, tea had a stimulant effect; it focused the minds of the workforce, helping them to concentrate better on their demanding jobs.

Fermented drinks, such as alcohol, also have the benefits of killing parasites and bringing liquid calories to the diet, but by the start of the eighteenth century beer production was eating up nearly half of the wheat harvest in Britain. There was no possible way for Britain's domestic agriculture to feed the rapidly expanding population and keep them in beer too; there just wasn't enough farmland for every new mouth in the industrial era. Calories had to come from an outside source, one beyond the boundaries of the British Isles, from the wider shores of the Empire. The pursuit of food has always shaped the development of society, and in the days of the Victorian Empire, the very start of our modern industrialised global food-chain, tea with milk and sugar became the answer to Britain's growing need for cheap nutrition.

Other benefits accrued from the choice of tea over beer, particularly for the young. Pregnant women drinking tea, rather than beer, would have significantly improved the health of the infant British population. Tea also contains anti-bacterial phenols, plant-based chemicals that act as natural disinfectants. Since it was typical in Britain to breast-feed babies for the first year, mothers opting for tea rather than beer meant British babies were no longer drinking alcohol at second hand. Tea reduced infant mortality, if it did not measurably increase overall intelligence, and gave an immunising boost to the population when industrialisation was demanding more and more bodies to help swell the booming economy of Great Britain.

European countries that continued to choose wine and beer as the staple drinks, such as France and Germany, lagged fifty years behind Britain in the process of industrialisation. It would be a stretch to lay the entire credit for this on tea, but its tea culture must have helped Britain forge ahead in the global race for economic dominance.

Taking tea in the afternoon followed the gradual democ-ratisation in the price of tea – first in the higher orders of society, and later in the lower. Tea time was a period of enjoy-ment, of visiting, for talking in the long hours between noon and the evening meal. By the mid-nineteenth century, 'tea in the drawing room' marked the first time that the ritualised notions of tea drinking took root in British society. Tea, as noted before, takes time, a certain amount of leisure and wealth to truly appreciate. The industrial revolution, which tea helped spur, created enough excess capital such that Britons could finally enjoy the fruits of their affluence.

In times of wealth, tea's cultural symbolism shifts from that of a stimulant to a balm, a relaxant, though chemically it contains both properties. The Eastern ritual surrounding tea is focused on relaxation, not buzz. Today in the West it seems there is a new study released every day examining the health benefits of drinking tea – from its anti-oxidant and anti-carcinogenic properties, to its role in stabilising diabetes, raising metabolic rates and lowering the risk of obesity, or boosting the immune system. Big claims and perhaps still to be proved in scientific terms, but any regular tea drinker will confirm that tea drinking increases mental alertness and short-term memory as well as lowering stress. Experts are examining tea from every direction as a magic elixir for respite, recreation, and a better, longer life.

England's great tea experiment in India was a phenomenal success. More people now drank more tea for less money. Tea exemplifies the grand theory of Empire: it could create a new class of consumers for British products while simultaneously expanding access to foreign products for Britons. Within twenty years of Fortune's theft of Chinese trade secrets, the tea trade had shifted away from China to the British dominions. When a single species was transported out of home soil, the world was never again the same.

19

Fortune's Story

To finish Fortune's story, it helps to imagine a day at Kew. Having sailed down the Thames, Fortune, in his sixties, arrived at Kew to pay homage to his botanist friends and colleagues – among them the current director, Joseph Hooker, the man once imprisoned in Darjeeling by the Rajah of Sikkim along with Archibald Campbell. Hooker was a great friend of the naturalist stirring up the scientific world, Charles Darwin. Fortune had a gay old visit, chinwagging with other botanists about new discoveries, remembering past scrapes, counting himself – at last – man among equals.

In truth, we have no idea what Fortune felt on this visit, or precisely when it happened. What we know of Fortune's adventures comes from his published works on China, India, and Japan, and from the copious records kept by the faceless, dutiful, admirable Company clerks and peons. Though much of the East India Company records were destroyed and thrown away when the charter was revoked after the Mutiny, there is, thankfully, ample Company material left in the British Library. However, none of Fortune's private papers survive.

Given Fortune's taciturn nature and his ability to keep his own company for years on end, he might well have excused himself from the distinguished company of other botanists after finishing his tea. He would then have taken a walk through the exquisite gardens that had once been the play-things of royalty but were now, rightly, a hothouse of scientific development.

Fortune would have walked up to a great greenhouse, the Palm House, gloriously situated on a hill. Kew's first director and Fortune's former boss, the father of the current director, William Jackson Hooker, had the Palm House constructed with a roof sixty-six feet high, since palms cannot be cut back, making it the focus of Kew Gardens. The tropical giants grow until they hit the ceiling. The all glass Palm House employed the principals of Ward's discovery, its engineering was based on developments in shipbuilding – it was, essentially, an upside-down glass ship's hull. Nestled amidst the palm trunks were further examples of tropical Imperial explor-ation – spices, fruits, timber, fibres, perfumes and *material medica*, the prizes of previous plant hunters.

Fortune would have wandered on, to a part of the garden that might have been his very favourite: the Chinese Pagoda. The pagoda was built in 1761 for a dowager princess amidst a growing enthusiasm in Britain for anything exotic and Chinese. The East India Company had made the country rich through trade, and China had been at the centre of that trade. A notice-able Chinese influence decorated the country: in the furniture designs of Thomas Chippendale, in textiles, in fine porcelain, in the Kew pagoda hewn from red English brick. Fortune saw China in everything he looked upon. And the pagoda, more than anything, reminded him of his long years of travel.

Following his first tea theft, Fortune returned home to his wife and children – but only very briefly. He barely had time to write up his memoirs and see to the younger Fortunes' situ-ation, reacquaint himself with his loved ones, and impregnate his wife again, before the Company called for the last time.

Fortune's discovery of the colouring of green tea prompted

a change in the tastes and preferences of the British people. The unveiling of the chemical greening of green tea at the Great Exhibition of 1851 marked a turning point – Britons now wanted their tea black and only black. The Chinese did not bother to adulterate the colour of black tea. Fortune's first tea makers to the Himalayas were versed in the art of green tea. But the results of his findings about chemical dyes so altered British tastes that he was sent out again. On his second trip for the Company – his last for that employer – he went back to China again, this time with explicit instructions to hire black tea experts.

Fortune's next trip to China included a different level of spying than his first – he became a drug smuggler as well as a spy. In the mid-nineteenth century the British Empire in India and the Qing Empire in China functioned as two vast nationalised drugs cartels, their fortunes dependent on the cultivation of two plants. We have seen the way in which Britain purloined the tea trade, but China too was bent on a quest of botanical thievery, planning to raise a domestic opium crop to compete with Indian Patna-raised opium. Just as tea could find a second home on the other side of the Himalayas, *Papaver somniferum*, the opium poppy, could be transplanted to the rolling lush hills of China. Plant stealing worked in both directions.

In the years after the First Opium War, although Britain had won the right to deal opium to China, its native opium was busily supplanting this trade. Chinese opium was cheaper. The Company had created a nation of junkies. Now, like any addict, China exercised all its ingenuity on discovering less expensive ways to get its fix. The Company, a dying multinational in its last throes, feared that China's own domestic crop would one day squeeze them out of this lucrative market. Since they had a prominent horticulturist already working undercover for them there, what could be easier than expanding his remit and asking him to obtain for them as much information as possible about China's nascent opium crop?

Fortune returned to the Company the following high-risk and ultimately rewarding details:

2 dried specimens of the Poppy from which Chinese opium
    is made
1 Opium knife used by the Natives in collecting the Poppy
    Seed
1 Paper of seeds of some poppy

'The seeds and specimens I send now will give the means of ascertaining . . . what those differences [between the Indian and Chinese varieties] are and whether they account for the difference in quality between Indian and Chinese Opium,' Fortune wrote to the Company. Botanists in India soon studied what, exactly, those differences were. In his popular and scholarly published works, Fortune made no mention whatsoever of his drug smuggling and opium investigations.

The tensions bubbling between China and Britain during Fortune's trip erupted in to a Second Opium War. The two empires came to blows in 1857, shortly after Fortune's second tea-hunting foray and at the same time as India was in the throes of mutiny. Britain, ever-eager to expand its markets, wanted even greater access to China, to penetrate past the treaty ports and into the interior. China, ever-reluctant, wanted to keep the predatory foreign devils at a safe distance.

When the Indian Mutiny ruined the East India Company, Fortune found himself, for a brief time, a new employer: the United States Government. By now his fame was secure; his accomplishments celebrated. He had made his reputation as a man who could monetise the botanical glories of the Orient. He was the father of a whole new industry in India, and the United States wanted its share too. It has always been supposed that the US has been a coffee-drinking culture ever since the Boston Tea Party, when a gang of patriots dressed as Mohawk Indians threw an entire shipment of East India Company tea into Boston Harbour to protest the high taxes imposed by the British Crown. But nearly a century later the American Government in fact had big plans for tea. It was thought that the agricultural regions of the American South would make the US a fierce competitor in the lucrative world tea economy. Uncle Sam asked Fortune to assess whether or not tea would take root in the hilly and humid southern Appalachian states of America, the Carolinas or Virginia. Labour was still cheap in the South.

In 1857, the US Patent Office hired Fortune to bring tea seeds to America. He was offered his standing rate – £500 a year and all expenses paid – to commit tea espionage for Washington. Caught up in the frenzy of industrialisation, the Patent Office believed American engineers could harness steam power to automate the processing of tea.

Fortune sailed for China again in March 1858, arriving in the Chinese interior in August. By December he had ready two Wardian cases of tea seeds and plants for his American employers. After many years of trial and error, he had become an expert tea hunter.

As soon as the cases arrived in Washington, the Commissioner of US Patents unceremoniously fired Fortune. Presumably the bureaucrat believed that American gardeners could take care of the by now flourishing seedlings. Indeed, the tea thrived in the Patent Office's gardens. By 1859, some 30,000 well-rooted plants from Fortune's haul were available for distribution to plantations in the South. By 1860, the dispersal of tea seeds and plants was a significant portion of the work of the Patent Office's agricultural division.

When Civil War broke out between North and South in 1861, the newly formed US Department of Agriculture lost all communication with the areas involved in the tea trials. By the war's end, without slave labour American tea could not compete with the cheaper overheads in Asia. The price of picking a pound of tea in the US was six times that of tea picked in China. Though there were a few more attempts at an American tea industry, it died stillborn. Fortune spent much of the Civil War trying to recoup his lost fee from the Patent Office – which, it seems, he never accomplished.

His final trip to the Far East in 1862, to both China and Japan, was the only one he undertook as a private citizen, working for nursery firms and paying his own freight. Fortune could finally keep a share of each and every discovery, and all ensuing profits, for himself. Japan, a previously closed country with a latitude similar to Britain's, was thought to possess botanical prizes that would adapt nicely to the climate of England. Fortune made a mint from his finds there, and so in his final years became very wealthy. His botanical prizes hit their target amongst the enthusiastic plant collectors of Britain. Moreover, in his years of living in Asia, meeting Mandarins and farmers, peasants and poets, Fortune had developed a good eye for the arts and decorative objects of the East which were so prized by the Western aristocratic and merchant classes. His eye for detail, essential in a plant hunter, would in the end make him a very rich man. When he died in 1880, his estate was valued at over £40,000, at least $5 million today (£2.5 million).

Fortune left a series of discoveries in the wake of his Chinese travels – the kumquat still bears the botanical name *Fortunella* in his honour, for instance. The plants and flowers Fortune 'discovered' in the Orient number in the hundreds: the bleeding heart, the winter jasmine, the white wisteria, twelve species of rhododendron, the chrysanthemum. He corrected Linnaeus's definition of tea's taxa by revealing that green and black teas were one and the same, and improved the health of Britain by pointing out that the Chinese were colouring green tea with poison. Fortune's experiments with transporting tea seeds in Wardian Cases made it possible for the great trees of England to migrate – prior to Robert Fortune's improvements on the Wardian box, England's towering oak and chestnut trees could not be replanted in the colonies as acorns and chestnuts, like tea seeds, did not travel well. His work made it possible for entire agricultural economies to find new markets and new homes.

But Fortune's world of plant hunting receded fast. Once the Suez Canal opened, ships were able to travel between China and England in little over a month, avoiding the treacherous temperature changes of travelling around the Horn, and minimising the threat to plant cargo. Telegraph cables were wiring from one part of the globe to another, so the street-smarts and improvisational bravado that marked his time in China faded into the past.

It might have seemed to Fortune that all the grandeur of God's earth had been completely catalogued and numbered. There was now new work to be done utilising Charles Darwin's theories of evolution. Natural History was no longer the mere act of cataloguing; it became a hunt for the narrative of how species evolve adaptive characteristics, through competition and natural selection.

There would be no more Robert Fortunes: the East India Company was gone, and with it the profit-hungry institutional desire for botanists. There was no longer any giant corporate monopoly willing to pay for research and development on the scale of the Honourable Company. Fortune had played his part on a grand stage as a younger man. As an older one it seemed to him there might be nothing left to discover, and certainly no one to pay for it. In his time he had done his part to enrich Britain; he made it more green and pleasant still. So many of Fortune's precious seedlings, so delicately packed and intimately cared for in far away Cathay, found a home at Kew, under the shadow of the great pagoda.

By the time Fortune was an old man, the tea plantations of India had outstripped those of China whose tea would never again be as competitive for the Western market. Fortune's tea theft would be repeated over and over again; tea would be brought to Ceylon, to Kenya, to Turkey, and it would be judged fine, high quality, good, even excellent. When Robert Fortune stole tea from China, it was the greatest theft of protected trade secrets that the world has ever known. His actions would today be described as industrial espionage, viewed in the same light as if he had stolen the formula for Coca-Cola. Any number of international treaties now police foreign exploitation and protect national commercial treasures. It could perhaps even be said that today the Chinese are wreaking revenge on the West for its previous thefts and earlier 'unequal' treaties. Frequent headlines about copyright violation and intellectual property theft make it plain that China, in its turn, has become adept at stealing trade secrets.

Today there is only measured enthusiasm for the mass globalisation of indigenous plant life. We know now that when species are taken to new habitats, without any natural predators or competitors, they overpopulate and decimate local ecosystems. Entire islands have been overrun by the kind of botanical frontiersmanship that Fortune and his contemporaries routinely practised.

Fortune was comfortable on the winding paths of Kew. He had grown up amongst the mighty bowers of the British Isles, and found himself at home in her pastures. Fortune was never an overly happy man, but as he walked through Kew Gardens, he would have felt – in a small and not overly proud way – happy with all he had accomplished. He had not saved the East India Company; it died by its own hand. But in green and pleasant Britain and in the high hills of India, Robert Fortune made new things grow.

Robert Fortune died in 1880. It is unknown how he spent the very last years of his life. For reasons of her own, his wife Jane burned all his papers and personal effects upon his death. She may have burnt his journals in response to a local scandal: in 1877, another man named Robert Fortune, a lunatic in Edinburgh Asylum, killed an inmate for his shoes. That Robert Fortune was tried for murder and later hanged in the same year as her husband died, a coincidence that might have made Jane fearful for his reputation. It is also entirely possible that she was swayed by the Temperance Movement of Britain, powered as it mostly was by women left alone while their husbands promoted Empire business abroad. These women were a harsh and puritanical bunch who would have frowned on any evidence of Fortune smuggling opium samples or indulging in the 'rank poison' of Chinese wine. It is not hard to imagine other skeletons in the cupboard: a Chinese girlfriend, a child – men alone in the wilds of Empire were well known to stray. Fortune makes little mention of the rampant sex trade in Chinese culture, a glaring if prudent omission. Had his personal papers been less circumspect than his professional writings, they might well have raised the ire of a wife left alone for too long with too many children.

But there is another possible explanation. Alone for years at a time, raising a family by herself, six children in all, surviving on letters and the occasional visit from her husband, Jane Fortune might have grown jealous of a different kind of mistress. Even when Fortune was home, his heart was still with his beloved plants, in China. He was hardly ever truly with Jane. So when he died, even the most devoted wife could well have felt resentful. She was alone again, this time for good. To be sure he had left her a great deal of money, but little of himself.

So Jane purged the remnants of Fortune's life: his worn-out gardening shoes, his collars, coats and gloves. In the process, she probably imagined what might have been had the man she married been more firmly rooted in Britain. Perhaps, in those first moments of her grieving widowhood, a jealous Jane Fortune eliminated all evidence of Robert's true infidelity – his great, enduring and impossible love for the flora of China.

Notes and Sources

As this is a work of popular history, not a scholarly undertaking, I have avoided the use of footnotes and tried to steer clear of mentioning sources in the body of the text. Nevertheless, this is a work of non-fiction and anything in quotes comes from a letter, memoir, newspaper or other contemporaneous source.

I have relied heavily on Robert Fortune's three memoirs, his letters to the East India Company and other Company documents housed in the British Library. Over 500 books and documents were consulted in putting this project together. Each of the broader themes – Fortune, the Company, China and professional botany – have been the subject of inquiry by minds greater and more learned than my own.

The exhaustive work on tea is William H. Ukers' aptly named *All About Tea* (The Tea and Coffee Trade Journal Company, 1935). For a more narrative tale, there are several excellent popular histories, but I most enjoyed the spirited *The Great Tea Venture* by James Maurice Scott (Dutton, 1965).

It surprised me how much fun it was to explore the world of the naturalists and botanists in Victorian England and the Empire, and I can't find enough praise for the scholars who got there first: David E. Allen's *The Naturalist in Britain: A Social History* (Princeton University Press, 1994), David Arnold's *The Tropics and the Traveling Gaze: India, Landscape, And Science, 1800–1856* (University of Washington Press, 2006), Fa-ti Fan's *British Naturalists in Qing China: Science, Empire, and Cultural Encounter* (Harvard University Press, 2004), Sidney W. Mintz's spectacular *Sweetness and Power: The Place of Sugar in Modern History* (Penguin Books, 1986), Donal McCracken's *Gardens of Empire* (Leicester

University Press, 1997), Henry Hobhouse's *Seeds of Change* (Harper and Row, 1986) and Sandra Knapp's *Plant Discoveries: A Botanist's Voyage Through Plant Exploration* (Firefly Books, 2003) were all tremendous resources. I am indebted to *The Apothecaries Garden* (Sutton, 2000), as well as the pamphlets published by the Physic Garden and to the Garden itself – among London's most splendid treasures.

As any student of China might, I depended on masters to instruct me in Qing history: Jonathan Spence, John King Fairbank, Immanuel C.Y. Hsu, Philip Kuhn and Fredric Wakeman all wrote brilliant and breathtaking works of expansive history which I eagerly devoured. For further reading on the Taiping Heavenly Kingdom, I recommend Spence's *God's Chinese Son* (W. W. Norton & Company, 1996). On Opium, Zheng Yangwen's *The Social Life of Opium in China: A History of Consumption from the Fifteenth to the Twentieth Century* (Cambridge University Press, 2005) is excellent. For life in rural China, Nancy Berliner and the Peabody Essex Museum's *Yin Yu Tang: The Architecture and Daily Life of a Chinese House* (Tuttle Publishing, 2003) is a generous resource.

I fear there is less compelling historical work on the East India Company than there should be. No text captured the grandeur or complexity of the Company in a way that satisfied me as a researcher. Nevertheless, I leaned on several solid works, among them Peter Ward Fay's *The Opium War* (University of North Carolina Press, 1975), Nick Robbins' *The Corporation that Changed the World* (Pluto Press, 2006), John Keay's *The Honourable Company: A History of the English East India Company* (Harper-Collins, 1993), Patrick Tuck's *The East India Company* (reprinted by Routledge, 1998), H.A. Antrobus' *A history of the Assam company, 1839–1953* (privately printed by T. and A. Constable, 1957), as well as David Macgregor's *The Tea Clippers: An Account of the China Tea Trade and of Some of the British Sailing Ships Engaged in it from 1849 to 1869* (P. Marshall, 1952).

In learning about Fortune, China and tea, I benefited from the able advice of tea experts, Mr Lu Shun Yong, his partners, Mr

Wang and Mr Shi, as well as Allen Stokes and Michael Harney; China scholars, Carsey Yee, Jan Wong, Hayes Moore and Susan Thurin; the peerless Richard Morel and the staff at the British Library Asia collection, and the entire University of Chicago library system – my favourite library on earth.

Beijing was previously known as Peking to English speakers. In 1949, the Communist government replaced the anglicized Peking with the official pinyin, Beijing, but it did not come into common usage until the 1980s when the government began using Beijing on official documents. Many of the older China hands whom I first met during the handover of Hong Kong still use Peking to refer to the capital. It retains a kind of colonialist hue that I decided to keep throughout the text, as anachronistic as it is.

Fortune was often the first, or among the first, Westerners into a rural area and it is not always clear what location or object he refers to in Chinese since he travelled at a time when there was no systematized Chinese to English transliteration. Where possible, I have strived to include the pinyin. But I am not, alas, a Chinese speaker and I was dependent on translators throughout. All mistakes, of course, are my own.

Acknowledgments

First thanks belong to my agent, Joy Tutela, who, with gentle guidance, helped me broaden a story about a gardener into a book about his world. Joy has fought for me, nurtured me, and put me in my place ever so gently. She and her colleagues, David Black, Susan Raihofer, Leigh Ann Eliseo, Gary Morris, Johnathan Wilber, Caspian Dennis, and Abner Stein are the noblest, kindest and, dare I say, best agents in the entire world.

Warmest thanks to my editor Paul Sidey, whose enthusiasm for Robert Fortune frequently outpaced my own, and to James Nightingale.

Lord, make me worthy of my friends:

Weidong Fu is my honoured teacher, translator and companion whom I miss terribly – I can only hope this book is a fitting souvenir for our travels together.

Scott Anderson brought me Robert Fortune one very dark winter and, with bottomless patience and generosity, weathered my tantrums. He read every word many times over and then told me, quietly, to make them better. I would not be the writer I am without him. Moe, Donna and Kelly Anderson taught me to love gardens. Donna died before she could read this book which owes a tremendous debt to her delight and skills in the garden – every tomato I eat reminds me of her.

Kim Binsted is my fellow traveller, it is entirely her fault that I ever lived in China; she welcomes me to Hawaii each winter, no matter how tragic I become. I would follow her anywhere.

Joel Derfner is the most talented man alive, a girl could not find a more generous, sexier, funnier companion on the terrible road to publication.

My first readers, Rachel Elkin Lebwohl, Victor Wishna, Saul

Austerlitz, and Joel Derfner provided my first moments of reward in three long years – in addition to sterling line-edits.

Megan Von Behren was my genealogist and Daniel Von Behren was my cheerleader and I am thrilled to be their wife.

Much of this book was researched and written far from home and I am grateful to those who gave me shelter and friendship in beautiful places. In London: Julian Land, Miriam Nabarro and Coco Campbell; in Tuscany: Henry, Tory, Elizabeth and Joe Asch; in Maine: Marc, Lauren, David and Delia Laitin; in Delhi: Janaki Bahadur and Christopher Kremmer; in Hawaii: Kim Binsted.

Other friends of Sarahworld who deserve a kiss and baked goods: The Magnificent Seven kept the wine flowing, Karen Bekker, Catharine Clark, soulmate Tammy Hepps, Charlie Paradise, Adina Rosenthal and Shana Sisk. I have been blessed with wonderful teachers: Darlene McCampbell, Earl Bell, Richard Ford and Alan Richman. Chicago would never be warm without Maria, Sergio and Pierralberto Deganello, Tino Palacio, Mindy Graham, and Rosie Humphries. Hawaii would be warm but no fun without Jennifer Baker, Jason "Big Red" Jestice, and Walter Eccles. Laila, Talia, and Mia Veissid and their parents, Marco and Phyllis, cheered me through dreary revisions and continue to do so.

Special thanks to Barney Rose, Clare Hollingworth, Evan Cornog and Lauren McCollester, Richard Bradley, Stephanie Jordan and Adam Brown, Shai Ingber, Burt Friedman, Elaine Land, Elizabeth Hamilton, Anita Fore and the Author's Guild, and the late Gladys Kenner, who always said China was no place for a young lady.

Lastly, tea and I share a birthday, the first flush picking is celebrated on the third day of the third lunar month, which corresponds to the 3rd of April (or thereabouts). If I have expressed that happy birthright, it is in no small part thanks to my parents, Helen Cohen Rose and Gerald Rose, without whom this book (and I) might never have flowered.